VALLEY OF THE
GIANT BUDDHAS

By the same Author, published by The Octagon Press:

MY KHYBER MARRIAGE

Valley of
The Giant Buddhas

Memoirs and Travels

by

MORAG MURRAY ABDULLAH

THE OCTAGON PRESS
LONDON

ISBN 0 863040 65 9

Published 1993

Photoset, printed and bound by
Redwood Books, Trowbridge, Wiltshire

Contents

1

His Majesty

Cairo: Any Egyptian will tell you that this city is the most fascinating, and the most maddening, he or she has ever seen. Not only Egyptians say this, travellers of wide experience say it and I rather agree. I don't think that even Calcutta runs it close for such a title...

Cairo is a microcosm – if such a word can be used of a place harbouring fourteen million people – a microcosm of all the elements of the country. The nation is undoubtedly an Arab and Muslim land, yet it has millions of Copts – Christians tracing their ancestry to the ancient Egyptians.

A highly nationalistic country with a proud history, Egypt has seldom been ruled by her own people. It is a deeply religious people this. Yet one where, in spite of great sufferings, smiling faces are everywhere to be seen.

And the name of the country in Arabic – *Misr* – is the name of Cairo as well, even though it was originally named *Medinat El Qahira*, the Victorious City.

I first arrived there with my husband as King Farouk's guest during the latter days of the monarchy. Characteristically, Farouk was of Albanian, not Arabian, stock, and very proud of his 'white face'. Many of his Pashas, the grandees, were of Turkish origin.

One of the first things he said to me was, 'Madame, your distinguished husband is here to be honoured because of his lineage, wisdom and advice. But you, wise in the ways of the West, do you not think, Madame, that if I puff out my cheeks, I become more pink and my sunburn does not show?'

'You certainly do look pale, your Majesty,' I replied, looking at his fleshy and greyish face.

And yet he could be astute. The next moment he said: 'I have just been receiving the British Ambassador. He actually asked me to do what I could to stop Egyptians attacking members of the British Army stationed here. I said: "Excellency, I have the honour to represent all my subjects, including those who do not approve of your troops in our country. Opinion, here, is free!"'

Farouk was a strange mixture, of cleverness and childishness, of baby and adult. He loved almost anything novel, and had a curious way of expressing himself, though in excellent English: 'I have a Jew in America; he sends me gadgets...'

If Farouk had not had so many drawbacks, which one soon glimpsed, he could surely have made progress in many kinds of ways. He was not, however, too supportive of women.

Once, when I asked him why he collected so many European artworks, if he was so convinced of the superiority of the East, which he constantly praised, he said: 'Because I respect the West. Its traditions, now unfortunately forgotten, are to put women in their place, which is second place.'

In one breath, he had damned with faint praise and put me down. He now proceeded to administer the *coup de grace* with more than the usual cunning of the male chauvinist, and – this was totally unexpected – all the verve and knowledge of a university professor:

'Aristotle, after all one of the founders of Western culture, is on record as saying, "The virtues of a naturally higher class are more noble than those of a naturally lower class: thus the virtues of men are nobler than those of women."'

All I could stumble out in response to this extraordinary quote (which I later verified as accurate) was,

'And what does Islam say about women, your Majesty, if Western culture is anti-female?'

He was ready for this; in fact, I could almost feel him anticipating it. 'Islam, of course, as in the Holy Koran, says "Verily, women are the twin halves of men!"'

The King's sycophantic courtiers, too, had to keep on their toes when faced with this kind of erudition. On this occasion one of them with a smirk, said: 'And, as your Majesty will know, that other Western icon, Sigmund Freud, said that the female sex is the lesser of the two. This assertion is in fact in print, in his works.'

I have seen worse performances by dons at High Table.

Farouk had an enormous Intelligence Service, but I soon gathered that everyone told him only what he wanted to hear. We were lucky in that. The spies must, surely, have known that we were meeting, in addition to such as the sheikhs of Al Azhar University, a wide variety of the rest of the populace.

The Muslim Brethren – strongly suspected of plotting revolution – sent representatives to pay their respects. So did the 'Free Officers', later to produce Gamal Abdul-Nasser who took over the country. He sought my husband out, to the frustration of Afghan ministers, when – as Egyptian President – Nasser visited Kabul.

The Officers did much to restore Egyptian self-respect after they got rid of the monarchy. Abdul-Nasser's successor, Anwar Sadat, and then Hosni Mubarak, exerted prodigies of effort to help the country and its people. Even to maintain the *status quo* was a major headache.

With an antiquated infrastructure and a burgeoning population spread along a tiny strip of fertile land beside the Nile, the problems were – and remain – enormous.

As *Al Hakim al Azim* – the Great Wise One, my husband Sirdar Ikbal Ali Shah was always surrounded by suppliants, informants and others during his Eastern travels and visits. Sometimes, I was convinced, they cancelled each other out in the eyes of the local *Mukhabarat* –

Intelligence Services. Such people often referred to this activity in these terms: 'Dogs and men alike need nutrition'.

This consultative function was the result of the long tradition of the family. Descended from the Persian Emperors and the Prophet, they have a natural constituency in the billion-strong Islamic world. As Sufi teachers of the greatest repute, they command reverent respect.

In Egypt, particularly, they are looked upon with especial regard for their family connection with Jamal Ed-Din al-Afghani, inspirer of Sheikh Abduh, father of the country's independence struggle.

In thirty or forty years, I had become quite used to this. Such is the significance of this family that I was no longer surprised to meet, arriving in Luxor for the first time, a man who knew more than six hundred years' names of the Sirdar's predecessors. Surely an equivalent event in one's own culture would be almost inconceivable to a Westerner...

Farouk himself owned some dozen night-clubs in Cairo. All were run at a heady pace and he was an inveterate first-nighter. He quickly tired of faces and the Pasha whose job it was to provide a constant stream of new talent for the boards had a particularly unenviable time. It was said he never knew what it was to have a full night's rest.

The telephone at this be-fezzed grandee's bedside might ring at any minute, from Paris, London, Rome, Cyprus or Beirut, informing His Excellency that a very special little number had just performed and the speaker personally recommended that she be invited to appear before the highest society in Cairo.

The engagement was usually made on the spot. Next day, several odds and ends had to be attended to, such as the first-class air tickets, as well as 'something extra', a gift of money to ensure that the artiste might be suitably arrayed to appear before the *bon-ton* of Cairo.

4

Farouk loved sequins, and if the Pasha chanced to forget this little particularity over the telephone, he would have to ring up whichever distant capital his informant was in to pass on the information. The rest was left to the dancer. The result was usually startling, as was intended.

From the time the invitation was extended until the arrival of the young woman, her progress was entirely triumphal. On the day of her arrival in Cairo, the Pasha would be borne in his car to the airport in good time. He was known to be a timid and restless person and spent the time until the plane arrived walking agitatedly backwards and forwards. His state of mind may be imagined.

The Pasha had once almost lost his job when a ravishing but black chanteuse tripped down the gangway instead of the expected French performer. The mistake had occurred because the lady had a French name. The spotter had not seen her personally, but relied on the knowledge that French entertainers were Number One on the current royal Cairo agenda. The name had nearly turned out to be his undoing.

One of Farouk's cronies (they giggled about him in discreet company) said that for the next few times he made any engagement, the Pasha usually rang up the scout at least three times, to be positive that the lady was of the right colour.

The Pasha eventually recovered from the shock, but it had left a weakness; he was unable to remain seated at the airport until the lady had been seen by him personally.

There were few of these mistakes, because the talent-spotters in foreign parts knew the tastes of the Egyptian monarch to a hair's-breadth. They found their work irksome but remunerative. In fact, so well had some of them performed their tasks over a number of years, that they had at times been invited to stay, as the guests of Farouk, at a famous Cairo hotel. These trips and the emoluments they received were considered by all to be highly satisfactory. This, at any rate, was the verdict relayed to me by an ambassador sitting next to me at a serious dinner-party.

By the time the plane landed, the Pasha was generally in a state of near collapse and his mood could only be improved by the appearance of a particularly presentable young dancer.

It was the Pasha's duty to accompany her to the hotel where, as became a guest of such importance and high promise, a private suite awaited.

If the young lady was considered by the Pasha to be extra special, he was allowed the privilege of playing a childish game with Farouk. He would report that the dancer was not quite what he had been led to expect. The King knew quite well that if she had not been better than usual, the Pasha would not have dared refer to such a disappointment on pain of being reduced to utter despair.

However, the little game went on until the evening, by which time the dancer had modelled all her garments for the Pasha, who advised her on the suitability of this flimsy garment or that. When the King arrived at the place of entertainment, everything was perfect. That is not to be taken lightly in a place such as Cairo was then, where satiated appetites were not easily whetted.

The King made a rule never to see the dancers before they appeared on the stage. He explained his reason for this to a Pasha. 'It adds to the anticipation in a world where excitement is so rare.'

Farouk's progress to and from his night clubs was quite a performance in itself. One such occasion was described to me by another member of the Diplomatic Corps: who freely admitted that this kind of despatch was regularly sent to London and elsewhere, for the amusement of the home authorities:

Round about the time when the cabaret was at its height, when the star was about to perform, a cordon of police armed with machine-guns and revolvers took up positions in a double row leading from the street to the entrance door of the club.

Presently, the air was rent by the screaming of sirens, and there was a flurry of police on motor-cycles, dashing around at top speed. Usually pedestrians kept out of the way; sometimes blind or lame people were not so fortunate.

As soon as the mobile police arrived, they threw themselves from their cycles and raced helter-skelter to one of the club entrances at the end of a cul-de-sac. At once a fleet of red cars appeared, travelling at still greater speed than their predecessors.

The front cars came to a grinding halt, and their occupants dashed for the cabaret entrance. One was Farouk, the others doubles. The whole incident looked like the shooting of a scene in a gangster film.

The police had to remain where they stood, like the faithful sentries at Pompeii, until such time as their royal master thought fit to leave. If the show was good, that was not soon. It must have been a thirsty job on those hot Cairo nights. When Farouk left, the same flurry took place; the party threw their arms in front of faces, so that nobody knew who was who.

Before the onlookers, who had usually not gone for the purpose of looking on, but by mistake or out of ignorance, had recovered from the shock of seeing police and cars, guns and racing figures, the putative guardians of law and order were blazing a return trail through the streets.

At other times, when Farouk made one of his frequent outings, he took a party of pashas and A.D.C.'s with him. Sometimes the King was in the first car, sometimes he chose one of the others. Occasionally he tricked the party and returned to the palace alone, by way of a joke.

The cars would race to the agreed destination before the

King's absence was discovered. When it became apparent that he was not there, the police would hare back to the palace, where Farouk would perhaps be sulking. The return journey was more like a rat-hunt through the streets than the progress of a royal party.

Nobody ever knew in which residence the King was spending the night. It was said he went to whichever one he chose, without consulting anybody.

I watched one of Farouk's progressions through the town one day as we were leaving our hotel. The Nile bridge was blocked and machine guns stood on tripods, as though the place was in a state of siege. People anxious to cross the river were hustled away by the police.

Next came the roar of police on motor-cycles followed by a fleet of scarlet motor cars madly zooming along. In the back of each car was Farouk: or a look-alike, for the benefit of possible assassins, who would have to take a split-second decision as to whom to attack.

So great was the pace that the vehicles almost looked as though they were joined together in one long blur. They actually created a wind as they passed.

A cat which had been amusing us by washing its face in the middle of the road, suddenly made up its mind to cross, just as the cars appeared. By the time the last one had passed all that remained of the cat was a sickening flat splotch.

The unseemly progress of the scarlet royal cars and the mangled body of the small animal made a horribly sanguinary impression on the mind.

This kind of behaviour, especially in the face of growing poverty, religious agitation and – it must be admitted – outside interference by the superpowers, boded ill for the 'F's'. (Farouk's family were superstitious about this letter, and gave all their children names beginning with the sixth letter of the alphabet.)

Our submissions on such points were fruitless. A member of the staff at the French embassy, obviously relying upon an intercepted document, warned me to avoid 'political entanglement' at all costs. 'A Belgian colleague has, in fact, just been forced to flee, Madame: and that was not due to any personal problem . . .'

While we were still in good odour, we were, one night, given a special invitation to attend one of the cabarets.

I had a good look at the King as he entered. I could not help noting how ill this gross, sensual-faced man now looked compared with the tall and handsome Prince Farouk we knew in his student days.

His present appearance was startling and arresting: that of someone who has seriously gone to seed. I wondered if he was on drugs. He looked fat and frail at the same time, and wore a non-slimming white tuxedo, a fez and the usual dark glasses.

It was a rule to pay no attention to Farouk's presence at any of the night clubs, for he liked to think nobody noticed him. And yet, on such occasions, the greatest care was taken as to the identity of those present.

That night, in spite of the supposed informality, the whole place seemed charged with furtiveness and unease.

No sooner had Farouk taken his seat than the lights were lowered, except for the limelight upon the stage. There was dead silence. No actress appeared. Farouk became impatient and snapped his fingers.

From behind the curtain, the Pasha made a sign and a dancer floated on to the boards. She was tiny, with a shock of golden curls and wore a scarcely perceptible garment of gold sequins. Farouk threw back his head and laughed huskily, deep in his throat, perhaps guffawed would express it better; he clapped his hands and showed high approval.

The Pasha, watching his master through a curtain's chink prepared for the purpose, mopped his brow and allowed himself the privilege of sitting down.

After each short dance, the artiste prostrated herself, practically touching the ground with her forehead, as though she were a bondmaiden being dragged by some slave-master into the presence of a depraved sultan in ancient Khorassan.

The artiste appealed immensely to Farouk. It would almost have been possible to have put her entire garb into a small envelope, hardly straining the flap. Nature had endowed the lady with a pair of bold blue eyes – and the ability to make the most of them; a gift she never missed the chance of using.

Farouk was now enraptured. He applauded constantly. He made the motions of jumping up and down in his seat. He might have been a boy of nine at a pantomime. Every now and again he shouted: 'More! Oh, more!'

The rest of the audience did not seem to share the King's undiluted enthusiasm. The dancer was recalled by Farouk until she had been almost an hour on the stage. Eventually she made a most captivating curtsey and ended the act. But Farouk kept on clapping.

Each time he stopped she curtsied again. The entertainment looked like going on indefinitely.

The girl was so overcome by the royal approval that she tripped fairylike almost in front of the King and made a special impulsive curtsey to him. Her eyes rolled and she looked so demure that Farouk jumped up and down in his seat and clapped the nearest pasha stoutly on the back. He was an elderly, thin man of small proportions and etiquette demanded that he show his pleasure at what sounded like a fairly heavy blow.

The order was given to a nearby Bey to get 500 gold sovereigns to give to the little lady at once. It is a night which must live in the heart of the dancer as all too rare in a hard profession. At the time of writing, this bonus was worth some $60,000.

Farouk thus paid well for his pleasure, but he was correspondingly unlavish when he was displeased. The European diplomatic circuit rang with tales of the distressed entertainers shipped home after Farouk had kicked them out...

And only the previous day, as a member of our party whispered to me; while driving, around dusk, along the lovely bank of the Nile, the King had passed a peasant and his family trudging wearily home to their village.

They had been up at perhaps 3 o'clock that morning in order to get their produce into Cairo. They were too poor to own a donkey and the husband and wife pulled the heavy cart all the way there and back.

They had stood in the market-place all through the heat of the day, selling their vegetables and were exhausted. The peasant failed to notice the royal car in the growing darkness – he was probably wondering whether the ailment he had, known as Nile foot, would get better; or how long he would be able to walk if the disablement became worse.

All unknowingly, the poor honest *fellah* had insulted the King. He ought to have thrown himself on to the ground as the royal car passed. Farouk had the car stopped, stepped out, and the man was shot dead before the eyes of his wife and two children.

The previous week, we had attended a reception given by his Majesty to a really third-class troupe of Western dancers. Abadin palace in Cairo, no less, was the scene of the festivities. The pashas and beys, sycophants of all kinds, were in full court dress, their chests strung with medals. One of the pashas, whose decorations included the Legion of Honour, had pinned it awkwardly underneath his left arm.

The women guests were from all ranks of society. Different though the backgrounds were, the only topic was the King. They referred to his goodness, his devout religious observances, and his greatness. The King could do no wrong. And the guests did full justice to the fare. To call the meal anything but an Arabian Nights banquet would do it less than justice.

There were stuffed chickens and glazed chickens. Whole animals and whole fish, treated to look as they did in life. These latter interested me and, on having some, I discovered that the outer skin was real, although it must have been cooked, because it was soft. The inside was of the consistency of potted fish, and delicious.

When I praised the food, an equerry brought forward the head chef. Well-briefed, he gave a long speech. French cooking, he declaimed, was wholly derived from the Arabian cuisine, learnt by the Frankish campaigners of Outre-Mer during the Crusades, before which no French cooking had ever been heard of...

'Even if it's not true, it's a good story, and well founded chronologically,' the Italian Ambassador said to me. Coincidentally, he had been saying how good but underrated Italian food was.

There were jellied soups, dozens of meat pastries, ice cream chocolate-covered *bombes*, pistachio and rose-flavoured ice creams, puddings, meat and fish balls, immense baskets made of spun sugar, filled with whipped cream and glacé fruit.

There were fruits and vegetables such as full-sized pineapples, potatoes, cabbages, carrots and cauliflowers: all in marzipan, looking so realistic that unless you saw them cut, you would not believe they were not natural.

There were dozens of different kinds of salads, as well as over a hundred other elaborate and more recognizably Egyptian dishes.

Farouk enjoyed himself immensely. He liked to put his favourite foods on the guests' plates, measuring their appetites by his own.

I thought of the emaciated Nile boatmen, the scraggy *fellaheen*, the malnourished children, as I memorised the fare.

There were literally thousands of sandwiches, small gateaux, and a table with all kinds of fresh fruits, jellies and drinks.

There was what a pasha called correctly 'heavenly trifle'. In it, was more than the usual allowance of sherry, judging by the scent which was wafted to me when the Pasha spoke.

On a table nearby, which ran the whole length of the great room, there were stuffed eggs, and dozens of dishes I had never heard of. There were immense golden platters of French chocolates, and colossal silver ones containing Egyptian nougat, marzipan, and delicious Turkish delight in mounds of white, red and green.

This was followed by black coffee, cigarettes and cigars. The Egyptian appetite is a thing to be wondered at. It just does not seem possible for a human being to be able to eat so much.

The results, in the form of the grotesquely rotund members of the Court, spoke for themselves. I wondered, for a terrible irreverent moment, what the food writers and gourmets of the West would make of such a display. I even went so far as to ask a young man standing nearby. 'Their grandmothers have never even heard of such things,' he said, equivocally I thought.

In spite of the guests having done extremely well during the three hours the banquet lasted, there seemed scarcely any diminution of the amount of food as we left the dining room. I tried to guess what the stricken waifs and strays of the Cairo streets would think if allowed to come in their thousands and help themselves.

As Farouk said goodbye to each guest, he seemed genuinely happy to have been our host. How long, I wondered, might such gargantuan feasts continue to be held without some retribution, some reaction? I had temporarily forgotten the crusading look in the eyes of many of our young Egyptian friends – a look that said we were witnessing one of the last orgies of its kind in Egypt.

Every shop in Cairo, without exception, exhibited at that time, a large framed picture of the King, usually in a prominent position. This was not the law, but if any shopkeeper thought to disobey, he had as a caution the tale of the day the police came to the shop of a man who had failed to observe this custom. For six days the shop remained closed, nor was the man seen. Then some days later he was observed being led about by his small son. His face was bandaged. Others spoke of the tortures he had endured. His eyes had been burned out.

Later this man became insane from the pain. Nor was he the first to suffer this. Nowhere in the world, even in the least so-called civilised place, was it possible to see such pitiful misery as in the streets of Cairo, any and every day.

Fragile wisps of humanity, whose ages ranged from six years to eleven, ill-clad and dirty, begged all the time. Their faces were scarcely human. The skin was drawn so tightly over their ancient-looking faces that they showed hardly a human trait. From dawn until dusk they haunted the streets. Some hawked lottery tickets, and at night they fell into whichever hands would give them a bite of food.

One small child, I remember particularly, used to sell lottery tickets. Her hands were bones covered with wrinkled skin and her eyes had the hostile, beaten look of a hunted criminal. Her face was no more alive than a plaster cast.

I took some clothes and food and walked along where I used to see her every day. At last she came, and I told her the parcel was for her. I handed it to her, but she refused to take it, replying as though I had asked her to jump into a fire. Suddenly she turned and ran as fast as she was able.

I spoke to a woman in the street about the child. She explained that these children had no parents. Some of them had been stolen when quite young and there were houses that were 'home' to a dozen or more of them. Sometimes there were as many as five men in one of these houses living on the earnings of the children. When clothes were given to one of them out of pity, the child was afraid to take them back to the house in case the men thought that other men had given them the things, which would have meant a beating for the child.

They returned to these houses at night with what they had earned, and were then sent out to beg for food. If they got any they were allowed back to these houses to sleep. Everybody, including the police, knew this and nothing whatever was done about it.

Near our hotel, there was what appeared to be a meeting-place for girls and boys. It was really the place where girls handed over what they had collected selling lottery tickets during the day. The boys were not more than fourteen. The girls queued up in front of a closed shop, and the boys counted their takings, checking them against the number of tickets left.

I have seen a teen-age youth banging the head of a child of about eight against the wall; seen children kicked and thrown viciously onto the street. The passers-by took no notice, except that some of them would give the child an extra kick for getting in the way. Had I interfered, I would have been seen merely as another of the hated foreigners: and that was enough at that time in Cairo.

Was not the cause of all this trouble and hunger and cruelty, the mismanagement which took place during the period of British hegemony, when London effectively filched Egypt from the Ottoman Turkish Empire? That at least was what everybody was told. Quite a number of people believed it, too.

In fact, it seemed more than likely that the dreadful oppression of the people by the Faroukian monster-state had simply hardened many of them to such an extent that they did not know what they were doing.

For instance, no foreigner surely had taught the Egyptians to belabour their animals – quite unnecessarily – to such an extent that they died? People were so callous that they were destroying their own property in ways such as these. More, when I shouted, in Arabic, 'Don't beat that animal!' quite ordinary, respectable-looking citizens clustered around me, roaring with laughter . . .

Again and again the noise of shouting and drum-beating brought us to the windows. We had our first taste of what became an everyday experience within hours of our arrival. The shouting rose above the din of raucous klaxons, above the compulsively flailing whips, senselessly lashing the already tractable, sometimes even choice Arabian horses and the general din of the street. The hotel manager had all the window shutters closed.

Presently a mob of hundreds of youths packed the streets from side to side, carrying banners and sticks. All were shouting at the tops of their voices.

In the centre of the crowd, a coffin was being borne on the shoulders of six young men. Many of the boys were weeping. The waiter who brought my tea explained with a compassionate shrug that it was only a student who had been killed in an affray with the police, because last week a policeman had been killed by the students. It was a case, he said, of an eye for an eye. The police and the students were old enemies, he said.

'But won't the police now break up this crowd?'

'The police will come presently,' he replied, 'at a safe distance.'

And so it was. Ten minutes later several truckloads of steel-helmeted police passed. The vehicles were moving slowly, and the police, never very stalwart, looked very afraid. Some were biting their nails, while others looked around furtively, as though expecting to be ambushed in the middle of the street: something which had, indeed, happened before.

'What do the King and the Chief of Police say?' I asked.

'The Chief of Police, madame . . .' and here the waiter raised his eyes, lowered his lips into a half-crescent, and shrugged his shoulders. 'The King,' he continued, 'knows nothing about what goes on that the pashas do not care to tell him.

'But one day, by Allah's mercy which is over all, this will cease. It *will* cease. Give us time.' It was the first of many times we heard this expression.

Many college students had no respect for discipline. If they wanted to strike they did so. Al Azhar is the oldest university in the world and its ways are still mediaeval. But at least all its students, from every part of the Islamic world (and in contrast to custom at the secular universities), got free lodging and a loaf a day. According to Muslim tradition, to charge for imparting knowledge is forbidden and something practised only by infidels.

Sudanese students had been imported to receive tuition at various institutions which, in the case of Cairo at least, offered little in the way of useful education. The rulers of Egypt, as had many of their predecessors, coveted the southern Nile Valley country, with its million square miles of often lush land.

The Sudanese youth, brought to Cairo, were to be converted to Egyptian ideas. They were to return home 'educated'. Many eagerly accepted the bait. Then, apparently, they were simply forgotten. A deputation of them told me they had not received any allowances for months, and they were almost starving. No application to the heads of their institutions was ever heeded.

Yet Farouk's propaganda was so thorough in the Sudan that when I told the students there what the real conditions in Cairo were, they would not believe it. All they could speak of were the tantalising 'wonders' of Cairo! They had seen films, they had read articles, they had heard lectures. I wonder whether those many Egyptian 'journalists' who crowded the Grand Hotel's bar in Khartoum had anything to do with these opinions.

The pashas, we were told, were the real evil geniuses of Egypt. Most of them, although there were exceptions, had risen 'for services rendered' to Farouk and his late father, King Fuad. The 'services rendered' must have been considerable, since they warranted palaces filled with expensive replicas of Louis XIV furniture, 'Arab elegant' as it is sometimes called in the West...

Many a pasha was for some reason indispensable to Farouk; or he had been a friend of the late King. The wealth of these men grew. They purchased lands, or were given them by Farouk in his generous moods. They owned the latest American limousines. Their lordly feet scarcely ever touched the pavements. Their parties outdid any except those of the King. Their wives were often in seclusion but those who were not were as important to social climbers as the air they breathed.

A small gift such as a diamond ring or a pearl necklace, or a trifle like a sports car, given to the lady, was known as the shortest route to the pasha's ear. After that anything was possible. The gift led to the first rung of the social ladder. A present could even be essential before an ambassador could obtain a meeting with the Foreign Minister.

Several of the pashas gave parties for us and they certainly knew how to dance attendance on a woman. To begin with, a flowery invitation would arrive. The house of the pasha, it proclaimed, awaited. Naturally, one always went chaperoned...

On the day of the dinner or luncheon party a monstrous chauffeur-driven car would appear and whisk the guest through the dusty rubble of the Cairo streets with hardly more sense of motion than there is on a down cushion.

If unable to exist without sustenance for the twenty minutes the journey to Heliopolis took, one only had to push a gold button with diamond centre, and thereupon sandwiches of half a dozen kinds revealed themselves. There would also be bottles of fruit juices and iced water.

At the palace, the car would glide through the gilded gates, up to the door, and the car door would be opened before one realised the vehicle had stopped.

My first such visit laid the pattern for all the rest. The Pasha, handsome and immaculate in well-cut English clothes, received me and my lady-in-waiting. A perfect rose was given with a courtly bow, such as Queen Elizabeth the First might have demanded as her right.

There were many neatly-turned phrases of welcome as we climbed the few steps into the house. We were taken into the reception room, stiff with brocaded French furniture. A beautiful antique Persian carpet covered the floor. I was careful not to admire it; for custom dictated that, had I done so, it would have been sent to us as a present.

The flowers in the silver vase, I was told, were plucked by the hand of the pasha himself; that only the best might be placed there in my honour.

There was a massive servant in pale blue uniform standing to attention nearby, probably to promote confidence, since no other ladies were present and none had been mentioned so far. This was a country where women of the moneyed class generally went about together in droves.

Yet could that have been a whiff of Chanel as we came through the hall? Was it imagination, or did I see the toe of a gold slipper peeping from behind the curtain?

Coffee was brought. It was black and bitter. I do not like coffee, but this is to the East what a cocktail is to the West, and I drank it. It is a pity I could not appreciate it, because it must have been the best. 'Real Mocha,' beamed my host, 'the berries are picked especially for me from certain bushes on the Red Sea shores . . .'

Luncheon was announced. We passed into the dining room, a beautiful and spacious hall, its furniture and floor all of polished walnut. A table groaned with silver and Venetian glass, against a perfect eau-de-nil lace tablecloth. The napkins were equally grand; there was but a tiny centre of linen, or was it cambric? The plates and the cutlery were crested.

There was a spray of rosebuds and maidenhair fern at my place. The Pasha noticed that I was wearing beige and said the flowers would be wonderful pinned near the collar. The servant held them while he performed the operation. It is wonderful, he said, how flowers may be complemented. This made me rather embarrassed, because I did not feel I deserved this remark.

I said that he must have had great fun choosing all the crockery, furnishings and so on in Europe and America. For a moment the Pasha looked puzzled. 'Oh, that!' he said, 'I have people to do all that for me. I am glad that you approve'.

One course followed another. The cooking was all French. It was delicious, and I regretted that my appetite was not capable of dealing with every dish. Fleet-footed silent servants waited upon us. Like our host, we had to wave away fully three-quarters of the twenty courses.

By the time we reached the point where the finger-bowls were distributed, (these had two perfect velvet damask rose leaves in their depths), we knew we had eaten too much. The sight of more black coffee and a large box of 'selected' chocolates seemed excessive.

It had been a wonderful meal and the pasha made an interesting and informative host. We drank even more coffee, then were invited to see the rose garden. It is a difficult job to grow roses in Cairo. The grass too, which is usually brown and coarse, was here emerald green of the richest hue. It was quite an oasis in the sunbaked surroundings. That grass alone and those roses must have cost a small fortune to produce. Meanwhile the Pasha was telling me touching anecdotes about the King.

'He is a wonderful man . . . so honourable . . . so kind . . . The King calls me by my first name.' The climax came when he fixed me with a stare which he must have reckoned to be of the most aristocratic kind and declaimed: 'His Majesty has actually employed me as his *Porte-parole*. I have spoken his very own words to others!'

When leave-taking came, I was handed into the car, where a giant box of chocolates had been already placed. I was given another rose and told that the garden would miss me, and would look for me again.

My companion was seated in the front of the car by the butler, and I was thanked for having loaned my presence to the luncheon. Then the pasha bowed low and the car slid away, bearing us back to the hotel. What more courtesy could any woman desire?

At the pashas' parties the food often came from Groppis, the famous restaurateur and confectioner. The Cairo restaurateurs were the most understanding in the world. In the middle of dinner, perhaps, or during a cabaret performance, the lights would suddenly fail. The manager would apologise. He did not need to trouble because everybody knew the reason. However, he insisted, it would take but a minute to put right. '*Mesdames, Messieurs, un moment, s'il vous plaît!*' And that is just about the time it took to convey two anonymous diners to a remote palm-shaded corner especially reserved for them.

Anonymous, that is, until the waiter whispered the names: it was good for business. 'It is a matter for regret,' said our waiter once, 'when the husband of a lady with power and money finds himself too occupied to act as her chaperon.' Very dangerous talk indeed, when the escort is the King: but this man was one of the myriad Greeks living in Cairo, and braver than most.

Professor Yusuf Shawarby, the Sirdar's representative in Cairo, related to us the true story of the shoes for the fellaheen, of which he had personal knowledge. Every now and again the King had moments when he was moved to think of the poor of his country.

One of the pashas, whose job was supposed to be concerned with the land-workers, reported that the fellaheen were nearly all suffering from 'Nile foot', and that this was due to their going barefoot. Nile foot causes deep ruts in the soles of the feet, bringing great pain and general discomfort. Farouk listened to the tale, and gave the order for a large sum to be put aside to provide for footwear.

21

Every fellah was to have shoes, good strong ones. Shoes, though, are to the fellaheen of Egypt what a mobile telephone would be to a beggar in England.

The narrator said that the pasha had named a large sum because after all there are many, very many, fellaheen. The pasha, it was said, began to turn things over in his mind. Fellaheen after all were fellaheen; never in their lives had they dreamt of a gift of shoes, let alone from the King. In cooler moments, it appeared to him to be ridiculous to give shoes to such people. Still the King might remember to ask and it was not wisdom to stutter over a reply to royalty.

Then the pasha had an idea. He would carry out the King's orders and yet hold back the steed of extravagance. He would supply the fellaheen with sandals. Sandals would be a fraction of the cost of leather shoes.

These fellaheen, he said to a close friend, are but slaves. If they leave the service of their king, nobody else dares employ them. How wise a man was Farouk to have made this unwritten law! Anyway, the Professor confided, although pashas were all supposed to be equal, they were certainly not: that idea, like history, was a fable agreed upon.

It was no secret that Farouk favoured some of the pashas above others and gave them handsome presents. The poorer ones had to mix with these wealthy ones, and how was it possible to dress, give parties, dress one's family and provide dowries for numerous daughters unless there were little perquisites? Anyone could understand that without over-exercising the mind.

The pasha gave an order for a colossal number of sandals, which were duly delivered to the fellaheen. This footwear was never worn. One does not give dancing shoes to deep-sea fishermen.

What mattered most to the pasha was that even after (so far as he knew) every land-worker had been supplied with sandals, there was a very satisfying sum indeed left

22

over. It was a sum which the pasha, it was said, needed and could usefully employ himself. He was also able to report to the King that his order had been carried out, and the Arabic saying that 'little by little the bird builds its nest' proved its truth.

The Professor added that the sandal pasha was 'as well-known as the Devil, and for the same reason'.

The lot of these shoeless small farmers did not end with their toil. Every morning at 5 a.m. they entered Cairo with their wares. Early as was the hour, their carts were piled with vegetables; all clean and artistically arranged.

Sometimes at a given point in the city they would find a mounted policeman waiting for them. Each peasant was required to have certain papers, allowing him to sell his crops. We used to watch the drama – of little consequence to us but far from little to the peasant – from our window. It always followed a similar pattern.

The mounted policeman would order the man under examination to untie the strings fastening the threadbare saddle of his scrawny donkey.

The expression on the face of the poor man was always pathetic: he seemed to be saying that he was late and that the knots were many.

The policeman urges his horse forward and kicks the peasant. Then the knots are untied. It takes a long time. The man is old. How he managed to get the immense load from his village to Cairo is another story. He is obviously tired and nervous.

If, as is usually the way, there is a large hidden sore, the man does his best to hide it by raising only an end of the saddle. The policeman motions that the saddle is to be removed. This is done and the awful sight exposed.

But the policeman does not see this now. He is examining the man's papers. He hands them back. They must be in order, but he looks at the donkey's back and waves energetically along the street from which the peasant has come.

Evidently the man is to return, and will not be allowed to proceed to the market. He is ordered to go home. The poor villager places his hands palms up and hands together and raises his eyes to Heaven. Heaven is far, but the policeman is on the spot.

There are some minutes of argument and supplication, until the peasant puts a hand into his garments and pulls out a few scraps of dirty, tattered paper money. He gives some to the policeman, looking at it as he hands it over as though it were his death sentence. The policeman takes it, thrusts it into his tunic, and waves him on. He'll get to the market after all . . .

After the policeman had dealt with half a dozen of these fellaheen, he would draw his horse to the side of the street where we could see him counting the various sums he had extorted from the meagre store of his victims.

This was the very same policeman who, the night before, had passed when I watched a vicious mugging actually being carried out – and had taken no notice.

The result of all these abuses was the rise of a number of secret societies. The leader of one was shot on the steps of the Young Men's Muslim Association. The matter was hushed up. The other members were imprisoned.

There were concentration camps to which anyone might be sent without trial. These places were out in the desert, miles away from anywhere. The heat was awful, and the treatment worse. I spoke to some young men who had been in one such camp.

Their only crime was that they felt the inhumanity to millions as though they themselves suffered, and they had declared that they were willing to give their lives to alter conditions.

Some of their friends died, and they returned home more dead than alive themselves. Their eyes had seen horrors that their demeanour made all too evident; they did not need to speak. Yet these young men still held their high ideals. They wanted their country to be respected and they were willing to give everything to bring this nearer.

The Cairo police did not inspire confidence in any single respect. They were dirty. Their clothes were put on just anyhow and, as a citizen said, looking at a particularly unappetising specimen, 'they are worse than their friends, the criminals they are supposed to apprehend'. They kicked and struck the homeless children of the streets. And they held all the aces.

A woman lunching at the hotel was telling me how she had to tip the local police patrolling officer to look after her house, which was in a lonely part. She said her radio had been stolen, and she knew the officer had taken it; there were even witnesses. She hadn't paid the man enough.

She asked how much we gave our police for similar duty in England. When I said we dared not tip our police, she said, 'Of course not officially, but I mean when nobody is looking!'

All the letters we received had been opened, and clumsily gummed up again. Whoever did it was not in a hurry over the matter. We received some airmail letters in the middle of January which were postmarked in England in November. Registered parcels and letters we never received at all. As to the letters sent out by ordinary unregistered post, only about five per cent were received by the addressees.

That was before we were warned not to write anything against Farouk or Egypt. I have realised since how near I came, by some of my references to the condition of Cairo, to a visit from a certain young police captain. I knew that he was charming, for he told me so. He said that although he was a married man, the ladies treated him as though he were a bachelor. I am afraid if he spoke the truth he would not be able to add any remark made by me at the time.

The shopkeepers spoke with nostalgic reminiscence about the good trade they had, while the British and American soldiers were in Cairo. 'Your men know how to spend money,' they used to say, 'they throw it away, you have only got to catch.'

When I was house-hunting, an Egyptian woman showed me a tall block of elegant flats, fifteen storeys high. They belonged, she said, to her cousin. '*Wallahi!* – by Allah! there was a woman for you. There was a woman in millions. You would die laughing,' she assured me, amid peals of laughter, 'if you knew, and I am going to tell you, how she got that place.'

Madame was a very stout woman. All three chins wagged as she laughed, and she repeatedly wiped the tears from her eyes.

'Tell me the story,' I urged, thankful at the thought of there being something in Cairo at which to laugh. I felt I would survive whatever it was. 'You'll never stop me!' she roared.

The story was hardly hilarious, and could be retold in a few words, though it took this woman over an hour to recount it, no doubt with embellishment.

During the war, fighting the Italians and Germans in the Western Desert, British troops visited Cairo on leave. This lady 'sold' them large quantities of tourist gifts, knick-knacks, kaftans and so on for their families, and undertook to send them by post to Britain.

But – 'of course' she never actually posted the goods at all. I asked what would happen if one of the soldiers came back to say that the items had not been received.

'They never did. Perhaps they were killed. In any case, too much stuff was going to the bottom, torpedoed by the Germans. That would have accounted for the loss. As for this lady: a lovely block of apartments for nothing!'

Her English was terrible, but there was nothing wrong with her business sense:

All English and American boys always send to modder. We laff and laff. They say: 'This good scarab ring, my modder she like. My cousin say yes because a good ring.

26

Anodder boy say his momma she like what you call bracelet. Anodder say his momma want bag. My cousin say bag with picture of Pyramids is good. Boy say it is great. My sister say it is just right, it is she say ch---eep. He is soldier, bag is cheep to him. Other boys say lace. Lace cheep too. All boys buy lace. Big big lots. Huntrets soldiers coming buying everytink! English and American soldiers funny.

The be--u--ti--ful gifts those boys bought! Lace bedspreads! Lace teacloths! Silver necklaces! Scarab jewellery! They paid her postage, and a leetle for packing, they had plenta money. Spend! Spend! What you guess? My cousin never send no parcels. She put money safe away. Poor mommas no get pretty things from Cairo! No matter! They think nice boys forget mommas.

'But if the parcels were registered,' I said, 'they could be traced through the Cairo main post office.'

Nobody ever trace nothing at Cairo post office. They try, Cairo post office say, 'I let you know. We finding out.' Ha! ha! ha! Long time finding out. My cousin she take chance. Everything chance! Marriage! Life! All chance! Before war my cousin poor woman. Another war I take chance too. Nize nize boys English, American! I like!

After that I sent no more parcels from Cairo. Moreover, if I looked at souvenirs, I either demanded what was in the window, or bought nothing. Somehow the ones from the boxes lose a lot of the glamour of the ones exhibited. It's a way some items seem to have in Cairo.

The *Ikhwan* – the Brotherhood, was a powerful underground party. These young and not-so-young men sought to reform many things they knew to be wrong in Egypt. Their idea was to reform the entire Muslim world, by bringing back the simple faith of Islam.

They were against all forms of bribery or licentiousness, and stood solidly for religious principles. They were opposed to the elaborate way of living then fashionable in Cairo and other cities. Farouk had them sent to the desert of Sinai, where they were put in concentration camps, and treated with the utmost cruelty.

After many had died as a result of their tortures, Farouk allowed the rest to be released. We spoke to a number of these young men. They were all educated and intelligent, and if they had been given the chance, might have served their country with distinction.

As it was, some were so embittered that they had turned into religious fanatics, capable of terrible acts, as so often happens to idealists when they are unable to make progress towards their vision.

At that time Farouk's position appeared, on the surface at least, to be so secure that nothing could unseat him. It is necessary to know Farouk's Cairo to realise the almost insurmountable task that the liberators of Egypt had.

Shortly afterwards there was half a page in a Cyprus newspaper extolling the virtues of Farouk. He was said to be 'a good swimmer, strong as a bull, a teetotaller'. There were hints of abusive articles about him having been planted in a British paper.

Farouk and his queen, Narriman, were at that time honeymooning at Capri. Farouk recounted how he had given a fifty centimetre cigar to Winston Churchill and how that gentleman had demanded a looking-glass in order to view himself and his mammoth cigar from all angles. Farouk said he was 'much embarrassed' at the behaviour of Mr. Churchill, 'in the middle of an official occasion'.

Farouk continued that Oriental people had to be careful of their dignity. It is amusing to hope Farouk was explaining about that dignity to Mr. Churchill when the cigar was presented.

For the reason of this same dignity it seemed that

Farouk preferred to spend his holidays in Capri, although, according to the article, night life there had so far been confined to the house. However, he and Narriman did allow themselves a dance now and again and 'a glass of orange juice'. When the waiter removed the glasses, Farouk and Narriman would 'go for a walk in the moonlight.' What puzzled Farouk most, this journalist tells us, was why the British, 'who are neither Communists nor Jews,' disliked him so much!

Shades of Cairo night clubs! And of the dozens upon dozens of empty liquor bottles carried quietly out of the palaces in Cairo and Alexandria, and secretly disposed of.

Nobody at that time knew the value of the contents of the two hundred and fifty roomed Kubbah palace outside Cairo, where Farouk spent most of his time.

In the capital itself, the Abadin palace held a treasure trove of rare Persian rugs and carpets, Sèvres and Dresden china. Perhaps the Ras-el-tin in Alexandria was the more famous treasure-house, with its fabulous collection of jewels. There was a fine yellow sapphire necklace, jewelled opera glasses, diamond tiaras and full sets of first-water diamond jewellery, jewelled coffee sets and fantastic gold replica temples in minature.

The bathrooms had sunken baths and the walls were covered with nude paintings. There was a private theatre and cinema. There were telephones in every room. Farouk's private fortune was believed to total the current equivalent of six hundred million pounds in cash.

There is a magnificent ballroom in Ras-el-tin palace, where several hundred people usually gathered. The throne room had a wonderful mediaeval French tapestry chair. The walls were painted in seeming gold-filigree in the Moorish fashion. The carpet was a priceless Ghiordes. An immense carved gold star on the wall behind the throne chair enclosed the name of King Fuad, Farouk's father. The windows were curtained in beautiful satin and heavy silk mirror-like velvet.

One night after a banquet, the talk turned to the hobby of collecting stamps, coins, bric-à-brac, etc. and one guest after the other spoke of his acquisitions. I remarked that my coin collection was a humble one compared with some which had been mentioned, but that I had several of the first Afghan stamps from the time of Amir Sher (literally 'Tiger') Ali Khan.

These stamps are circular, and are intended to show the head of a tiger. The impression was made with a large sapphire seal. The seals were of immense value and remained in Afghanistan until recently.

Farouk was all interest. Were they for sale? The moment was an awkward one, because the King was always indulged. Farouk said he had almost every other stamp, and what offer would be acceptable? I said the stamps were in England. A Pasha said they might be brought immediately by air, and before I knew what was happening Farouk was being congratulated upon his acquisition. 'They are worth anything you ask,' cried some pashas to me. 'To sell to His Majesty is indeed an honour,' added others.

I told one of the pashas in an aside that I was a collector, not a stamp dealer. These stamps would eventually be given to the Afghan nation, for their famous collections. They were part of the patrimony of my adopted homeland.

I began to fancy that Farouk, staring at me, was looking like an epicure might on being offered fruit-flavoured yogurt.

Perhaps to change the subject, as the atmosphere was getting a little strained, the pasha now said that Farouk was the greatest ruler in the world, and the most beloved, and that his well-known generosity was about to take one of its most delightful forms.

'His Majesty,' said the pasha, 'will of course lead the way.' We fell into line in the wake of Farouk. We traversed long deeply-carpeted passages, all brightly lit. We passed sentries who presented arms. Not a word was spoken. Most of the artists responsible for the large canvases decorating the walls had apparently been of the opinion that the acme of beauty lay in the naked form although each appeared to have his own predilection for the feminine part he considered most worthy of his attention.

We must have been ten minutes on our winding way, or was it an hour? At last the crocodile of guests stopped. A door of some importance was evidently being opened. There seemed to be some difficulty about the key. Later we realised that there were four locks.

The door we saw was tremendously thick and solid. There were two sentries in the passage outside. The room was a blaze of light. It was a colossal place, and the lights were so powerful that it was like looking into the sun. Then all of a sudden the blaze from the chandelier was turned off and others sprang up. These were crystal candlebra shaded in pink, placed on tables throughout the room. But the lights, remarkable as they were, were dwarfed by the things upon which they shone.

Never since the days of Ali Baba, whose jewels were supposed to have been greater in quantity and quality than any before or since – has such a staggering collection been revealed to the eye.

There was not a word spoken. Farouk was pointing to a vast canvas depicting a full-sized figure of a nude examining a necklace. 'The artist who painted that,' he said heavily, 'committed suicide because he said he would never paint anything so exquisite again.'

We passed in wonderment through this room crammed with gold and silver, tapestries, Louis XIV furniture, jewels, china, other exquisite pictures and bric-à-brac.

More corridors, carpets, chandeliers, and again the line stopped. We had descended two flights of steps, quite an undertaking after the many delicacies of the banquet. One steel door was opened. Then another. Then a third. Another great blaze of light sprang up in the room we were entering. We felt like conspirators. It was like the old days in India when the Maharajahs had shown us their State jewels.

'Here,' Farouk was saying, 'is a statue of Minerva.' We crowded round politely. The Roman goddess of War and Wisdom was over five feet high. The statue was in fine gold, which looked almost liquid.

But Minerva was only one of many. Aphrodite was there, the goddess of love who rose from the foam at Paphos, across the sea in Cyprus. She, too, was of similar height and in the same material. Farouk touched each with the connoisseur's quiet pride. There were dozens of smaller goddesses – all in gold.

Beautifully executed Turkish gold tombak inkstands, flower vases, paperweights, cigar and cigarette boxes. Angels (baby and grown-up), ash trays, bon-bon boxes, trays, tea and coffee sets, epergnes. Everywhere feminine charms were revealed. Books which were in reality boxes, and boxes which were books. And a revoltingly-realistic cobra with diamond eyes, so naturally hooded that one was stricken with fear at the sight.

'That cobra,' said Farouk, 'is one of my jokes. I sometimes put it in the bedroom of foreign guests!' He demonstrated by placing the wretched thing on the ground, whereupon it wriggled across the floor, and then rose almost on to its tail in the attitude of striking.

The women screamed, at which our host clapped his hands and roared with laughter, stamping his feet like an excited child.

We passed into the next room, which was also brilliantly lit. Here the tables were in reality glass-topped showcases. There were immense glass-fronted cupboards, in which were dazzling displays of diamond jewellery. 'This,' said Farouk, 'is the collection of a favourite of Louis XIV.' There was an enormous stomacher in large liquid diamonds, which sent out every colour in long scintillating spikes.

One becomes used to seeing Eastern collections of jewels, and Western jewel emporiums, but our breath caught in our throats as we examined the necklaces, bracelets, rings and earrings. 'How much are they worth?' I ventured to ask.

'Some say thirty to fifty million sterling pounds,' a pasha replied. 'The workmanship is excellent.' We passed into another chamber.

'The stamps,' said somebody in an awe-struck whisper, as though he had been a worn-out traveller catching the first sight of Paradise.

My knowledge of philately is fair, but I had no idea how minute it was until that night in the Ras-el-tin palace.

Nobody seemed to have seen anything like what now entranced their eyes, although a number were collectors. There were immense cases and frames filled with stamps; cupboards too. Piles of rare postal covers, with every variation of postmark, lay stacked in one case.

The collectors among the guests pointed wordlessly here and there, and looked questioningly at each other, some of the stamps were such rarities that we had only heard of them.

The next room was devoted to sculpture. Many pieces were such as one sees only in galleries. Beautiful, without doubt, if one is an artist or sculptor. Considered rather daring by those not interested in art.

Around the room were placed beautiful gold chairs, upon which admirers might sit. There were other lovely pieces of French period furniture.

Millionaires and others in the West, with something on their minds, often broach a subject during tours of their art-collections – I knew that from previous experience. I was therefore not over-surprised when the King led me into a side-room and had me sit on one of his sumptuous sofas.

'Just a word while you are here.'

'Majesty?'

33

'Twice, during the ancient and Islamic periods, Cairo has been the centre of the world.'

He looked at me closely. 'Do you know what I mean?'

'Under the great Pharaohs, and again under the Fatimites, Mamlukes and others.'

'That is correct. Emerging from the desert, the Muslims carved out the greatest empire the world has known. They penetrated to China and India in the East, to Vienna and France in the West. They occupied all of Spain.'

There are a billion Muslims in the world today, more than a fifth of its population, still spread from Malaysia to Morocco, and from Bulgaria to Brunei. They all know the bald facts which Farouk was reciting. Why was he telling me, who might be expected to know this already?

He was now slightly breathless, his eyes flashed, and he thrust his enormous head forward, chin up, as if addressing an audience, Mussolini-style.

'Yes, your Majesty . . .'

'Islam introduced education, culture, science and art to the West. Today it has no overall leader, no Caliph. It needs someone like Haroun El Raschid, like Saladin, like Ataturk of Turkey.

'And I am that man! Tell your husband. Assure him that all facilities, in money, in personnel, in training, in anything, are available. Just tell him I, the King, said so! He will know what to do.'

I nearly laughed, but Farouk's little red-rimmed eyes behind their tinted glasses were fixed on my face. Fat, ridiculous Farouk a Caliph! Ruling from Sarajevo to Sarawak? With night-clubs and pashas in Damascus, Samarkand and Bukhara . . .

'Naturally, Majesty, your remarkable message will be passed on as you instruct, in the fullest detail.' I had been present at enough diplomatic occasions to know the terminology.

The tubby King looked at me and grunted. 'Good. Now we can join the others.'

To me it was the last room which was the most memorable. As we entered it there was before us a larger-than-life figure of Nefertiti, seated upon a gem-studded throne. So lifelike were the features, so full of expression the eyes, so soft and appealing the mouth, that one halted, almost expecting to hear her speak.

All around were heavy ornaments and jewellery in gold: gigantic pure gold sarcophagi; gold chairs with lions' feet and lion heads; statues of the gods of the Pharaohs; magnificent figures of the kings themselves, of their sons and wives; hundreds of effigies of slaves, and Nile boats; exquisite Egyptian-blue beads and other jewellery.

Looking at this glorious collection, whether at modern items or those thousands of years old, one felt the drama of present-day existence slip away. The museum in Paris, or the one in Cairo, have not the beauty nor the power of this collection to transport one into the very life of those far-off days. Here one felt a member of the royal house of the Pharaohs.

The extraordinary 'feeling' of that room in Ras-el-tin palace and the presence of those mute but expressive things which had once accompanied those legendary kings to their last resting places and had kept company with them in their tombs for two thousand years, was one of acute resentment.

I had the weird impression that the figures had become animated and looked with loathing upon those whose contemporaries had had the temerity to disturb their rest. The beauty seemed to fade from the gold figures, and there was a feeling of warm, damp suffocation, as there is sometimes during the Indian monsoon.

I made my way to the door. There seemed to be unseen hands behind, propelling me forward. Fortunately the party was leaving. Later, when speaking of all this to an old European egyptologist, he said his opinion was that some of the evil which he believed was embodied in these ancient relics – evil practised by the priests at the time of the Pharaohs – had been invoked through the presence of a reincarnation of those times, present as a contemporary person among the guests.

All the way back I had that nasty feeling of being followed. Only when the last steel door was securely closed did I feel free from whatever the thing was.

I see from my diary that I did all I could to collect information about the supposed ancient curses and hauntings of the tombs and artefacts of Egypt.

People, it seems, get the ghosts they want: no Egyptian I spoke to had any idea of the images and imaginings which Western people harbour about their country. They all claim that the innumerable tales, books and films about evil mummies and the like are entirely invented or imagined.

There is plenty of occult lore in Egypt. What makes it all the more interesting is that none of it coincides with Western reports and beliefs. In other words, we carry our own ghosts with us.

As our car sped us homewards I kept wondering about the colossal wealth in Cairo and the abject poverty and I wondered whether, after all, things had changed so much after all in Egypt.

The words of a Muslim sage to whom I had spoken the day before came to me too, 'Islam does not forbid the accumulation of money, provided there is a good proportion of it given to alleviate poverty.'

That night I fell asleep thinking of how the proceeds from the sale of only one of those gold statues would have had the power to bring joy to the hearts of the thin waifs of derelict humanity who haunted the streets of Cairo, and that no collection of jewels or bric-à-brac would ever have the same power to interest me again.

We were told later that we had not seen the Secret Room, which was heavily barred. It was said that therein the heir to the Pharaohs kept all his 'choicest pieces', whatever that might have meant. After some exposure to the wonder which is Cairo, that could have meant anything...

2

The Nubian and the Locust

We arrived in Jedda in the afternoon, on one of those blazing hot, sticky days. We stepped out of the boat which ferried us ashore, vowing never to travel anywhere again, as long as we lived. Just nowhere. The wanderlust would have to be thrust away; definitely, positively.

We were now being shepherded to the Customs – called the *Jumruk* in those parts. I was tired of telling officials in half a dozen countries that we had nothing to declare. Nevertheless they were, as usual, as conscientious as terriers after rats. 'Where,' I wanted to ask for the hundredth time, 'since the last Customs rummaging, at an unbelievably underprivileged port, would it have been possible to collect dutiable goods?' Scarcely in the incendiary atmosphere of the Red Sea.

But it doesn't do to annoy officials in the East, any more than in the West...

We drooped against some nearby railings. We were tired and dirty. Suddenly, the whole atmosphere seemed to change. A handsome Arab, dressed in *agal* and *kafiya*, the Saudi headgear, and in a long gold-embroidered cream *mishla* (robe) strode up, positively radiating authority. He spoke shortly to the rummaging Customs man, whereupon that official quickly and respectfully closed our cases and turned towards other prey.

The Arab who had stopped the performance was joined by several others, who had come towards us. They said they had been sent by our host, King Abdul-Aziz ibn Saud, to receive us.

'*Marhaba,* – you are welcome, this is your own country,' they chorused. First they shook hands, and then they placed the palm of the right hand to the breast, over the heart. The greetings over, we were taken to a sleek Cadillac, into the depths of which we were grateful to sink and hide our grubbiness. I began to feel like a tramp might, on a charity outing.

In no time, we reached the guest house. It was a tall, white building, dating from the Turkish period, with lofty rooms, electric fans in the ceilings and with beautiful latticed windows. A graceful verandah ran around the second floor of the building, providing shade, a place to sit without being seen, and a touch of mystery: for it had formerly been the external dimension of the women's quarters.

Here there were more people, more greetings, in Arabic so flowery it made me wish I was attired in more than ordinary clothes, to appear to deserve the compliments.

It was at the building's entrance that we first became aware of Najib. Very tall, coal-black, smiling and dressed in a gleaming white, shirtlike robe with a broad sash, he looked every inch one of the staff: certainly a highly-trained servant. People even seemed to treat him as if he was working here. He certainly was, but working for whom was not clarified for some time.

The temperature was at a giddy height and we took a lot for granted. That included accepting people, especially anyone as useful as Najib. No sooner had we arrived than he was shouldering our luggage and asking where our accommodation was.

Later, much later, some stray remark of the manager led us to realise that he thought we had brought Najib with us. But the latter had apparently simply appeared and made himself indispensable. We then assumed that Najib had been sent by our host, as a personal servant. Anyway we wanted to keep him. The denouement was much, much later . . .

39

We agreed that Najib had adopted us. He was not a
talker, and his replies were trimmed down to a minimum.
He did tell us that he was born in Nubia, part of the
Sudan, just across the water from Jedda. We were to note,
he said with unaccustomed emphasis, that he was a Nubian, nothing less.

It seemed easy to appreciate how he dreamed his
dreams of coming to Jedda. For, we romanticised, is not
the opposite side of a hill or road or river always the more
attractive? How often he must have shaded his eyes as he
looked through the haze of the Red Sea and thought, 'over
there is the place for me'. Life on the other side of the
water, the Holy Land of Islam, held out promise which
the Nubian boy simply had to sample.

Having travelled confidently and arrived, full of expec-
tations, he must have found that work is pretty much the
same everywhere. What is more, it can be even more of a
disillusionment where one is alone and a stranger. All this
knowledge must surely have come to Najib slowly and
painfully, as to all those who are forced to face reality. Yet,
with the ingenuity of his worthy race, he had clearly
arrived at an agreement with himself; at least he was able
to do that.

Once there, he had not the money for the return trip,
nor would he have it until such time as he had saved
sufficient from his labours. He would therefore, doubtless,
resolve to get on with the job, and make the best of it.
Perhaps that was how he had come to turn himself into
our servant?

One might guess that, having come to this decision, he
had made another, equally binding: that of never allowing
the least relaxation of his masklike expression while on the
wrong side of the water.

He was honest, energetic and untiring. Whatever he
did, he somehow endowed it with importance and, often,
zest. He would knock and then enter a room as though
we were a beleaguered few, and he carried news of our

immediate deliverance. Najib swept the rooms and laid the meal table while creating a baffling aura of significance. Nothing he did was ever done in the ordinary way, but it was done as he wanted it.

When the other boy did things wrong I was always nervous lest the amount of correction, the ear-cuffing whose reason was almost never explained in words, might do harm to the boy. I do not think the victim knew half the time what the punishment was for.

Najib was tall and broad-shouldered, with a distinct air of authority. When on duty, the other servants were humble before us. Najib was never that; perhaps conscious that his name, in Arabic, meant 'Noble'. He would take orders from us, and carry them out to the letter, but one had the feeling that he kept saying to himself, 'it is only for a little while'. The Nubian people are a proud race. If one fails to show them consideration, which generally means no more than politeness, their pride immediately shows through.

We got on well enough with Najib. From 5 a.m. when we had our early tea – because it was cool then – throughout the long hot day of fetching and carrying, until eleven o'clock at night, everything was done with despatch.

Najib wore a small soft white cloth cap, whose position tended to indicate his current feelings. When he was annoyed, the headgear was pushed well forward. When delivering messages from callers, the hat sat straight upon the top of his head, almost as if it was a ceremonial object. On Fridays, when he was dressed for the mosque, there was a carefree latitude about his walk, and the cap clung somehow to the back of the head.

'Dressed for the mosque,' in his case, meant simplifying, not elaborating, his costume. I asked him why he removed his cummerbund before prayers. 'Allah approves of simplicity,' he answered. But for the midday congregational prayer on Fridays, he wound a white

41

turban around the cap. Was this not an elaboration? 'No, it is the Example of the Prophet, Upon him Peace.'

No time of the day was ever given to whistling or singing. If Najib had done either, it would have been like laughing in our faces; and that was unthinkable.

When the short afternoon siesta came, or his duty was over at night, Najib retired to the broad corridor, took his bedding roll from the window-sill, extracted the thin mattress and transferred it to the floor. Upon this he placed himself, wound his quilt tightly around his body, and lay thus mummy-like until the dawn prayer. This was signalled by the nearest muezzin, using the approved method to determine the break of dawn by distinguishing a white from a black thread, and giving voice from his minaret accordingly.

I sometimes wondered how Najib ever returned to consciousness from his torpor. When I reported to him about lizards in my bedroom or a shower of crickets on the bedspread, I seemed to sense his pity for me. Western education, he must have thought, has its drawbacks. He would tell me that lizards are harmless; that crickets are kept by many as fortune-bringers.

If I did not appreciate this kind of, to me, recondite information, he would instantly sense it and turn heavily away, emitting a sound midway between a sigh and a groan and pushing his hat farther back on his head. My lack of a proper cultural background must have appalled him.

A request for a less grimy or uncracked plate seemed completely untranslatable to him.

He would pick up the offending article and look intently at it, as if trying to observe the shortcoming, to see what I meant. As to the germs to which I constantly alluded, he for long kept an open mind.

'Germs – bacilliyaat,' I said, from time to time, pointing to cracks or a grubby dish. He looked, I think, upon these references to germs as remarks I could not help making.

He learnt that the best thing to do was to take the dish away, and quickly: perhaps lest I get a turn for the worse. I must have seemed completely mad, with my cries of 'Germs, Bakteriya, Illness!'

I asked him, eventually, what germs were, because the penny seemed to have dropped. He was a long time gazing at his toes, then he said he thought they were *afrits* – evil spirits, which only I could see.

'There is a woman in our village,' Najib continued, 'who can see spirits, when other people cannot.' I said that was almost correct, and after that there were no more cracked dishes.

One day he explained that the afrits were tiny but potent ones which lived in the cracks in the dishes, adding that there were now none of the demonic plates left. He said that they had all 'slipped to the ground' and been broken. I wonder whether the manager ever heard the story.

Before we left, I told Najib that it was better always to have plates without cracks. He said that this seemed to be a useful and unusual piece of wisdom: some of the staff who had been ill had recovered since the 'slipping of the dishes', and Najib told them that no cracked plates should be allowed henceforth to harbour trouble-making minia-ture devils.

As he said that, he looked so authoritative, so like the reincarnation of an ancient Pharaoh, that I felt like a slave whose work was to toil at the building of the pyramids.

When he swept the sitting room, if I happened to be there when he came, he pointed with his switch broom to the bedroom, indicating that I was to go there during the cleaning. If any of the other servants had done the same, I would have felt annoyed. When Najib pointed the way, it was as though an emperor of ancient times asked me to precede him, so much dignity did he invest into a mere gesture.

During the day, we passed and repassed through the

passage which was Najib's 'bedroom' on our way in or out. By day the space was empty, save for a roll of bedding placed on the wide window-sill. That and a large wooden cupboard comprised the furnishings.

Here at night, Najib slept. Here, at the five daily prayer-times he spread his mat, and gave account of himself to Allah. If he wasn't there at prayer-time, it would be a Friday, and he would be at the mosque. And there was no nonsense like days off for Najib. The two annual festivals and most of Fridays, and that was it.

At the end of each day, when duty was over, to his bed he repaired, and before he slept we sometimes heard the clink of the heavy silver riyals, the Maria Theresa dollars, thalers, which were the local currency.

These were counted and put carefully away, no doubt against the day which would bring the excitement of buying the return ticket to the Sudan. No Western blandishments in the souk, such as cola or cigarettes, caused Najib to rob his savings of one riyal.

One never saw him chewing surreptitiously, like the other servants, who were mesmerised by American 'candies' or those sweet refreshments which acted as magnets to the hard-earned riyals. 'I have to save,' he said, 'until I return home.'

This only excitement of the day over, we heard him intoning passages from the Koran. This would be followed by the final prayer of the day.

Usually he was punctual with the early tea. Sometimes he was not. On such occasions I used to awaken him by banging on the wall. It was then that I learned to envy his sleeping abilities. Sometimes the knocking was loud enough to bring the porter hurrying to see whether the place was on fire or murder was afoot.

In Jedda the doors of the old merchant princes' houses – which this one had once been – were solid and heavy, with strong fastenings – long, two-inch thick iron bars, fitting into stout metal hasps. I soon discovered that it was possible to make a noise loud enough to wake Najib, and, I discovered later, everybody else in the building.

This was accomplished by banging the bar of my door up and down on its hasp. It was no pleasure to make the din, and I indulged in it only when the heaviest of ordinary knocking failed.

One day I realised there were rats, or at least one rat; and one is too many at such close quarters. It gnawed away somewhere inside the huge window frame, kept quiet for a while after we made a noise to frighten it, and then carried on. There was simply no way to dishearten that rodent. During the night it worked like a cross-cut saw, hour after hour, giving the idea that there might be dozens of its kind.

It was not a fast worker but a thorough and determined one: probably, I imagined, a Najib of a rat, devoted to duty . . .

It was obvious that its destination was my bedroom, and it was correct in its estimation that eatables were to be found there, such as biscuits and chocolates most of the time, and that the result was more than worth the labour.

Najib was summoned, with much hammering, and told. Yes, he pronounced, it was a rat, but there were many such in Jedda, owing to the proximity of the ships. The rats, he said, had 'tee--th! s--o long! They often bit children in their beds. Only last year . . ! .'

'Yes,' I interrupted, 'but what about this one?' He looked at me with a puzzled expression. Perhaps he was wondering what the country I came from was like, when people made such a fuss over just one rat.

However, he left the room saying he would get something or somebody. By and by he returned with the boot boy, who was carrying two large bricks; there was also a boy with a sack, and a man with a ladder which was clearly never intended for use in cramped indoor quarters. He had the look of workmen the world over, when they seem to be present for ceremonial reasons, or to provide moral support.

'Why the bricks?' The bricks, said the lad, were for the killing. One was placed on the ground, like this, then the rat...

'Please!' I begged, 'not here.' (The killing, I meant.) The boy explained that some rats had red hairs in their whiskers, and a very few had completely red whiskers, all red! This was lucky, because it was possible to sell one single red hair from a rat's whiskers for a riyal.

These red hairs were money! And the more red hairs the more riyals! The small boy asked whether I might be expected to claim the rat, on account of the red whiskers. I quickly reassured him on that point, and the crew now looked as if they were going to get down to work.

The boot boy said that, if there were red hairs, he would carry them for the time required for the magic to work and would then sell them.

'What kind of magic?'

'Riches, winnings at gambling games; enough money to build a house, and live without working.' In short to become a Sheikh, not forgetting the automobile. The ladder man now said that some people were too fond of their own voices.

'How,' queried the bootboy, ignoring the remark, 'was anybody to know the magic was gone?' He would have emptied all magic out of the hairs before he sold them. And he laughed, 'Hee! hee! hee!'

Thus would he have both the money and the luck! And that, he considered, was a full cup.

Najib broke in upon these pleasant surmises by saying that the one who brought about the death of the rat got the hairs. No doubt he was thinking of the counting of the riyals that night.

Besides, Najib continued, hammering away at something at the same time, the rat was really mine. I told him quickly that the animal surely belonged to the manager. This, they all agreed, was not to be considered. The manager already had more money than most people, owing to the fines he imposed on such as themselves. '*Na'uzbillah* – we take refuge in God. Everyone there had been "let blood" – done out of money – by him.'

I asked what a magical whisker was worth. One said there were those who had money and only required good luck. His voice rose as the hammering became louder.

The bootboy said he thought money was good enough luck in itself. The man who had brought the ladder asked who knew what a headache such a thing as the possession of money might not give, and that only those who were short of tooth (young) spoke without thought upon such a burden. The small boy said he knew a man who would give him a riyal, for even the smallest red hair.

The ladder-minder held that young men who were heirs to fortunes were always the ones to approach. They had money, but were foolish with it; and if they were foolish to the extent of believing that a red hair from the whiskers of an unclean rat had the power to divert Allah from what he had willed, they deserved to lose their fortune.

The boot boy said that people with ailments were good buyers. He said too that during the last pilgrimage a man with red hair stayed here, and that 'there were many riyals in his hairbrush'. I knew now why there was always a scrimmage for the wastepaper basket in my bedroom.

He continued that some of the purchasers who bought the combings in all good faith had an intuitive feeling that something was unusual, and said they thought the hairs were rather finer than usual, and was the rat a new kind? These sagacious enquirers were told that it had been a bad year for rats; food had been scarce, and the animals were thin, thus making the hairs likewise. In the end, only half the usual price had to be accepted – because thin hair must betoken thin power.

All the time, Najib had been working away. The rat took little notice of the opposition. Not wanting to see the use to which the bricks were put, and knowing the excitement which was rapidly growing would not consider my feelings when the catch became imminent, I went to another room.

Much later on, I asked about the rat. It had been caught, Najib said. It was a black rat, not more than a foot long, just an ordinary rat, with black whiskers. Yes, with black whiskers. Later, another servant told me that there was a *hakim* – medicine man is as good a translation as any – in the souk who would bleach the hairs and then henna them. Then they would be quite red.

He and the bootboy were to divide them. What about Najib? Najib, he said, had the last rat all to himself, the one which had gnawed the two babies. That was a one of some boldness, and it had quite a few red whiskers, which had saved the middleman's price. There was a lot of expense with the black ones, while there was no hesitation in asking as much as two riyals for each really red hair.

'Why not ask the same for the dyed ones?' I asked. Ah, the dyed ones would be examined, and people were clever, whereas if you quickly mentioned a small price, they thought they were getting a bargain. Even rich people always preferred bargains. They were greedy, you see...

Najib appreciated that the few pieces of jewellery I had with me were precious. One day a ring rolled somewhere and being in a hurry to go out, I had no time to look for it. On my return, I found it placed conspicuously on the dressing-table. A half-opened matchbox stood upon its end, and the ring was put therein.

So far as Najib was concerned, it had no value or interest for him, except what must have seemed a peculiarity of mine. He had his riyals and I had my playthings, and that was that. He had an amusing way of hanging my hair-nets on nails on the wall, and my stockings in the veranda.

He had the poorest opinion of chests of drawers and wardrobes, and his philosophy regarding them was simple. Rats, he believed, not to mention moths and cockroaches, liked these places made of wood, got into them and worked unseen. Thieves, too, were encouraged to open doors, and drawers, whereas if things were left in conspicuous places, the rats and cockroaches were afraid of the daylight, and the thieves had the same kind of fear. This was a long explanation for Najib, and he ended by saying that only Allah's mercy had been responsible for the rat making a noise and being discovered.

Then a locust arrived on the veranda. He was almost the dusty colour of the wood and so streamlined, so beautifully compact, that he looked like a new type of car, in miniature.

His eyes were round and sparkling black, which added to the resemblance of a streamlined limousine, for were they not the well-protected and cunningly placed head-lamps? He sat perfectly still: probably he had come a long way. In any case, whatever had caused the parting from his swarm, there was nothing repulsive about this older-than-time pest, which, with millions of its kind, flew in invincible formation, miles in length and breadth, and landed here and there upon the green crops, leaving the entire countryside completely devastated.

Often on our travels in India and Arabia we had seen what appeared to be a dark airborne mass coming nearer and nearer; denser than any cloud, and quicker moving. Presently we had seen the cloud near enough to recognise it as myriads of locusts. I thought at such times of the locust-control men in their lonely tent near Jedda. Cut off from everything, choosing to live like that, far away from other human companionship, farther away from ease and any semblance of comfort, because they had made it their job to study this practically undefeatable scourge.

Najib told me that a number of these insects, toasted over a fire in a shovel, were a tasty bite, and that he had often eaten them when he was a boy. I did not encourage the conversation.

Carefully, he took the creature from the veranda window. He held it in a peculiar, certainly expert, way, so that its wings were pinioned. It was about three inches long. I had not much interest in it, realising that its relatives were probably stripping some orchard far away. After their long flight through the dusty heat, the agricultural patches must indeed seem green and pleasant.

Later, we had occasion to visit the Locust Extermination squads, which are doing a great job, under the worst possible circumstances. Passing through great stretches of thousands of miles which is the territory of these squads, one realises how colossal is the task they have undertaken.

No wonder one of those men living in the tent said there were days when they got on each others' nerves so badly that they never spoke a word to one another. The aim is to attack the laying grounds. There are thousands of miles of sand, baking hot, to be negotiated, and only by trekking through that vast expanse, can one begin to understand a little of what they are up against.

Why, I kept wondering, do they do it? One seldom hears of them. There are no advertisements which encourage young men to join the Locust Extermination Service and see the world. There are neither drums nor uniforms. Just heat and dust, loneliness and sand, everywhere. All the time. How and why do they do it, I ask myself.

Najib liked to shop. He was happy to be sent for English and American goods. He liked the packings; the rustling paper, the pieces of fine string, but most of all he liked the tin boxes in which the biscuits came.

The opening of the tins was always interesting to him. First the transparent outside paper was carefully removed, then a knife was run round the lid. Then, when the top was taken off, there was the excitement of removing the tinfoil. This was done with a key supplied for the purpose.

Najib would stand, scarcely breathing, while the foil was cut all around. Every now and again his fingers would twitch as though he longed to do it himself, and then, happy moment, both foil and key were given to him. 'Is it silver?' he asked. No, it was tin.

He pursed his lips and turned his head to one side. 'It looks like silver.' Then he would be given a few of the biscuits. These he wrapped carefully in paper and tucked into his cummerbund, rolling each separately, for the eating was a private affair. When the box was empty it was given to him as well.

Once when we passed through the corridor where he slept, a cupboard door was open. There, in a trim stack were the empty boxes; beside them was a neat pack of the tinfoil, and the straightened-out papers which had been used to protect the biscuits were all likewise carefully piled and tied with the precious thin string.

Najib kept an eagle eye on the biscuit box, and as soon as we reached the last layer, he reminded me to get more. Soon he began to bring boxes of starch, and other products in only marginal demand. He did not understand why some boxes, such as biscuits and chocolates, were so important and others not. As he had got the boxes of starch and the like on approval, no harm was done.

Later, he said that when the pilgrims came to visit the holy city of Mecca they had need of empty boxes and he sold the stored ones to them. They did not give much for them, but it all added up, and eventually he was able to change the Egyptian *qurush* (pence) they gave into riyals. Not often, he said, but gradually.

As there was no green to be seen anywhere, he one day put a rhubarb leaf – only one – in a vase on the dining table. It took me some time to recognise in this ordinary leaf, the family to which it belonged.

I had never noticed, it seemed, the delicacy of the

veining and the sight of a large green leaf where no leaf might be expected excited me. If obtainable elsewhere, I resolved to work a rhubarb leaf into future table decorations with striking artistic benefit. But when we arrived in a place where there were flowers in plenty, the implausibility of the idea became manifest. Circumstances alter cases.

When we left Jedda, Najib wanted to come with us. We asked him why. He said he would like to see flowers and trees, as he had seen them in our magazines. Besides, he had done all he could do in Jedda.

Some years later, visiting the Aliens' Office in Khartoum, in the Sudan I was delighted – if at first amazed – to meet him again. I was more than interested to hear that Lieutenant Najib of the Special Branch, formerly on undercover duty in Saudi-Arabia, was now a Captain.

How had he played the part of the houseboy so well? 'We have servants of our own, you know,' he said. We had many a laugh about rats, afrits, cracked dishes and silver paper . . .

3

Woman in a Man's Town

The words of an acquaintance in Cairo came back to me as I sat at the breakfast table in Jedda one day. He had said, 'Why on earth do you want to go to a place like Jedda? It's as hot as blazes now, and by the time you get there, midsummer, phew! It will be sizzling! There's only one hotel where a Western woman can stay and anyway, it's just no place for a woman.'

The man was right about the heat, but I was on my way to Mecca. At that time, foreigners – even diplomats – were not allowed to the capital, Riyadh, so all the legations, consulates and embassies were (supposedly) located in Jedda. In fact, as I learned from my many friends in the diplomatic community many of those accredited to Saudi-Arabia, chose to reside in neighbouring countries and visited Jedda only occasionally.

Jedda – ancestress, is so named because an enormous, probably prehistoric, burial-mound was touted – until the end of the Turkish occupation, early this century – as the tomb of *Umm-Hawa*, Mother Eve. People made pilgrimages there, especially women seeking fertility. The Saudis, Islamic puritans of the Wahabi sect, soon stamped that out and it took another fifty years before Jedda yielded to the pressure of events and became the thriving metropolis it is today.

Now, of course, you have sweeping highways, glittering shop-windows, air-conditioning and hygiene, under a prosperous administration; then, one of the sights of the

53

town was a large goat, climbing like all his kind to the top of a pile of something or other...

Not so very many decades ago here, my English breakfast here consisted of two eggs as hard as golf balls – of course I had asked for them soft-boiled – served on a meat plate with no sign of an egg-cup, and accompanied by a knife and fork of large and workmanlike proportions.

On another large plate, there were several inch-and-a-half thick chunks of bread, badly singed. The butter had liquefied and was served on a soup plate. It tainted the hot air with a pungent effluvium. On a small saucer, there was what the flies recognised before I did as jam – and they intended to have it.

Breakfast over, the table was cleared and the problem of ventilation presented itself. The heavy wooden Venetian-like shutters of the beautiful old Arabian mansion which formed the hotel were, as always, down.

Would it be advisable to put oneself to the labour of raising these, for the sake of some oxygen? Open, they would surely give free access to the flies, the anger of the sun drinking in the sky and the loud noises emanating from the nearby school...

Then there was the acrid and choking smell of tar, which was being spread over the road below by a scarlet-faced American guiding a huge yellow machine performing the modern miracle of asphalting. All that, or just leave things as they were and be darkly asphyxiated? The noise filtered through the windows. I listened to the regularity of the corporal punishment from the school – it decided me upon asphyxiation.

As early as 10.30 a.m. the absence of outside air won. The gradual decrease in this necessity of life, you might think, is in itself an unbearable discomfort but when accompanied by odours seeping under the four-inch gaps which are left under doors here to encourage ventilation, it is even more problematic. That is to say, there was undoubtedly ventilation; but it came from the smallest, but not the least obtrusive, room in the house.

After a few futile attempts at raising the window slats I determined to go in search of Abdallah, whose work it really was, even though energetically-minded women like myself thought they might like to try.

At that time, my knowledge of Arabic and Abdallah's grasp of English might well have been described as painful. We communicated most of the time in dumb-show, which rarely meant the same thing to both of us at the same time.

With my handkerchief acting as a buffer between me and the 'sanitation', I discovered Abdallah already sound asleep on the window-ledge of the room where he slept.

Calling loud enough to wake Abdallah is not one of my accomplishments. There was nothing left then save to do the job myself. Those windows had to be opened, and at once.

The first stage is to step out onto the wide outside balcony (which later on, at the height of the crowded pilgrim season, will be used as a bed-space). Next, firmly grasping two frighteningly-corroded semi-circles which may have been brass in days gone by, one takes a deep breath and heaves with both hands.

Some considerable agility is required, and a pious incantation quickly spoken. If these have any power, you find you have raised the thing to a place where there is, on each side, (or is intended to be) a folded down iron 'arm'. This nasty rusted object, I saw, ought to have been pulled out, gate fashion, before starting the hauling.

If you forgot, or did not know, you must now lower the shutter with double the care you took to raise it. It now feels as though it weighs a ton. If you have not forgotten, then you are the proper person to deal with Jedda windows; and you will have the necessary dexterity to place the weight of the shutter on those extended arms.

There are three windows and four shutters to each, so that there is plenty of time for excitement – and practice.

Still what has been achieved once can almost always be done again.

There was no doubt a time when this particular window arrangement was new; high-tech even, perhaps oiled, and the process more simple – but it could never at any time have been easy.

Those must have been the days when the security of the window-arms were a thing to remark and depend upon. Now the hinge-fastening hung on a few rusty nails and a prayer.

After breaking two finger-nails, barking a shin and receiving a thick cloud of pre-Turkish occupation dust in my face, I tried to assess what had been achieved.

I also admit to a feeling that I would be able to report victory to friends, in the form of, perhaps, an amusing letter home. This vanity was soon punctured, however, when I mentioned the matter to a local Sheikha, wife of a grandee.

'Servant's work? I don't advise it, *habibi* – darling ... Where was the houseboy?'

'Asleep.'

'You should have beaten him!'

I only managed to retrieve that situation by reminding my haughty friend what the Holy Prophet's widow had said, immediately after his death. People were collecting every scrap of information about him, so that it would never be forgotten. Someone asked: 'What did the Prophet (Upon whom the Salute!) do at home?'

The widow answered: 'He helped in the house...'

It was no use expecting cool air to come off the Red Sea at that time of the day. Light there certainly was, blazing at incandescent strength when all windows were opened; there was also a wide view of part of the town, houses, the street and the sea.

To the left were streets bordered by sunbaked, ancient, Arabian merchants' mansions, for all the world like a series of giant dusty honeycomb sections placed on end, and just as securely sealed. Did the inmates, of whom there must have been thousands, breathe happily through all the surrounding miasmas, or had they some form of gills, through which non-oxygenated air became cool as mountain breezes?

Away to the right, the Red Sea shimmered. To the left there were some half-dozen stubby minarets, not like the graceful and extravagant ones seen in Delhi, Istanbul or Cairo, because this is the Muslim Holy Land and the Saudi Arabs do not allow the ornate in religion.

To them, minarets (classified as *bida* – innovations, since they did not yet exist on mosques in the 7th century, at the time of the Prophet) are tolerated for the five daily calls to prayer.

The houses remained closed and tight shut, as a ship's hold is battened down when rough seas are expected, and never once in weeks, did I catch sight of so much as an attempted flicker of an opening.

I found myself, isolated in my rooms, becoming so inquisitive about those distant windows that I seldom lost an opportunity of staring at them. Watching became something of an obsession with me. I began to think perhaps there was some rite of communal window-opening at a certain time, which I would not have missed for anything.

I became like a marooned watcher on a desert island, afraid to lose time searching for food lest a ship come and go during his absence. Perhaps the windows had all been opened, and the people had come out and waved, during my siesta?

Just in front of my range of windows was the road, on each side of which European-style shops were being built. Jedda might be old-fashioned so far as sanitation goes, but even then it was up with the latest where limousines – they can hardly be called mere cars – were concerned.

As soon as the heat of the day was over, round about five

p.m., there was an inundation of cars, in all the delicate colours of an English flower garden.

The explorer, (H. St. John B.) Philby, was the local representative for an American car manufacturer. At that time he was frenziedly selling cars in pastel and two-tone colours to young sheikhlets, both the camel-rich ones and those beginning to benefit from the trickle-down of large oil royalties through Aramco, the Arabian-American Oil Company.

He called himself Abdallah – Slave of God, and spent as much time as possible trying to please the venerable King ibn Saud. Everyone was sure that he was a British spy. He was the father of Kim Philby, the British intelligence officer who later defected to the Soviet Union. People blamed old Abdallah Philby, however, much more for the nuisance caused by the cars than for his putative spying.

One Saudi princess, surrounded by handmaidens and visitors, explained at a party, some of the Arabian attitudes towards such 'spies' as Philby, which she had gleaned from her husband, who had been educated in the West:

'You see, my dears, we must try to understand these infidels, these *kafirs*, who are becoming more numerous and intrusive. They have peculiar ideas.

'There are no military and no political secrets here; but western people are obsessed with collecting information nevertheless. They publish it in books, booklets, and in journals of all kinds.

'I would not be surprised if Abdallah Philby was collecting information on five-legged camels, which he would then write about. Once in print, such information causes these people to give each other awards, much as we would to battle-champions ... Philby and most infidels are misguided, but harmless.'

The khaki-clad policeman who stands, it cannot be comfortably, in stiff laceless leather boots, whistle in hand, just outside the hotel, has a busy time. But he is never too occupied to receive friends who thread their uneasy way through the cars, to shake, and sometimes to hold, hands.

Intricate salutations are exchanged, bows, hands on hearts and foreheads, and occasionally embraces. Some of these greetings are sedate, as becomes the status of the traffic director, whose chief has the power to order a man to be beaten almost to death. That he is said to be not averse to the proceeding is the purest gossip.

Other greetings are less formal. Sometimes at nights, from the shelter of the veranda where I sat, with only the hotel lights to disclose their presence, the policeman and his friends indulged in little games with boyish lightheartedness.

Sometimes they snatched and blew the policeman's whistle; sometimes he left his point-duty and chased them; and sometimes they would be standing talking when another would stamp heavily upon their feet.

Saudi-Arabia is an 'appearance culture': one in which appearances count most, not inhibitions. For this reason, childish pranks are all right providing people who might disapprove do not see them . . .

When the traffic regulators were otherwise engaged, the press of vehicles directed itself as best it could, and cars could be seen running along the pavement, while pedestrians had to dive for shelter. Cats and goats fended for themselves miraculously.

Slim young men passed on their way to drink coffee or cola at one of the cafés. In the half-light, one might have easily mistaken these youths for girls in evening dresses. They wore long white *galabias* and their dainty bobble-edged headcloths were caught to their heads by the traditional black, double-corded rings supposed to be derived from the camelman's hobble. Their thin, delicate hands fluttered as they talked; and their laughter was soft and musical.

Sometimes on the hottest days they wore, cloak-wise, a

black, semi-transparent, gold-embroidered *mishla*, which gave a distinctive air and graceful look to the wearer. Such a garment is often awarded as a robe of honour; and it is believed by some to be the model for the original of the Western academic gown.

The world's oldest university is in Cairo and in the Dark Ages, Arabian places of learning kept knowledge alive even for western scholars. When such seekers-after-truth returned to Europe, however, whether from Andalucia or Baghdad, they were often, like Pope Gerbert, called magicians by horrified churchmen. In the Middle Ages, the great Roger Bacon wore, like other alumni, a mishla at Oxford, as a sign of his graduation in the East.

At a café, preferably in the open in front of it where one could be seen, the youths would vie in outward signs of sophistication. To order tea was rather ordinary, while coffee should for preference be of the straw-pale, Nejdi kind: as drunk at Court, powerful and spiced with cardamoms.

It was, however, the height of sophistication to call for a bottle of cola and then – as if accustomed to such a treat every day – to take a mere sip and leave the rest to the admiring glances of the less fortunate. It could cost a labourer a day's work to buy a bottle of the magical drink, as seen in American films . . .

No Arab woman ever accompanies a man outside. Simply not ever. It is generally believed that women thus neglected, by western standards, get up to unwelcome pranks. Much, if not all, of this image is due to European fantasy in fiction, but many Arab husbands take no chances.

The simplest, probably oldest, and still the most effective method of masculine control is to place a chosen woman servant in charge of the ladies. This woman prefers to tell all to the husband, rather than have her wrist twisted beyond a certain point.

If she dares to tell any woman whom she watches of her

role, there are always others under her who have their eyes on promotion; servants are plentiful and easily sacked. The mistress of the house usually confides in her personal maid, yet she may well be – unknown to the lady – the house detective. Sometimes the wife who thinks she is too clever to be caught finds out that the walls have ears and can speak as well.

An Arab is allowed four wives by law, if he can afford them, and if he finds himself capable of treating them all alike. Few find that they can share themselves successfully among four women.

This legal caveat has been taken to mean that there should be monogamy: since complete equality of treatment is never possible between people. One is the rule, yet two wives or three are not unknown.

Therein lies the power of the mother of the first son. If she is fortunate enough to be the mother of Zayd or Kasim, the others had better not forget it. If they have no sons and have been disagreeable to her, or just if they have no sons, she will taunt them in the hundreds of ways the flowery elasticity of the Arabic language allows.

It is not a case of telling hubby when he comes home; he is not interested in womens' quarrels, and in any case it is an unwritten law that each woman fends for herself. The maids, like their kind the world over, are not averse to accepting hush-money if things become difficult.

Sometimes unpleasant situations arise when the older wife, married some years, and mother of the first son, finds out one day that a young sprite of a beauty with wealthy connections is to share with her and two other nondescript wives, the remaining quarter of their husband.

Any woman can understand the feelings of Halima in this unpleasant situation, falling as she does between the two stools of man's instability and the moneyed witchery of number four. Small wonder the coffee houses are always man-crowded.

Small wonder that the coffee is strong and black and

61

pungent and that the sound of the trik-trak counters can be heard, although not always seen, for most of the day in the cafés. These are the ways the men adopt of working off the tensions which have arisen or are about to arise in the domestic field.

Jedda was a man's town first and last. There was simply nothing for a woman to do, or anywhere for her to go. There were shops and interesting old houses but one could not spend very long seeing these. You would soon be labelled mad if you did.

Only a few servant women, closely veiled, make their way to the bazar. I put on an all-enveloping *burqa*, with a woven grille in front to see through, and glide into the souk. Merchants, mostly small grocers, avoid looking even at my muffled form. The heat is intense. Tins of Huntley & Palmer's biscuits vie for space with luminous ninety-nine-bead rosaries from Japan.

I look into the magician-chemist's shop, with its stuffed lizard dangling like a shop-sign. The magician-chemist acknowledges my presence only by repeating his litany of offers, face averted from the apparition which must be someone's housekeeper:

'Beauty in a bottle, oil of Java-Sumatra! Become a husband's delight for only five riyals! Energy pills, contain crushed pearl ... one packet only is left. Purgatives like demons! This badge will destroy the Evil Eye...'

A tremendous pale blue car which might be anybody's dream cruises past, driven by a handsome sheikh. It does not cause the slaving Yemenite housebuilders to raise their eyes one inch from their work.

An aircraft glides to the airport. Where from? Cairo, or El Riyadh? Who knows? Who cares? Perhaps, like the three which came last week, the planes are loaded with yet more French furniture, straight from Paris; fresh fruit and delicacies for the palace of a sheikh.

It could, of course, contain a grand piano, like the one

consigned from London the other week, and now the subject of intense discussion in the harims.

Saudi-Arabia is 'dry', and not a drop of alcohol may legally be consumed there; though British and other Western expatriates manufacture a really noisome drink called *Sadiki* – my friend.

But when a certain pungent, yellowish liquid started to seep out of the piano destined for the British Vice-Consul, Mr C. Ousman, he received a telephone call from the Chief of Customs: 'Perhaps you would be so kind as to collect your diplomatic baggage. Your piano appears to be leaking...'

There is delicacy for you in these matter-of-fact days!

Shortly afterwards, Mr Ousman was assassinated, though I was assured that the religious police, whose brief does not extend to infidels, were not responsible.

So far as the local men were concerned, before there were videos and television to watch all day, they had certain relaxations. There was hunting with tame hawks, endless feasting ('Tonight I shall take my dinner with you, O Sheikh' was the oft-heard formula) and religious harangues.

For women, gossip, children, clothes and a fair amount of (unauthorised) clairvoyance and the like were the main time-fillers. In the East, there is not the same chance for all women to cook. Work of any kind is definitely degrading; a woman who works is instantly regarded as relegated to the servant class.

Nor in most parts, is a perm possible, nor a smart coat worn. It is understandable that something must take their place, and why not the turn of a phrase, the polishing of a gibe until it has reached the final stage of undefiled sarcasm?

The power of the religious police was very great. It was also unbending. It was just not right for a woman simply to walk abroad in Jedda. She would see next to nothing, in any case, if she did. There are no fashions locally: clothes are made here or bought from Paris houses, to show off in the harims. Gadgets for home or kitchen were not required; after all, what are servants for?

There are no women's clubs, which are considered such a blessing in places far removed from Jedda. Those new cars take cargoes of women out when darkness falls. They must not drive themselves. It is a man's job to drive a car. Everything is a man's job in Jedda. Woman's place is definitely behind those closed shutters.

When the heat is over, our driver takes us along the shore road. It is beautiful. We get out and walk, watching the stars come out. After the jolting of the car, we enjoy the peace around us. Away ahead we see other cars, parked close by the sea.

There are a few veiled figures in the dark, but faces? Never. Just an indeterminate mass of drapery merging circumspectly into the coming night. An ant would have its work cut out to get between the mass of cars and the sea. Otherwise I would have been tempted to make a detour and prove for myself whether those figures indeed had faces.

Since the days of the Prophet, the holy men of various Muslim communities have interpreted Islamic teachings in different ways. Some insist it intends women to be completely invisible; others take a more lenient view, and say circumspection in dress fulfils the law.

Jedda is near to the holy city of Mecca, and there life is expected to be lived on more rigid lines than anywhere else. This cannot be otherwise, because there is something one can almost feel, as though the sanctity of the place were solid. So no woman who wants to be thought respectable goes out, except for an errand of absolute necessity. If she does go, she is veiled from head to foot.

When women go to Holy Mecca on pilgrimage, they wear the long white pilgrim garb, yet there, while they encircle the Kaaba, at the moments of deepest spiritual significance, their veils are discarded.

In the Holy of Holies of Islam, veils are *forbidden* to the pilgrims. Why? Because the veil in the form it is used today, was a badge of hauteur, not one of repression, worn so that the common people could not look at the lady.

4

To Allah's Gate

Jedda was blazing hot, even in the early morning.

I dressed in my simple pilgrim garb: a long-sleeved white cotton dress, belted. It was as plain as an overall and reached almost to the ground. The head-dress, a white nun-like veil, I tied across the forehead and secured at the back of the neck. White canvas flat-heeled shoes and white cotton stockings completed the ensemble.

The men wear a single, bleached and unstitched, cotton sheet wrapped round their bodies, exposing the left shoulder. The idea of these simple clothes, in the case of both men and women, is that all pilgrims enter the sacred precincts equal.

Today the excellent wide macadamized road between Jedda and Mecca makes the journey an easy and pleasant one, and motor buses cover the fifty-odd miles at a trifling cost. Distant and near, high ranges of rocky mountains hem in the valley road, round which there are great stretches of yellow-grey sand.

One catches glimpses of nimble glossy black and brown goats, surely the most attractive of their kind anywhere. These are attended by shepherds wearing trailing Arab garb and long black curls, such as were worn by their forefathers in the days of the Prophet.

Although I subsequently made the journey many times by air-conditioned car, on this, my first pilgrimage, I joined a traditional camel caravan.

At sunset the cool air descended. All around were spread the desert sands, which, so short a time ago, had been a rich saffron: but now the glory of the sunset was gone. For a short moment the setting sun had saluted them in parting, glorifying them in a mantle of royal gold. They had responded as if in farewell, showing here and there unexpected flashes of mauve and emerald, pink and delicate blue. Now the blanket of night rapidly covered their loneliness. We rose from our knees as, facing towards the Holy City, we ended our sunset prayer and began the quiet invocation:

Labbayk, Allahumma, Labbayk!
Labbayk, la-sharikalak, Labbayk!
Inna al hamda, wa an-niamata
La-ka w'al mulk!
La-sharikalak!

Here I am, O God, here I am!
Here am I, there is no partner to thee, here I am!
Verily praise, and kindness, are of thee!
There is no partner to thee!

In the desert, the hours of direct, blazing heat are long and the chill which comes with sundown is somehow always unexpected. It can feel like an eternity from the cool early morning until the sun sets. Hours when the simple necessities of life are understood better: water from a cool spring in the hills; a cool wind, perhaps rustling through a few trees. I would, I knew, never take them for granted again.

Even here, in the prosperous southern part of the Hejaz, a breeze may herald a sandstorm; and we soon found ourselves in one. As this devastating enemy rolls, the only thing to do is to wrap a blanket around your head and crouch down behind an obliging camel, until the sand-devils have danced themselves to exhaustion, by which time everything is filled with, invaded by, tasting of – sand.

I was on a Saudi camel, which is really a one-humped

67

dromedary, much slower-moving than the local steed which I found in Oman, but very like those of Afghanistan, where we had Bactrian (two-humped) ones as well.

Some women pilgrims travelled to Mecca in a *shagdaf*, a camel-litter: a sort of square house of cane over the hump. It was covered with matting, or even Persian rugs and shawls.

You have to make at least one desert journey to understand what this experience is, and how it somehow adds, for ever, to one's resilience.

The desert Arabs say that those who have lost the art of such travelling are cursed. They are not complete human beings, they aver. Further, they point to all the settled Arabian and Semitic civilizations which have, unarguably, collapsed and died. My caravan-leader, who had driven a taxi in New York for some years, said: 'We people of Father Ibrahim are always cursed and destroyed when we make cities our homes...'

When night had fallen, all at once I became aware of the powerful presence of the sky. The great, black shroud was now glittering with diamonds, flashing blue and yellow. They appeared so low as almost to be within reach.

As I looked back towards the woman beside me, a complete stranger, we both smiled, as if sharing a secret and yet, did not know what it was. Something seemed to come to life in me which, in the city, is deeply hidden. Modern civilization has no power to awaken this: which seemed a pity, because the feeling was one of such beauty and radiance.

I felt myself thinking, 'What a pity! In the West we have only literature, art, science, music, food, comfort – when we could have this...'

As we camped beside the road, a small fire, over which a shepherd cooked his evening meal, sprang up, then died.

We slept, and were woken as if in minutes, by the dawn, the call to prayer, then marshalled by the caravan-leader's cry: '*Rahla, Rahla!* – On, On!'

Many large cars, driven by sheikhs, went by at tremendous speed, going to and from Mecca, as well as wagons carrying merchandise.

The thanks and gratitude for this improvement in the safety and speed of travel along this road goes to the credit of the maker of Saudi Arabia, King Ibn Saud, who turned the once brigand-infested area into a peaceful highway.

Before the road was built, pilgrims negotiated this treacherous valley on foot, or by camel or donkey, oppressed by heat beyond description. On top of that was the danger of brigands who lived by plundering the unfortunate pilgrims. So unsafe was the journey that those about to undertake it said farewell to their friends and families. The chances were against ever seeing them again.

Now, although the journey is still just as hot, pilgrims are forbidden to walk during the worst of the torrid daytime.

There is a police post past which all intending visitors must go, and all must be examined before proceeding. Non-Moslems are not permitted in the holy city.

There is also a half-way house where food, soft drinks and petrol may be obtained.

The desert sand has immense beauty. Some stretches are smooth and golden, giving the impression of great waves of golden syrup. Others are so dark as to look like black treacle. Some are in sculpted waves, like a petrified sea.

Here and there, groups of camels seeking the sparse feeding provided by the desert, merge into the colour of their surroundings. The animals are often tended by women, who, as bedouins, refuse to veil their faces, this custom having been imported into Arabia after, and not with, Islam. I spoke to one nomad beauty about this, and she said, 'Such arrogance is for town-dwellers, not for real people!'

The camels are both clean and healthy and, remembering

their overworked and pathetic relatives in Egypt, look as though they belong here, which they do. There are flocks and flocks of trim goats which are sold to the pilgrims, to be used in ritual sacrifice.

The sun picks out the colours of the stones, the greens, blues and purples. The desert has few flowers, but the stones are of every colour when the sun shines on them. The rocks are so burnished by sand drifting that they appear to have been recently and laboriously polished.

An odd tree here and there adds to the loneliness. The small sage bushes along the sides of the road add their soft hue to the surroundings. Peace stands guard like a sentinel. The thought of holding on to it as long as possible comes softly to a mind beset by too much civilization. The tiny *Yarbu* – Jerboa, scuttles to and fro, seeking insects, in turn hunted by a desert fox . . .

If only life kept before us things like this, which are so necessary to us, perhaps its mad race would lose whatever meaning it has.

The silence fell softly on noise-assaulted ears, and it came as a precious and too-fleeting benediction. The tawdriness of present-day living, the meanness of humanity, marched in front of the eye like convicts on parade. If only – if only . . . ?

Recently-built houses of spacious and attractive appearance are now to be seen along the Jedda-Mecca road.

There is also a first-class garden which has literally made the desert bloom. Dr. Badkuk, the pioneer spirit who brought it into being, needed more than the usual courage of his nomad forebears to do so. Although many times his labour met with cruel disappointment on account of drought and pests, one being the dreaded locust, he carried on with still more labour.

Eventually a water pipe was laid, from a distance of forty-five miles, and now this government-sponsored project has more than compensated for all the difficulties.

The Director of this Experimental Farm relates, as he

shows wondering people around the grounds, how this and that grew and after how many disappointments. People drive out from Jedda and Mecca after the heat of the day and drink coffee under the trees, having seen the rare sight of tomatoes, aubergines, melons and other vegetables growing luxuriantly, surrounded by sand and bare steel-hard rocks.

In the past few years, based on this experience, thousands of hectares of vegetables have flourished.

As such pioneers have shown, the desert is not sterile at all, and needs only water to flourish again, as it did so many years ago.

I was long past the garden, but still thinking about it, when suddenly, around a corner, the Holy City appeared. It might have been any ordinary place; no notices, or advertisements, no adjectives worn threadbare by hopeful advertisers, just a grey quiet city. So quiet.

It seems strange now that somebody did not say: 'There it is', as would have been the case in Naples, or Rome when a famous building was first seen. None of us spoke. Only the pilgrims' whispered recitals of verses of the Koran were heard. Then we were entering the city gate, slowly and circumspectly. A few moments later we were being received courteously by the hotel manager.

Bathed and refreshed, we dressed and went by car to the main gate of the *Haram Sharif*, (the Noble Sanctuary) a magnificent enclosure which has 19 doors and in the centre of which the granite-built cubical building, the *Kaaba*, stands.

There are now electric fans which are used when the pilgrimage falls in the hottest weather, at which time the temperature reaches 130 degrees Fahrenheit.

We mounted the steps and, removing our shoes, entered in stockinged feet. The huge rectangular arena enfolds one immediately in its peace. The turmoil of the world which is 'too much with us' is easily left, along with our shoes, outside. Fears and sorrows, disappointments and griefs, melt away. There is a feeling of being a child again, without responsibilities, with that happy sensation of contentment and simplicity which only the child experiences.

Reverently we approach the Kaaba. Whatever we are or own in the outside world counts no more. The feeling of purity and spiritual uplift, with, strangely, no feeling of emotion, is uncanny. Perhaps this is the acuteness the spirit knows when it is freed from the trammels of the body? If it is, death should hold no fears for even the most timorous.

There are hundreds of white-clad pilgrims, who have come from every corner of the globe. At the time of the annual pilgrimage, they are numbered in millions. Nobody raises his eyes to the face of another. The crowds are orderly. Only peace is here and the feeling that this is the very door of Allah.

No pictures, no images, no chanting, no fakirs, hawkers, fuss of any kind. This place must surely be unique on earth . . .

To each one this is the moment of fulfilment. To thousands it is the satisfying culmination of long years of scrimping and saving. Even to the rich, to those to whom there are the bowers and the scrapers in the world outside, there is a feeling of brotherhood. Coming here is, for the Moslem, one of the Five Pillars of the religion: Prayer, Fasting in Ramadan, Charity, Struggle and the Pilgrimage to Mecca.

Here nobody knows who you are. Nobody is thinking about you. For once income is not a matter for speculation. For once, and the feeling may have to last all the years that life holds, there are hearts at peace.

The stones upon which we walk are smoothed by the feet of such pilgrims. Pleasantly warm too, because the top of the structure is open to the sky.

Without noticing, we have taken the hand of the nearest pilgrim in our party, and in this manner, as is fitting to such purity of feeling, we reach the black-draped Cube. A covering, rather like thick tapestry, is spread over the Kaaba. High up, we notice the name of Allah embroidered skilfully in gold. This needlework is executed by pious Egyptian women on a new covering each year.

While I was in Cairo, I had watched the very interesting ceremony of the *mahmal* – a litter containing the Kaaba's curtain – which was at that time presented by the Egyptian monarchs, and is now sent by the republican Government.

Crowds gathered long before daybreak, and filled the streets leading to the city square, where a huge pavilion had been erected for the more fortunate guests. From this, there was a splendid view of the proceedings.

A volume of cheering heralded the arrival of the King; troops presented arms, and the National Anthem was played. The bright sunshine added lustre to the brilliant scene.

The camel bearing the mahmal proceeded slowly to the arena, where its bridle was handed to the Egyptian Minister to Saudi Arabia, who was every year named as *Emir el-haj* – Leader of the Pilgrimage.

Then the curtain, the *kiswa*, made from eight immense pieces of black and green silk of superb quality and embroidered in gold and silver with texts from the Holy Koran, was carried forward.

The name of Allah is woven all over the carpet. And each year it is possible for pilgrims to purchase small pieces of previous carpets. Large pieces are given, as a special honour, to holy personages, heads of state and the like.

Refreshments were then taken in the pavilion, consisting of soft drinks, tea, coffee, cakes, sandwiches, trifles and the like.

This was followed by a military parade, and the playing of the National Anthem.

The camel carrying the palanquin circled around the parade ground, symbolising the seven times the pilgrims circumambulate the Kaaba at Mecca.

A cavalry detachment and the mounted police moved slowly with the mahmal towards the mosque where the carpet would remain until the Emir el-haj set forth upon the journey to Mecca.

The streets were densely packed with people, and every balcony, roof and doorway was crowded with a cheering mass of humanity.

Later when the mahmal and kiswa left Cairo, the populace gathered in thousands. The sunlight caught the gold and silver embroidery and the mahmal sparkled as though diamond-encrusted. The simply-garbed devotees who surrounded it made a striking contrast. Thus the hanging started on its way to distant Mecca, as it had done yearly for the last eight hundred years.

Some months later, when on the pilgrimage, I saw this carpet in the sacred precincts covering the Kaaba itself.

We began the first of the seven circumambulations of the Kaaba. The famous Black Stone is set in silver into one corner. Each time a round is finished the pilgrim kisses the stone. It is worn smooth as polished amber.

Having kissed the stone, each pilgrim raises his hands and says '*Allah ho Akbar* – God is greater.'

Just in front of me there is an old man. He looks ninety. The years have been hard upon him. He has difficulty walking. Some relative offers a protecting hand. He lays his upon it as though saying, 'Some other time I shall be glad of support, but here at Allah's gate I am strong.'

The expressions on the faces of the pilgrims are not easy to describe. There are perhaps no adjectives for spiritual contentment. The event is too precious to describe, and too beautiful for imagination.

We know that here we are better off, somehow, than we are in the world outside. Here we can forgive that which we may not forget. All petty-mindedness has been cast away. We cannot harbour any malice towards anyone, friend or enemy. Such feelings have left us, vanished: as are all outward signs which in the ordinary world are used to assess our material value to others.

The old pilgrim now stands with his hands and face pressed against the Kaaba.

There is a look upon his face which the artists who paint the pictures of saints have never produced. The old man is oblivious to everything, it seems. There is so much beauty and power in his contentment that I feel as if it were my own. Perhaps he feels near the end of his earthly pilgrimage and has come to Mecca to die. This many aged people do, happy that they may rest near the Holy City.

Now we have completed the seven circumambulations. We are given a drink from the holy well of Zamzam, which is some yards from the Kaaba. There is no charge for this. The office of keeper of the well is an honorary one and of great honour, and descends from father to son, its origins lost in antiquity which goes back, in legend, to the search by Hagar, in the wilderness, for water for her son. This, continues the belief, was why Abraham built the Kaaba here – in thanksgiving, when the spring appeared.

No mementos may be bought either outside or inside the sacred precincts. There are no programmes, nothing which reduces spirituality to materialism, or even to emotion. Here spirituality and emotion never seem to be confused.

No hawkers could exist around the Mecca shrine.

We return to the main entrance to put on our shoes. We notice that although we have been walking in our white stockinged feet there is not as much as a speck of dust on the soles of our stockings.

Now we must traverse seven times at a fast pace the path Hagar took when she sought for water. This is between two points called *Safa* and *Marwa*.

On each side of this road there are shops. Yet not one of

the shopkeepers comes inquisitively to look at the spectacle. As we finish for the seventh time, we stop at the door of the barber's shop.

The ceremonies are now over. The pilgrims may now style themselves *Al Haj* – the Pilgrim. Many, however, refuse to take the title, which is often considered one of vanity.

Apart from the spiritual experience of the Mecca pilgrimage, there surely is no city in the world in which one finds such helpful consideration. Other cities in the East seem tinged with a kind of fear and distrust of the present day, similar, as though they had caught the infection from each other. There is nothing like that in Mecca.

It gives the lie to those who say that religion is dead and that men no longer believe. I would that those who voice such opinions could have the experience of a visit to Mecca.

The first thing which comes to one there is the peace, which can perhaps only be experienced there. The West, one realises after this experience, has, perhaps fatally, confused emotionality with the spiritual; fervour and excitement for higher understanding.

Just as there can be few people in the West who would know where to go to experience this atmosphere, it is an atmosphere which would certainly escape the howling fanatics, poseurs and others who make up most of today's 'fundamentalists'. In Islamic terms, they may be religious, but they lack spirituality.

As we left to make our way back to Jedda along the desert road, just as the sinking sun was gilding the scene, I felt that it was going to be difficult to fit myself again into the world outside.

I felt ashamed for having taken part in the hustle and bustle, the hurly-burly, which is called modern civilization. I dissected my feelings as the car sped along the way. Back to ordinary life I would have to go, and again become one of the teeming, mindless millions who thought so much of themselves.

I closed my eyes and prayed that when such time came I might never forget this experience. Many times since, when pain and disappointments have descended upon me, I have been able to draw courage from the memory of the Mecca pilgrimage. May it be so to the end.

5

Boys Will Be Boys

Every morning except Fridays, boys of all ages, shapes and sizes trooped into the Imam's school, just across the road from our house. Aden might be better known to the world as a Socialist country, before the Communists were driven out: the people were still overwhelmingly devout Shiah Muslims.

Soon there was a regular babble of voices as the pupils intoned passages from the Holy Koran.

'All--ah!' pronounced the teacher. 'All--ah!' yelled the boys. 'Ho--akbar.' 'Ho--akbar!' (is Greater than all else!) repeated the class. The noise was certainly great, and the cane came much into use. 'Whack! Whack!', it said repeatedly as it came in contact with this or that part of a scholar's anatomy.

This continued, monotonously, all in the same tone until the words had the correct stress. It was obvious that only the approved musical pitch satisfied the teacher. By the time the children had a passage word perfect so had I, and it and the whacks rang in my ears long after the boys had dispersed for lunch.

Halfway through the morning the pupils had ten minutes' break. They tumbled out into the street, and seemed to take up old differences of opinion where they had been obliged to leave them before going into school. The bigger boys teased the smaller ones, and any cause for displeasure on the part of the former was considered a good excuse for ear- or arm-twisting.

Presently the lemonade- and sweetmeat-seller – the

Limonata Man – appeared, and was immediately surrounded. The bigger boys had first innings, and quickly drained the glasses of red and yellow sherbet set out on trays suspended round the neck of the vendor. Sometimes they bought unhealthy-looking sticks of what looked like rock.

Next came the turn of the little boys, who showed considerable anxiety, because the precious minutes spent by the older ones had not left much time for the joyful appreciation and selection of the goodies. But their concern was better understood when they had made their purchases; because the big boys noted what they had bought, and if they coveted the sweets, as they usually did, they simply helped themselves.

Although the younger ones' anticipation turned to bitterness in their mouths instead of the expected sweetness, there were neither tears nor complaints. The small fry knew that here, might was right.

At times it was both pathetic and amusing when the younger boys were out some minutes before the older ones. They raced down the steps, exhibiting a joy of anticipation which the older boys never saw. They hopped along to the allowed limit of their territorial freedom, eagerly looking out for the Limonata Man.

While they waited they watched the school steps, scanned the road, and hopped about on one foot, anxiety growing as the minutes passed.

Sometimes, to their joy, the man came early enough: and they were able to buy and dispose of the sweets and drinks before the other boys appeared; then, as though suddenly overcome by the enormity of their offence, they proceeded to hide behind the school wall. Such success was seldom theirs, but the very rarity of the occasions caused the younger boys to make every use of them, hugging themselves with joy.

If the bigger boys came out and thus dashed the hopes of the younger ones, the ear-twisting seemed almost to become vocal and ask, without the need for words, why the small boys had hoped to cheat the big ones; and that they, the juniors, had better realise that when such hopeful practices were afoot, so also was the immediate correction thereof.

Some mornings it was obvious that a different feeling permeated the school. Money was more plentiful. Perhaps a relative had visited some pupil's home, and administered largesse which the recipient felt he wanted to use to show his riches.

On those days, even a small boy was allowed to choose and eat what he wanted and everybody else was allowed to do likewise. First of all, he showed the coins to the others before giving them into the ready hand of the trader whose 'name was written upon them'.

Sometimes, if one of the younger ones had provided the wherewithal, it might be noticed that he blossomed under the hand which the bully had condescendingly – and hopefully – placed upon his shoulder.

Sometimes the windfall, if it had come to one of the younger boys, was not enough to include everybody. It was then that the bully appeared in his true colours. He was not so big but he had some fighting prestige or other commanding quality which set him apart. It seemed that etiquette required him to take the money, do some rapid brain work then order everybody away, except his four best friends – at least so one understood from the dumb show.

These four and the bully completely forgot about the others, and applied themselves to choosing from the tempting selection.

The rest stood apart, mouths slightly open, scarcely allowing their eyelids to drop over their eyes, lest they missed one detail of their sacrifice. One turned quickly away from the scene. On the days when the sum was fairly large – and therefore important – everybody received something.

Even though the bully could not resist twisting the ears of the littlest ones, everybody was happy. The ones whose ears had been reddened by the bully's attentions were allowed to remain sufficiently near to him to hang upon the words which fell from his lips; and when the break was over, the small boys followed, hand in hand, in the wake of those whose power over their comings and goings was so complete.

What matters of State, upon which we older people felt ourselves to be engaged, could have been of more abiding interest and importance than the Time of the Limonata Man?

6

Ali: The Prince's Brother

A few days after we arrived in Oman, my husband was invited to an assembly of sheikhs and other notables. Just as he was leaving, a young man introduced himself as Ali. His father, he said, was a greatly-respected Imam, a religious leader, at present in Malaysia.

After dinner he asked, with great politeness and fluttering of eyelids, if he could have the great honour of riding in our car as far as the guest palace where my husband, and I, together with our son Idries and a small entourage, were installed. Ali's own car, it seemed, was out of order: it needed a spare part, now being flown by courier, from the United States.

The Sultan himself, he said, with a flutter of the eyelashes, looked upon him as his own son. Altogether Ali was, we gathered, *persona grata* at Court.

When I met Ali, he appeared somehow too polite. He was more like a timorous girl than a man; tall, with an oval face, and of very small build. I argued myself out of my dislike: I was being foolish; Ali was young – too young for deception...

Somehow it was a relief, though, when he went, after bowing low with his slender hand placed in an artistic gesture over his heart.

Next day he was our first visitor again. He enquired solicitously whether we required anything, no matter how small, that he might have the honour of hearing our commands, and carrying them out.

When we said there was really nothing, he pouted a

little, and said the Prince had ordered him to come, and
what was more, to attach himself to us during our stay in
Oman.

I was suffering from fibrositis at the time and was
unable to go out. At once Ali was all concern. The Prince
must be told. The Prince would be distressed. Doctors
must be summoned. The royal doctors must come. I
assured him that I had medicine, and that the ailment
showed signs of lessening.

In any case he asked whether he might borrow the car
and the chauffeur, because he must report to the Prince
how we were faring.

He did not return for six hours. The Prince, he said, was
filled with anxiety, and only the fact that he was indis-
posed himself kept him from calling personally. There
was no mention of the departed hours.

The Prince was anxious for us to accept the hospitality
of his yacht, moored nearby. If the following afternoon
suited us it would await us. There would be a cool breeze,
and the Prince knew we would appreciate that.

As His Highness awaited our verbal reply, Ali proposed
to return at once with it. I sent a message thanking His
Highness, saying that the pain made movement impossible, and asked whether another day a week later would be
equally suitable. Ali took the car again and the delivery of
the message occupied him, once again, the whole day.

I could not help harbouring unflattering opinions about
Ali. I knew the Prince would not detain him if he had been
placed at our disposal. Neither would the Prince allow
him to keep the car, without which getting about in Oman
was, and still is, not easy.

Yet, being guests, it was impossible to question the
integrity of a man who said he was the friend of the son of
our host.

After that Ali went everywhere with us. Sometimes we
drove along the shore road in the evenings, when it was
cool and quiet, away from the bustle of the city. One

evening the chauffeur referred to having taken Ali to some desert oasis, where he had spent the night. It is not my way to question one person about another, but I asked the man when this had happened.

He had taken him, he said, the day before yesterday. Strange, Ali had told us he had spent the time with the ailing Prince. Strange that he had not mentioned the oasis, considering he had borrowed the car. Someone was prevaricating.

Next morning Ali arrived, to say that the Prince had ordered him to stay in our suite, so that he might be at hand if required. I could not think of any eventuality which might arise to make the presence of Ali indispensable, yet the royal wish was an order.

Ali was to go with us everywhere; the Prince, he said, insisted. The idea was far from pleasing to me; frankly Ali's ways were too mincing and artificial, and there was that unexplained visit to the wilds.

The rest of our party, the secretary, aide-de-camp and so on, seemed to have a similar opinion, although little was said.

Ali now fawned upon us, and had the most unpleasant way of prefixing all he said with, 'The Preence says ...'. Our position was difficult, as I have said, and the room to be provided from our suite for Ali made it distinctly awkward. Just how awkward we did not guess at the time.

The most suitable bedroom for him was a small one, through which one had to pass to get to the veranda of the guest palace unless one climbed through the high windows. Still, however inconvenient, we could not take exception to arrangements made by our host's son, the Preence, for our comfort. Ali appeared most of the time to be so young, so inoffensive, so anxious to please, that I began to doubt my instincts. Surely, I argued with myself, such a small matter was not worth thinking about.

That night many visitors came to see Ali and we heard the sound as of counters upon a wooden board – such as greets one at every open-air café in Cairo – during the engrossing game of *trik-trak* – backgammon.

There was the more easily traced sound of riyals being counted, more of them than Rafiq, our secretary, had ever needed to have at his disposal.

The partitions between the rooms were of thin wood, and because of the heat there was a space left open high up in the walls. It was after 1 a.m. before the clicking of the counters ceased, and much later than that before the loud whisperings and the clink of silver coins stopped.

Next day no mention was made of the visitors; Ali said the Prince's yacht would await us at the jetty nearby. The Prince had sent his salutations and hoped we would excuse his absence, as he was not yet well.

After the heat of the day was over, we drove to the jetty. There was no sign of the luxury yacht, nothing save a fairly clean, small fishing boat in which a few rough cushions had been dumped.

Four immense burly unkempt sailors jumped out when we arrived, and salaamed. There was a hurried whispered conversation between them and Ali, while we took our uncomfortable seats. I, at least, felt like an unwelcome visitor in a boat of Penzance pirates.

When he sat down, Ali explained that the Prince apologised for this boat, but that his yacht had developed some impediment in its workings and rather than disappoint us, he had sent the fishing boat. The explanation did not satisfy me. I knew the Prince would never have done such a thing, whatever had happened.

The outing was not a success. The spray sometimes played to its own amusement with the little boat and won. We asked presently to be taken back. As soon as we returned to the palace, Ali borrowed the car to report to the Prince how much we had enjoyed the trip!

Next day Ali returned with another car, saying he had told the Prince that the first one was not big enough for our requirements. The new one – a stretch limousine – looked almost like a weekend cottage, and I was annoyed with him for taking it upon himself to give orders or even requests in our name.

We went for a drive along the shore. Ali sat as usual in front with the driver. There appeared to be some tension between them. The chauffeur was not speaking in his usual polite manner, and several times he raised his voice, in reply to the dulcet tones of the youth.

When we returned from the drive, the chauffeur carried our bags to our apartments. When he left the room, he met Ali and I felt rather anxious when I overheard the chauffeur's words: 'I know you, Ali, son of Jamal. I am not going to drive you any more.' There was much more, but eavesdropping never explains any situation, and I negotiated the window and reached the veranda. There I saw the driver was using what force he was capable of to prevent Ali from entering the car. He succeeded by pushing the latter violently against the wall, jumping into the car and driving furiously away. How many rounds there had been between them before I did not know, but the last one went to the chauffeur.

What those ominous words meant, I wondered. 'I know you,' can mean so much. Years of intimate knowledge of a person, or just the phraseology of a man who thought he had discovered something new?

Every night guests came to Ali's and played trik-trak until the small hours. Sometimes he accompanied them when they left. Those nights he seemed to spend out, because we never saw him until late the next morning.

Nowadays he lay in bed a great deal, saying he was ill. We spoke of getting a doctor, whereupon he said he would confide in us very privately.

The Prince, he said, had had a turn for the worse, and he had remained the night with him. What else could he do for a prince who never called him Ali, but always 'brother'. The Prince was only content when this 'brother' was near him.

I asked him to take a letter to the Prince wishing him a speedy recovery. Ali decided against this, because he said then the Prince would know he had abused his confidence. Anywhere else it would have been possible to make enquiries about Ali, and find out what was what. It was the royal element which made it impossible to ask. The Arabs are a polite people. They do not discuss their king or their princes, much less the servants appointed by them. Suppose Ali *had* been appointed by the Prince?

My husband and I had both formed the opinion that there was something wrong somewhere, but where? Each of us was equally tired of taking Ali around with us everywhere. We began to plan how to get away without him. How was it possible to manage this when we had to pass his door, which was always open?

One day when Ali went off to see the Prince, or so he said, an Arab friend proposed a fishing expedition. This sounded just what we wanted. We packed hampers with tinned fruit, biscuits and chocolates, and breathed happily. Our friend produced fishing rods and tackle, and we felt like a bunch of children playing truant, which we were in a way. Ali was nowhere to be seen and we left no word as to our destination at the palace.

We reached a pier and fished for about half an hour, then divided out the sandwiches, watching the smart little coloured fish which it would have been a shame to catch, so much did they seem to enter into the spirit of the chase.

Some of the little two-inch long ones were blue as sapphires, some were rose-pink, and they swam about in the happiest abandon. Near the moored boats, we caught sight every now and again of immense dark brownish-black fish, which seemed immune to anglers' wiles.

We were laughing happily when we saw Ali gliding towards us. Someone said in a depressed tone, 'How did you know where we were?' To which he replied, 'It is my job to know; the Preence must hear everything . . .'

Everybody rose, nobody felt equal to the fishing picnic

now Ali was there. We gave the food away to the several small boys who had been watching us.

Next day I asked Ali not to take the car as we were going out. He looked crestfallen, as a schoolboy would when told the Head was displeased with him. The Prince had told him to go on a 'private mission' for him after lunch. I told him to ask the Prince to give him another car, and feeling like it, asked him where his own was – of which he had spoken more than once. I said I was sure the Prince would stretch a point for his 'brother'.

Ali smiled, and his long lashes sprayed upon his cheeks. He had a provoking way of showing very even white teeth, which somehow conveyed less than transparent honesty. By all means, he said, he would ask the Prince, only His Highness was difficult when he was ill, and would be 'very angry'. That was the first we heard of the Prince's frequent displeasure.

The change in my attitude to Ali was noticed by everybody, and hints were diplomatically dropped that as we were guests, we must not cause any displeasure. The Sultan was an old friend. The orders were not from him, we knew. Not that we thought the Prince had given them either, but Ali seemed so confident and sure delivering the messages, that we could not understand what had happened to the erstwhile courteous and hospitable prince that he should now show 'anger'.

From that time on I began to order Ali not to take the car. When he prefixed his childish request with those words 'The Preence ...', I said: 'Not at all, I am going to call on the Prince today.' For the ghost of a second Ali showed fear. I saw it because I was looking for it. I do not think he even knew he had shown it. 'Everybody here,' I said, 'treats us with courtesy except yourself.'

'You do not understand me,' said Ali, in the petulant way a film star used to say to her leading man.

Several times after that we went out for walks asking Ali to remain behind. Soon we were aware that police, who acted like the old Keystone Cops variety, were shadowing us. They had the most comical way of passing us at a half-trot, looking in the opposite direction in an exaggerated way, then taking a quick look back at us, before diving into some doorway or behind some wall.

From this point of vantage they would observe us, with their eyes gazing over a wall, and the tops of their heads and peaked caps in full view. Sometimes one or two would run alongside of us. I am not sure who or what they thought they were supposed to be: but their disguise consisted of covering the word *Shurta* (Police) on their shoulder-straps with adhesive tape. One had the impression of playing with children. Except that they carried guns.

The whole thing was half amusing and half annoying. As time went on, observing them from our veranda, I became aware that these policemen were stationed outside to follow any one of us, and see who came to the palace. Outside there was a row of shops being built, and here they hid, or thought they did. I used to watch from the veranda when either my husband or son went out, and sure enough these comic policemen followed. Sometimes they had sheaves of papers under their arms, sometimes nothing, but they had the idea that when they carried the papers they were unrecognisable as police – even when they were wearing their uniforms. We had so much fun with them that Ali lost much of his power to annoy us. Had they used the ordinary police methods of surveillance, nobody would have been any the wiser, but they behaved in a quite crazy manner.

One day one of them followed me. It is said that people born in any highlands do not like to be followed closely. I am not sure of others but I can answer to the truth of the assertion where I am concerned, and when I was conscious that there was a comic policeman just behind, I thought it would be fun to turn round and ask him where the paper shop was. No sooner had I turned than he dashed to the middle of the road, where he commenced to flail his arms, pretending to direct the traffic, which fortunately took no notice of his antics except to steer clear of him. I waited on the pavement looking at him, then, when there was a lull in the traffic, crossed over. As soon as he saw me approaching, he took to his heels and ran towards the police station, while passers-by stared unbelievingly, searching all round with their eyes for the thief or whatever else had caused the police to move so quickly.

When time hung heavily on these watchers' hands, such as when we were not out, they liked to take up their position where they had a full view of our veranda. Here it was possible to hear their conversation. Two of them were not by any means pleased with the treatment they received from Ali.

It was not surprising to hear them speak his name, because I associated these incidents in some way with him. Several times when he came towards the palace I saw a policeman approach him. This was not what he wanted, and once he struck one of them in the face. The man recoiled and raced away.

Finally, I could stand it no longer, and I asked Ali what it meant. Oman after all was practically 'out of the world', and as royal guests we had somehow been effectively isolated from all other contact.

Ali at once became all concern. Leave it to him, he said. 'The Preence' of course must not be told, because he would be too angry. For once Ali and I agreed. All the time this undercurrent in our lives ran so deep, the surface of our lives remained calm as they did before the advent of Ali.

I could not help worrying, sometimes, wondering whether these police, who looked so unlike police, were thieves and robbers, with murder in their hearts.

Whatever Ali said bore fruit, because afterwards the buildings under construction held nothing save the builders. Ali now took an insane dislike to a sheikh who came to visit us often. We liked him and looked forward to seeing him. We exchanged books and magazines, and in Oman one knew the value of both. Ali warned me darkly against this friend. He was a villain, and would harm us, he said.

Then Ali took it upon himself to forbid the man to enter the palace. We knew nothing of this, but when the Sheikh did not visit us for a week, we began to wonder what was wrong. The administrator of the palace told us that Ali had given the order 'from the Prince' not to admit the Sheikh to our apartments. Ali told me that Oman was a most unsafe place and he was only protecting our lives.

This had worried the Sheikh and one day he managed to send a note up to our apartments, by a houseboy, asking if anyone was ill. I sent the reply immediately, asking the visitor to come up. While we were talking Ali appeared.

For a moment when he saw who was there his eyes became mere slits, and his tightly drawn lips gave a most unpleasant look to his white teeth. He forgot his usual studied manners, then apologised for intruding and left abruptly.

The next day we heard that the Sheikh was in jail. It transpired that he had encountered Ali in the hall, and that Ali had warned him if he went to see us again there would be trouble. The Sheikh had enquired what kind of trouble, and Ali had said the police would see to that. The Sheikh, who knew his ancestry back for thirty-three generations of *Sharifs* – nobility, was disinclined to listen. He struck Ali across the face and said now it would be worth whatever was coming.

A secretary of an important man in Oman told us later that the police owed Ali so much money in gambling debts that he practically ran the police station. What he ordered was done. He said Ali had had dozens of people imprisoned, and that everybody was afraid of him.

It was several days before we discovered where the Sheikh was. My husband went at once to see the Chief of Police and the Sheikh was released. The Chief said Ali had reported that the Sheikh had disobeyed the Prince's command, and the Prince had given an order for him to be imprisoned.

We became emboldened, and were now fairly sure that Ali was using the Prince's name to further his own interests. Still, this was the East, and as it was quite possible that Ali was also a boon-companion of the Sultan's son, and we were still guests, we would be wise to tread warily.

Still nobody else spoke against Ali, and as he surely would not tell such lies regarding the royal family, we began to feel miserable all over again. Suppose? I kept thinking, suppose?

Meanwhile my husband and son were invited to visit the Saudi king, Abdul-Aziz ibn Al Saud, flying to his desert palace in Riyadh. There were no scheduled flights at the time, so a chartered plane arrived. The two spent a few days there, and came back praising the cordiality and hospitality of His Majesty.

I visited, as expected, members of the Omani royal family, but protocol did not allow me to gossip about such as Ali; so things dragged on. Arab robes of honour, titles even, were bestowed; not one word of any of Ali's dark hints was mentioned.

We had but to ask, and we could have anything we wished; we were honoured guests, it was hoped that we would stay for months, years, and so on. The Sultan himself sent me a message, assuring us, us of his pleasure at our presence in his country.

This Sultan had all the dignity and simplicity of the truly great figure he was locally considered to be.

But events were moving; a very different light was turned upon affairs. The drivers absolutely refused to allow Ali to enter their cars, and although he begged, they remained adamant. Our favourite chauffeur said he would rather leave than change his vow not to drive Ali.

We asked him why. He said that Ali had struck him

often, and that if he did so again he would kill him. This was straight talk, and the molehill showed signs of becoming a mountain. I said that perhaps Ali's own car might now be repaired. The driver said Ali had no car.

He hoped to win enough at gambling to buy one, and if the police paid all they owed he might get one, but Ali would rather they did not pay him, so that he could keep his hold over them. In fact he had refused to accept the repayment which one of the policemen offered him.

I replied diplomatically that as he often took the car with the Prince's orders, it was difficult for us to do anything without first consulting the Prince's private secretary. Ali had told us that the secretary was his true brother, so that road seemed to lead nowhere. I asked the chauffeur to continue for a few more days, which he promised to do.

Often when we opened the door of our sitting-room we found Ali there 'just coming in', or so he said, with that ingratiating smile of his. This on-the-spot spying annoyed me, more so because I knew he was searching for something, and I wondered what. It happened too often to be mere accident.

One night I stayed up until his trik-trak playing cronies had gone. There was a small hole which acted as a peephole in our door, and which commanded a full view of the corridor and the door of Ali's room. Our room was in darkness, the corridor was lit. I had a desire to have a look at Ali without the smile. Thus one may learn a good deal.

When the friends left, he stood with his back to the wall near his room. His lips were pursed and he was deeply engaged in thought. Every now and again a disagreeable smile crossed his face, and twisted his lips. A very dangerous looking individual, indeed. That expression betokened ill, and soon, for somebody. I could not help feeling slightly nervous when I guessed who it might be.

Presently four tall ruffians appeared, and some memory returned to me: ah! the fishing-boat men! Ali pointed to our door, said something under his breath, and then pointed out through his room to what I guessed, indicated the veranda.

Our windows, all six of them, were open. It needed quite an effort to lower them, and the rattling made in the operation was too great to be considered under present circumstances.

Imagination once awakened, especially in mysterious circumstances during the night, and more especially in a place where one is practically the only individual of one's own species, becomes scarcely supportable.

This looked like murder to me. Robbery first, of course. Memories of previous completely untraceable disappearances of foreigners flooded my mind. Here the whole procedure of slaying somebody seemed not just possible but easy.

I became my own detective, and reasoned, that to begin with, we had things which Ali had greatly admired; quite a number, in fact. Number two, Ali controlled the police. Number three, here were the ruffians, or should they have been number one? Number four, these men had a boat which might put out with a load of dead bodies and dispose of them in the sea. The whole plot in four uneasy stages.

There but remained for these accessories after the fact to return and forget all about it. There would be an enquiry perhaps; perhaps not. Enquiry or no, the thing seemed far too easy to me as I stood listening, on the isolated veranda, where I had crept.

The sound of stealthy footsteps came from Ali's room. I hoped to find a policeman on duty just outside; then remembered he would be Ali's man. Someone spoke in loud whispers, and was hurriedly hushed. Then a number of thick whispers came to me. I wondered why I had been so thoughtless as to go on to the veranda. Fear is a terrible force. It was fear and not bravery which had caused me to

94

do this, to step almost into the ruffians' hands. Courage has sense.

My heart thumped in my ears, and the support of bones and muscles seemed to leave my legs. My breath made gurgling sounds in my throat. Novelists have it that people shout in fear. Not if they are as afraid as I was. There must be depths of terror, and at the greatest one is mute.

There seemed to be a scuffle of some sort in Ali's room. Had these men come to murder him? I could not hope so – I was supposed to be civilized, but I own that at the thought I felt a sense of relief. Next I was aware that one of the men had gone, he crossed the road in front of the palace. He climbed rather than walked, with a rolling rounded bow-legged movement which one associates with baboons.

That left three and Ali. Still too many. Moreover why had the man gone? To bring something or somebody? What or who? Ropes? Probably. Now completely in the grip of terror I became bolder. I am not one who is capable of waiting. I like to know, never mind what, just know. The whispering went on. I crept along the veranda as near to the wall as possible, until I came to Ali's window.

Holding myself tight against the wall I kept my head well back, thus being able to keep an eye to the window-frame. The idea that I was eavesdropping did not enter my head.

The men were standing facing Ali, who was sitting on his bed. They were now listening to him. On the table were two bottles. I recognised one as being brandy. Its three-star label gleamed in the light.

Now and again I saw the face of Ali through the group. He had removed his *agal* and *kafya*, and I realised how this head-dress adds to the age of the wearer. As he sat there Ali looked about seventeen, and more like a girl than ever. He was emphasising some point, at which the men demurred. One of them now spoke, but it was difficult to catch any words, except *fulus* – money, and *sa'a ithnen* – two o'clock, which got us nowhere.

Why, I wondered at this point, did everybody sleep when murder was in the air? Now the biggest roughest man said, '*Ana awz falukia akbar* – I want a bigger boat.'

Ali said, ignoring the request: 'How long will it take to row to . . .' and '*Anta awz kam?*' which seemed to be getting down to business, for it means 'How much do you want?'

I did not hear the man's reply, but Ali raised his eyes deprecatingly at the mention of the sum. Upon which the men turned away. Ali touched one upon the arm and the argument began again. Then, with a horror that almost made me cry aloud, I saw a thick coil of rope lying at Ali's feet. They kept referring to it: '*Al habl! Al habl!* – the rope! the rope!' And each time it was mentioned Ali made such an evil face that he appeared as old as Adam.

Every now and again he said, 'Stop that whining.' He was not having an easy time with them.

And I reasoned that it did not look as though they were going to harm him. Not in any case until it was worth their while, because they looked like men who would stick at nothing.

Why not rouse the palace guard? I had thought of that, but decided that Ali would remember that at some other time, if not now. And he seemed to have so much power that one never knew who was who. Yet bloodthirsty as these piratical sailors looked, they seemed to question something.

They were now whispering again, and applying their hands to their throats in the motions of strangling. There was a good deal of altercation and Ali said three of four times '*Ishrab min al bahr*' (roughly meaning 'Go to hell'). He then applied the bottle to his mouth and took a number of gulps of the brandy. He appeared to be intoxicated already.

Suddenly he struck one of the men, who recoiled against the wall, although he was three times Ali's size. Whoever they were, they were entirely in Ali's power, as the Victorian writers would have put it.

One of the men now took up the rope and went towards the door leading to the corridor and our room. The others followed, looking backward fearfully at the tipsy Ali. The latter now put his feet upon the table and smiled happily.

Our door leading to the corridor was not locked! Hurrying back, I pushed home the bolt and stood against the stout support of the door. I knew that if they found the door locked, all they had to do was to return through the veranda, from where they could enter the room in one step through the open windows.

The even breathing of my husband was the only sound. I could not waken him now without making a noise, and even if I made none, he would be sure to ask loudly what was wrong. Looking through the peephole, sure enough, I saw the bulky figures approaching along the corridor.

The light had been turned off, but there was enough from Ali's room to illuminate all who passed. It may have been my fancy, but it seemed that there was a rush of air, like a hot breath, on to my eye from the other side of the peephole, and the door gave slightly as though perhaps a shoulder had been applied to it.

The door 'gave' again, so conspicuously that the bolt seemed to weaken. Still there was not a sound which might be called human. It scarcely seemed possible that these men could be so quiet.

The next push caused the door to bulge, after that a low voice urged the others, 'More'. I knew the door would give soon, I also knew that we were alone in that part of the palace, and that our bodyservant was not likely to be aroused by any noise we were capable of making.

I pulled the sofa across the door to bolster it up, and ran. Jumping through the window, I ran along to Ali's room. He was praying! Although it was not prayer time.

'Who are these ruffians of yours?' I shouted in Arabic, so loudly that the men were evidently frightened, and made a concerted rush to the door at the end of the corridor. They yanked back the bolts and dashed out into the night.

I raced back to the veranda to see the men pell-melling down the street opposite dragging the now-uncoiled rope behind them.

Ali now appeared, suave and as polite as a courtier, although obviously tipsy. 'You spoke, Madame.' Ali's English was spoken with that semi-lisp which is supposed to be so charming to the ear of the listener.

'Who were those murderers who were trying to enter my room?' For a fraction of a second Ali allowed his eyelashes to lower in a movement designed to convey shocked disbelief.

'I am sorry, Madame has been dreaming.'

'What about those men who took us out in the fishing boat. They were here talking to you, and then tried to get into my room. They had a rope.'

Perhaps for the first time the real Ali appeared. His eyes narrowed and his lips drew tightly over his teeth; possibly this reflex was so basic that he did not notice it himself. There was so much hate in the look that I felt Ali could have done well enough himself when it came to a matter of extermination.

Yet, like a fast cloud across the sun, the girlish smile took the place of the evil. Looking at this gentle expression, I wondered whether I *had* been dreaming.

'Madame must see a doctor. Tomorrow I will tell the Preence.' Fear is a weakening thing when it has gone, but I wanted to strike Ali as he stood there trying, and managing, to look like a choir boy.

'You are lying, and I know you intended to rob or murder us. I do not trust you any longer. I know the police are in your hands, and you need money. You will not get any from us.

'The other day you said you were going to build a house on the seashore, if all went well. All is not well, and you are a thief. If you are not gone in the morning I shall see the Prince myself and ask him what such behaviour means.'

'Madame will feel better after a rest. The intense heat here takes strange turns with people who are ill. Retire, Madame,' and here Ali made his most gracious bow. There was a curl on his lips as he said, 'Tomorrow I must tell the Preence that . . .'

'Say no more.' I was speaking in furious anger, and Ali realised he had gone too far. He now cowered in the corner, and sheltered his face with his arm, but it did little to save him from the thrashing I gave him, with a very stout stick I found in a broom-cupboard.

I left him sobbing, whether from pain or rage or both I do not know, but I felt more than pleased and wondered whether I had been the first woman to give an old-time drubbing to Ali, son of Jamal.

Back in my bedroom I wondered what would be the upshot of it all. It was only 3 a.m. and still dark. There was still time for the men to come back.

I lowered the windows. They made a great noise, but still my husband slept on. How was I to tell him in the morning that I had lost my temper and given a beating to the 'brother' of the Prince?

How would the Prince take the news? I spent three bad hours until the arrival, as usual and without anyone apparently having seen or heard anything, of the early-morning tea: over which the story was related, leaving out the beating of Ali. That, I felt, was a personal affair between us, and I knew my husband would take a serious view of it.

We sent our servant to see whether Ali had gone. He had not. He was sound asleep. He slept until 11 a.m. No conscience troubled him.

We reported to the palace administrator that Ali had behaved badly and we demanded his removal. The administrator, who also seemed subjugated to Ali, said the

Prince had sent him and only the Prince was able to remove him.

Here was the nub of the difficulty. The power of Ali was absolute. That day he behaved as though nothing had happened. For *sang froid* I have never seen his equal, and I have come across a few of the same type.

As soon as my husband went out, I went to the administrator's office and said I would remain there until Ali was removed from our apartments. The man was nervous, and assured me in honeyed phrases that he could do nothing.

He ordered coffee and persuaded me to sit in the lounge. He led the conversation into every channel but the one which contained the object of my visit.

I kept coming back to the unpleasant subject, and eventually the man said he would send somebody and ask Ali to leave. The servant returned to say that Ali had called him unforgivable names and threatened to throw him down into the street.

My husband returned and I persuaded him to write asking the Prince to remove Ali. What he said I do not know, but it could not have been the whole story. That night Ali left. We were told that the Prince had ordered him to go on a mission for a time.

We had a wonderful three days' respite, then discovered that Ali had returned. He was asleep in his old room. I called to him to come out but he refused to reply. Presently he dressed and went out, leaving his belongings. The palace administrator again said he could do nothing.

Ali insisted that the Prince had sent him back. This was not princely behaviour. It was the angry reaction of a man who tries to bluff and intimidate his victims. He was using the friendship of the Prince as his chief weapon, and it was easy to guess how well he had succeeded in the past, simply by telling any who fell into his hands that the Prince was displeased with them. He knew, of course, that the majority would be too afraid to communicate with the Prince.

We no longer drove at nights along the peaceful shore in the evening coolness. No longer did we feel safe driving along the then only surfaced road after the heat of the day.

The chauffeurs reported as usual and were obviously disappointed when we said we were not going. They thought the fault was theirs and asked what they had done. Like the other Arabs whom we met, they were always polite and helpful, and so unhappy did our chief driver become, that I told him we did not feel confident about Ali's behaviour.

At the mention of that name the driver broke into a spate of Arabic, then remembering my limitations, he spoke more slowly.

The gist of the story was that Ali was a drinker and a gambler; that money was as necessary to him as his breath. He had borrowed the pay of the driver, and any servant who was easily frightened of what the police were capable of doing to them. Ali did not want the money the police owed him; he wanted his fingers around their throats.

The floodgates were at last open. 'Why,' asked the driver, did the *Emir Al Kabir* – my husband, indulge the man?'

'Indulge?' I asked. Yes. Day after day, bedouin sheikhs, foreign oilmen and businessmen, notables of all kinds, were given huge banquets at the palace, and all was charged to our account, settled by the Sultan. Settled by the Sultan, yes, I thought, but not authorised by us.

The driver was almost incoherent with rage and frustration. Everyone had been given expensive gifts, some had been given bribes and all came from the Palace funds ... Why favour a filthy son of a camel; like that? What hold did he have over us or the Prince?

I realised at that moment that Ali was a particularly nasty conman. Everything he said or did was probably based on bluff. He was half-Malay. That, the driver said, accounted for his bad habits and his ideas of murder! He

101

was always threatening to murder someone and the driver knew there were men afraid enough of him to do even that at his bidding.

It was easy to hold a man by the throat, the driver said, when he owed you money. If you owed a man money, he became the dictator in your life. He said this owing of money, made policemen Ali's hostages. For two reasons did Ali gamble, because it was as his breath – he being half-Malay – and because he was determined to build houses.

'*Borreh! Borreh!* What a man!' On the very last day he had borrowed his pay he had shown the driver just where the house to be built with the winnings was to be situated; near one of the Prince's houses.

When there was a chance I asked, 'Why give Ali the wages? Why not say "No"?'

Because, he said, Ali was more powerful than the police, and anybody who disobeyed him was taken away to prison, with chains on his feet. He had frightened many important people with 'Malay sorcery'.

'But Ali is a friend of the Prince,' I mused. 'He goes to the Prince with this news and that – half of it untrue. He was a playmate of the Prince when they were boys, and the Prince is too kind to see what a schemer he is.'

What, I wondered, had he said to the Prince about us? How he had used us to further his own ends, we shall never know. This much I did know, and that was that Ali was going to leave our apartments even if I had to stab him to death myself!

He would show no fight; his cunning had always protected him. Next afternoon everybody was out except myself and Ali who, I could hear, was having a bath.

I heard the pitter-patter of his wooden sandals across the corridor, and then waited fifteen minutes for him to dress.

Making my way to his door which was half open, I called loudly, 'Ali!' – no Sheikh this time. There was no reply. I repeated the name. Still no reply, but I saw him back against the wall, obviously nervous as such cowards are. 'Come here,' I called, as to a servant. He emerged quietly.

I told him that he had returned after being ordered to leave. That he had caused a great deal of annoyance to us during our stay. That to save any more trouble I would give him two hours to get out of the apartments, and that if he remained here I would go to the Prince and tell him everything. Moreover before leaving he would be given another thrashing – a real one this time – if he stayed over the two hours.

He began, 'The Preence...'

'... will be very angry,' I finished. 'I know, but it might interest you to know that since the Prince offered us his yacht which you hired to other people, no report has been given to him about us.'

He replied that he could repeat the entire Holy Koran by heart; that he had never told an untruth in his life; that his whole existence was dedicated to Allah; that I was his respected sister, and that he had told the Prince how good we had been to him.

I replied by telling him that I knew he had lied about his father who had been dead for years. I knew that his mother had forbidden him the house in Muscat, and many other equally disagreeable truths, which we had learned. I also reminded him that he had asked us to give him all our valuables that the police might keep them safely for us. Another person had taken this advice from him when he stayed at the palace the year before. I told him that I knew that, when the man went to the police for his money and watch, the police had never heard of either him or his things, and the man was left penniless.

By now I had my own informants, among the women-folk of the Palace. Harims have their uses...

Within an hour he had gone. He did not stop to say goodbye. Knowing him as I do, I am sure he told the

Prince many things in his own favour, and precious few in ours.

We were later told, when asking why Ali behaved as he did, that he himself gave the explanation that 'the Pakistan special representative and certain British interests had told him that we were dangerous foreign agents', and that 'the Sultan should be informed and that we should be watched'.

Of course, even if any of such a farrago were true, murder is certainly not Arab justice, especially where guests are concerned. And, if 'The Preence' happens to read this, I hope that things are clearer to him than they could have been while we were there. Certainly, apart from the abominable Ali, the truly royal and hospitable treatment we received may be matched, but could not be excelled.

7

No Troubles? Buy a Goat

It seems a small thing in any language to order tea and toasted buns to be brought at once. One morning, not long after arriving in the Gulf, I smugly believed that I was doing just that, in Arabic.

But, shortly afterwards, a knock on the door revealed not Karim the houseboy carrying a tray, but a stranger who spoke no English. A stranger, moreover, in the garb of a holy man, talking volubly in Arabic and obviously expecting a reply.

There was nobody near to act as translator, and hospitality required that coffee be brought at once. Luckily, when visitors arrive, coffee follows as a matter of course. Happily, too, the reverend gentleman continued talking despite my apparent reticence. He must have thought that I was shy.

It transpired, after a telephone call to a friend, that Karim had thought that I had asked him to find a divine who would explain the Islamic legal position on the releasing of slaves held by infidels.

Amateur linguists, of course, are never put off by such trifles.

Another time I gave one of the porters a banknote and asked him to fetch me some change, pointing from the veranda to the shop where he might get it.

Sure enough, the man hurried off in the direction of the shop, with no apparent difficulty in discerning my intention. Now, it seemed, at last I was being understood. This was a wonderful and elevating experience.

Presently there was a sound of slipping and sliding outside the room. The servant appeared, hot and wild-eyed, dragging a most obstinate goat at the end of a rope. The animal wanted to go its own way and bleated loudly. The man dragged the animal inside the room, closed the door, and slipped out with a very odd look in my direction.

I had two of the worst hours I can remember with that goat. It was a beautiful animal, glossy black. Its coat was thick and smooth but it was not house-trained. It had been accustomed to the wide open spaces. It would surely have been happy in the Alps, bounding from crag to crag. Here, its natural exuberance led it to delinquency.

It had the most inquisitive turn of mind imaginable. Hardly was it within the room, when it jumped nimbly upon a chair and took possession of my hat, which was expensive and new. This was a bad beginning, and when I tried to take the hat away, it snatched it right back and began to eat it. It stopped only when there was nothing left. Now it seized my handbag containing my passport and money. I got this back, a little torn, but succeeded in annoying the goat in the process. He lowered his head and made straight for me.

There was nothing for it but to leap onto the table. I did so, sending a large bottle of cola crashing to the ground. Luckily, its fizzing distracted my uninvited guest; he sniffed at the foaming liquid, excitedly butting it with his horns, as he gathered courage to sample it.

This the goat did by making several half-frightened excursions round the wet patch, and then dashing away. It tried several times to reach a vase of dried flowers which I hoped I had put out of the way. Then, quite unexpectedly it made a plunge right through the liquid, slid upon its hind legs, scrambled up and retired to a corner dripping with cola.

Here in the most comical position, with its forefeet up in the air, it began to lick the stuff off its coat. Every now and then it bleated in short, contented gasps. Then, quickly rising, it lapped up the liquid that still remained on the floor, continuing to lick the ground long after there was a bald patch in the carpet.

Now the animal began a hunt round the room, returning every now and again to sniff the place where the drink had been. It began a series of attacks upon me, so I thought it best to get inside a large cupboard.

Robbed of its prey, it assailed the door with tremendous strength, whinnying almost like a horse. All seemed quiet for quite a while and I opened the door to have a peep. The goat was fascinated, it seemed, by the reflection of itself in a polished wooden cupboard door. Each time it backed for an offensive attack it flopped down on its haunches. Trying to regain its footing, it kicked out in all directions. It now dawned on me that the goat was perhaps stupefied by the cola.

Nothing else, surely, could account for the difficulties in which it found itself. Each time it strove to rise, its feet gave way and it made a peculiar sound, like a mixed groan and a whimper. The noises were oddly human and, approaching the animal, I saw that it was rolling its eyes in a dazed way. I began to wonder whether perhaps my hat had poisoned it and if it were dying.

Then I noticed that quite a large piece had been chewed out of a basketwork chair. This had been painted green, and I thought it must certainly have been poisonous.

My guest now rose with extreme difficulty, after falling in more ways than one would have thought possible, and staggered, head practically touching the ground, to the door, where it collapsed on its knees.

It surveyed its surroundings in a befuddled sort of way, but seemed unable to fix its gaze upon anything. Thinking it might now be possible to get it outside, I approached and just as my hand was on the door handle, the goat made a successful bite at my skirt, and held on. I did not know much about goats and was not expecting the snap.

However incapable it was of walking (and it could not even stand) its grip was like that of a vice.

I managed to slip off the garment, and the animal at once started to eat it. It snuffled all the time and seemed to be breathing heavily through its nose. If, I reasoned, it had been poisoned, it should not have had any further appetite. I stood watching my flimsy disappear as though it had been a handful of grass.

Would nobody ever come? I tried to reassure myself with the thought that this was just one of those dreams. It was no comfort however to remember the Persian saying '*Gham nadari, buz bakhar* – If you have no sorrow, buy a goat'.

Yet I knew it was no dream, and began worrying myself wondering whose goat it was. Where was the man with the change? It was obvious that the animal had been delivered to the wrong person. It was a beautiful, though destructive, beast and yet my early affection for it had become dulled when I thought of its depredations.

There was a footstep outside; the door opened, banging against the goat, and my husband entered, after some little difficulty.

Never one to show surprise, he looked unbelievingly from me to the goat, and then at the confusion. He hoped, he said a little anxiously, that all was well. He had returned because he met one of the hotel staff who told him that I had bought a goat, and he had just wondered...

We summoned the servant, who said that I had given him a note, telling him that I wanted a goat, and pointing to a man passing a shop opposite who was leading one. He was told to be quick – that part I had managed correctly. The servant said the man had just bought the goat and did not want at first to part with it, but when he saw the money he seemed to change his mind, and was quite pleased. This was easy for me to understand because he probably bought three goats for half the sum.

We kept the goat for a while on a plot behind the Guest Palace and named him Hitler because of his fondness for territorial expansion and his ability to bully numbers of people successfully.

Hitler followed me everywhere. We became good friends. If he got a chance, he came to my door and bleated loudly to be allowed to come in. He must have had happy, if hazy, memories of those first carefree hours and may have thought longingly of the sweet effervescent liquid, but Hitler was not encouraged to become an addict.

The porter was told that I did not understand Arabic and considering what had happened because of this fact, he was told not to address me in that language. For some reason of his own he could not understand or believe, experience notwithstanding, that it was possible for me or anyone else to be ignorant of his tongue. After that, although he spoke in staccato Arabic, my performance was in dumb show. Of course, I recalled, Arabs call people who don't know their language *ajami* – the dumb.

It is one thing to learn a language and another completely different affair to speak it in its own terrain and get anybody to understand.

8

Number Two, Special Ward

The plane journey from the Gulf had been one long memory of pain.

It became obvious that I would need treatment before I could continue the long journey to Afghanistan. I had taken pain-killers until my ears were filled with a roaring like a high-speed non-stop train tearing through a junction. I had hoped to get away from the Indo-Pakistan subcontinent before the monsoon – and I still hoped.

I was glad to see the doctor. He was a kind and jolly man, and listened to my entire medical history in the patient manner of most of his profession.

He examined me everywhere, prodding where it hurt most. Then straightening up he said: 'This will mean hospital for you. We'll put you in the special ward. After a few weeks' treatment you'll be fit.' He lowered my finances by a sum which made me gulp, said au revoir, and before I had recovered from the shock, his big car was gliding out of the hotel grounds.

I was tired. I'd not been able to lie down for three months. The eight months I had been away from my home seemed like years. I had reached the stage when I wondered why people travel at all.

My mind turned to the special ward and it cheered me up. At least I would have a good rest, when they had done something so that I could lie down. Special Ward. There seemed magic in the words. It was as though somebody had said 'damask roses sprinkled with dew'. My mind got to work on all that comprised the running of a special ward. Trim and efficient nurses, doctors with healing in their hands and the rout of this ghastly pain.

This, I thought, will mean the wearing of the Neapolitan embroidered dressing-gown, and those nonsensical ostrich feather mules which the handsome young Italian in the Naples shop had said were simply made for the Signora.

Those then, and the quilted dressing gown ... but a bout of pain put all other thoughts from my head. I quickly swallowed a tablet supplied by the doctor, and not included in the fee.

The next day I arrived at the hospital. It was a great rambling place, all on one floor.

First, the taxi man took me to the out-patients' department, around which crowded every condition of human being from the age of a few months, to several who appeared to be so old they were scarcely still human. Here they squatted or lay against the building, gloomily awaiting their turn.

The driver left me to make enquiries as to the location of the Special Ward. The sight of a foreign woman seemed to prove too much for those patients capable of dragging themselves alongside. They opened the doors of the taxi on each side and let in a cloud of flies, while they asked in various local languages whether I was a doctor.

Was I a patient? On hearing that I fell into the same category as themselves, they plied me with questions. Had I a stoppage? Heart disease? Stones in my kidneys? Cancer? Or perhaps an unmentionable disease? The driver returned from his reconnaissance, and treated the crowd to some particularly abusive ethnic oaths. They were hurled back by the crowd, with interest.

The driver called to them as we left: 'Scum, my passenger is going to the *Special Ward*!'

Next we stopped at what turned out to be the mortuary, where two men hurried out. Catching sight of somebody still alive, they called to the driver: 'Tell them to kill them first, will you?' and spent so long enjoying the joke that we had to wait to be told where the Special Ward was.

The place looked quite inviting as we drove through the grounds. There was a considerable stretch of grassy sward, the hospital in-patient wards were within a veranda covered with green creepers. The green wooden-latticed windows were open.

As the taxi drew up, an orderly appeared with a push-chair and wheeled me along the veranda to my room.

We stopped outside Number Two. This was not very cheering, because to me numbers have a significance, and I have never known two to mean anything but trouble.

By now I was being wheeled into my private room and, in those few shattering moments, I would not have noticed had the roof fallen upon me. The floor was cement and none too clean. No rugs. The walls were dirty, so were the doors.

'Is this,' I ventured, 'the Special Ward?'

'Yes, indeed, espeshal vard.'

The pink etceteras would never be worn here. A pair of clogs and a knee-length overall would be more suitable. I began to feel that it did not matter if I never walked again. Two revolting, goggle-eyed lizards clung to the ceiling. Previous patients had slashed at many flies against the walls.

The large-fee doctor came in breezily rubbing his hands.

'Ah! We have arrived.' Two mincing and highly inef-ficient-looking probationers hovered near. Neither appeared to have any interest beyond watching who passed along the veranda. Their eyes were kohled, and the blackened eyelashes did a good deal of fluttering. Their nails were heavily varnished.

When the doctor had gone, I expressed surprise that they were allowed to use so much makeup, and said that in the West nurses were not allowed to use more than a minimum of cosmetics while on duty. They seemed amused and said that once their three years' probation was over they planned to go to England. 'We'll liven them up a bit over there!'

Luncheon time arrived and a man brought a tray on which rested a cup of clerical-grey soup, locally known as Brown Vindser, said to have been a favourite at Windsor Castle in the time of Queen Victoria. Much of it had been spilled in transit. On a large thick much-chipped plate were two slices of underdone and indefinable meat, a few slices of slithery beetroot, without vinegar, and two yellowish potatoes. They looked rather like dirty soap. On a small saucer was a luridly-coloured red and green pudding, the size of an eggcup. This menu, I was to discover, never varied, day in, day out.

The greengrocer who had the contract to provide the hospital's 1,500 patients with beetroot and potatoes must have been in a flourishing condition, I thought. I said as much to a man, who was now identified as a 'Catering Officer, First-Class'. Not as much as you think, he said, since the administration took so much in backhanders from him – the Officer's brother-in-law, as it happened.

After a week of this diet, I could not look at the food. I thought the local dishes might be better. Aubergines, flavoured rice, and yogurt! I realised I was starving. The thought of the delicious meals we used to have long ago in the subcontinent came to my mind, but in pictures, yet almost visible, a mirage of wonder . . . Those of us who had friends outside, or resources to pay for food to be brought in, were warned to conceal this as much as possible, for 'food from outside was NOT DESIRABLE'.

Accordingly, it became difficult, almost impossible, to smuggle much in. Even bribery, to my amazement, did not seem to work. Still, most of us stuck it out because this was the only place for some sort of medical attention for many miles around.

Local food was ordered, though described by the nursing orderly in terms which would have been the despair of a Western liberal, so respectful was it of both the local population and the proletariat:

'You have chosen well,' he said, 'for it is the food of destiny. Former rulers, such as Moguls, ate it. It also gave British, God bless them, the strength to stand the heat. It is also product of middle class, and they are salt of the earth, as you know. Doubtless you are one of them, isn't it?'

My first Subcontinental middle-class meal was dinner. When it was placed before me it made the English-type food of the previous day positively appetising. Here upon a cracked plate was a mess of grubby-white rice, swollen to immense proportions and soggy. A bowl contained some dark browny-black gravy from which long meatless bones protruded. A large, dirty piece of unleavened bread lay beside the plate of rice.

Nevertheless, hunger is a force in itself and insists upon being satisfied. I poured the 'gravy', which I supposed was curry, over the rice. The first spoonful convinced me that the cook had an abnormally heavy hand with the chillies. The rice itself tasted like I imagined soaking wet paper would. Alone, or accompanied by its confederate, it was next to uneatable.

One of the 'houri' nurses, who was examining the things on my dressing table, said that the rice given to her and the other nurses was 'terr--ible reely'. That they paid too much each day for their food, and were going on strike.

'Strike!' I repeated. 'You mean stop work?'

'Of course, why not?' she replied, taking one of my letters out of the envelope, and beginning to read it in amazing English.

'I wass--so--o glad to--o re--ceef yo--ur let--tir.'

'Who is this purson?' she asked.

'A friend.'

'Is she married?'

'Yes.'

'How many children has she?'

'None.'

'Why?'

'I never asked her.'

'Why?'

'Because it is her own business.'

'Is she going to have any?'

'I have no idea. Please bring me some water, and something for gargling, my throat is burning.'

'Why?'

'Perhaps the cook can tell you.'

She took no notice of this remark. On her way out she met another like herself, and they began to converse in loud voices.

Somebody was calling for a cleaner. The cry was repeated until a member of that bone-lazy fraternity appeared. An ambulance tore along outside the veranda. Its doors were opened noisily. There were shouts by the nurses for blan--kets! stret--cher! The groans of my neighbour in the next ward who was recovering from an operation could be heard now and again through the din. It was a point of honour to speak English. It was, like the food, apparently very middle class.

I learned afterwards that the loud shouter was none other than the ward Sister: the terror of all lower ranks. It seemed to me that a voice like that went with an inferiority complex. Anybody with ability never needs to shout.

This nurse had a voice like a foghorn when raised, and like a dripping tap on a tin plate in ordinary conversation. Perhaps her voice had been perfected in a country village.

Here it had a way of ricocheting off the walls and being hurled back.

Sister came on duty at 8 a.m. when she marshalled the cleaners. The orders began, continued, and ended in a loud ringing voice. There were many replies, because nowadays menials have their rights. Moreover, as they told me, since the British went, the people who now had the power did not know how to give orders. In spite of that, any cleaner who thought he could shout louder than Sister soon gave up trying. She was not more than five feet tall, neat as a pin, and even if she was five hundred yards away every word was clear.

She liked to be mistaken for an Englishwoman, and often was until she opened her mouth. She preferred to hold forth in English which was unfortunate if you were used to a more Western form of it.

People who didn't know English had to learn it to work with Sister. 'You are lacy, vy you not here ven vanted? Go clean the so-and-so of Number se--vin.' A spade was a spade to Sister!

Twice weekly there was the laundry to be counted. This took place outside my door and if I had not slept the night before, the row was almost unbearable. It was still not so bad for me as for the newly-operated-upon patients.

The laundry tussle began with loud shouts for the orderlies – two of whom swore that one day they would hold Sister down and strangle her. They were saving up, they said, for a celebration afterwards.

This caused a riotous response from the others. Then the counting began in Sister's piercing voice.

'Tow--ils, how many?

'Show me tow--ils!

'Blankets! YOU fo--ol. Do--not--tell--me--you--can--not--find--it! Six, I say it is. It *got* to be six!'

'Five, please Miss,' (she liked this English appellation best).

'You *got* to find it. That is my order. I am bass here.

'Count a---gain.'

The count produced no more. This meant that one of the orderlies had not been to some ward or other, and another tumult arose.

'Ha--mid Ali! Akbar!--Lal--Din. You fo--ools! Do--not--tell--me--you--not--have--it. You go find it. Go--get--it. That is my order. You got to!' All at dictation speed.

Groans redoubled from one of the nearby wards. The patient who had had the brain operation was asking (or rather shouting above Sister's voice) for water. She called to a passing nurse to take a basin to Number Five whose 'stomach had turned against him'.

The stretcher passes noisily on its way to the ambulance. Last-minute orders are given by crowds of bystanders, apparently at random.

At these rather terrible times – for the other patients – many pairs of feet pass along the stone-paved veranda. Some because their owners have to accompany the patient; others because their proprietors will tell you they have never missed seeing a patient go to the operating table and return therefrom – like the cheerful old ladies who will tell you they have never missed an important funeral.

All the nearby wooden lattices are thrown open, and a fleeting, cursory interest taken in the unfortunate patient, as he or she is put into the ambulance. After all, a hospital is a dull place unless one is on the staff, and any happening whatsoever goes to the composition of an event.

The patients' relatives, who are allowed to stay in the hospital – I will tell you why presently – have a unique opportunity of seeing life in all its morbidness. They watch like vultures for the return of the ambulance and, if it is away for over six hours, added anxiety asserts itself. Never do they ask stray passers-by, 'Is the patient all right?' but always 'Is the patient dead?'

When I mentioned this to my doctor, he answered with the sort of surprising information – sometimes irrelevant, but to me interesting – that often appears in conversation in the East: 'It is Iranian influence. The Persian for 'hospital' is *Bemaristan*, place of the sick. The Arabic word, however, is *Dar al-Shifa*, Abode of Cure . . .'

The patients and their acquaintances, as well as members of the staff, leaned outside against the veranda windows. The diseases of everybody's relatives were described in loving detail. One had lived for a week without a heart; another had never had any heart, even at the beginning. She had died when she was twenty, because the doctor could not see her in time. A friend said it was God's will, and the narrator said with a snarl in her voice that it was.

Another said that everybody died who came to that hospital. While yet another remarked that that was to be expected, when people were put to sleep by *dawa*; medicine. The patients whose relatives these conversationalists were, must have spent some lonely hours, for many of the visitors seemed to choose my window to stand outside.

The reason why the relatives were necessary was because the nurses were few and patients often wanted water and had no means of attracting their attention. The bedside bells were invariably broken, and the din from the nurses' room was so great that they could not hear the patients' cries.

When there were no operations scheduled, the gossipers liked to visit neighbouring wards. No matter what you felt like, they would sit on your bed, and tell you of the last few days on earth of more than one who had died of your complaint. Their powers of recitation were tremendous, and the agonies of death fully reported.

The best plan was to pretend to be asleep, or to speak only English, but then the women who were supposed to make the beds, carried all particulars about everybody on their rounds. The fact that I was the only foreigner, and knew a good deal of the language, was most encouraging to them.

One visitor, who used to come every day and sit until I was forced to 'wake', was a mine of non-stop information.

There was simply nothing that woman did not know. She lost my sympathy the first day by telling me that she drank only water and ate dry bread. If that was so, she had discovered the secret of putting on unlimited weight. She was tallish and very stout.

118

She told me that the doctor said she ought to have her stomach cut out. She had replied to this doctor, 'If God says I am to have my stomach cut, he will make me willing. I am not willing. That was a year ago, and I am quite well, except for two or three days of pain in my stomach every week.' That was the burden of her conversation.

Meanwhile there was an almost perpetual procession into my room. Nothing is private in most parts of the East. Visitors stay for a long time, the longer the stay the more anxiety it indicates. They prefer to sit on the bed. There were never any nurses around to keep order. When complaints were made to the probationers they used to ask how things were done in England. I wondered where to begin to explain.

Visiting hours were supposed to be from 4 p.m. to 8 p.m. They always stretched to 10 p.m. Quite small children were sent to play in front of the wards on the grass. The tumult was indescribable.

Every relative capable of walking, and many who could not, came to visit their ailing kith and kin. The children yelled themselves hoarse and then cried. The visitors had to shout at the patients to make themselves heard. Loud laughter tore through the other noises and it can be imagined how the really ill fared.

This was the Special Ward; I used to wonder what the public wards were like. When any complaints were made, the nurses replied, 'You are luc--ky to be in private section. How you like pub--lic vard?' This must have been a joke because the nurses always laughed at its mention. 'He! he! he! It is terr--ib--le,' they would say.

There seemed to be only one or two qualified nurses, the others said they had had 'one or two years' training'.

At breakfast time, while the tiny, unappetising and aged boiled egg – always hard – lay untouched on the plate, two or three of these trainees came in. They were on their 'round of inspection'. They said, 'good-morning',

119

argued in chirrupy voices and tittered their way out, holding hands. By the time they paid the last inspection visit of the day, they were usually not on speaking terms. And the petty squabbles and the revenge each had thought out were all related in detail. Had my husband not come to stay in the hospital, and discovered how to smuggle in some food, conditions would have been completely unbearable.

After breakfast the newspaper man walked in. Morning was an uncomfortable time in that hospital – it was like being ill in a busy High Street.

Another newspaper man came in looking for the first, who owed him money. Would I tell the man that someone or other wanted to see somebody else? Next came a cleaner. In time we learned to be amused at his appearance, and called him 'Caliban'. He seemed made for the part. He was tall and black and bow-legged. His feet were very long and bare. He had a tremendous head of hair, like an immense crow's nest, placed rather forward on his head. When he looked round the blind in the doorway, his hair preceded him by about a foot.

His eyes were colossal, black and wild, and they had a way of swivelling round, showing nothing but the whites. He used them too much. He had a weird way of throwing his mane, or trying to throw it, out of his eyes. This occupied a lot of his time and seldom seemed successful.

His chief tools were a long fearsome broom, whose 'bristles' were foot-long rags. The other implement inseparable from him was a pail of water. The water was not clean. It was never clean. He made a fearful noise dragging the pail over the cement floor. He would dip an end of his broom in the water, hold it up while the water reached the other parts, and then make a sweeping gesture like a fisherman spreading his nets, until the whole floor was wet. He never scrubbed the floor, though it badly needed it.

Once the floor, the trunks, shoes and wardrobe had

been thoroughly splashed with chalky water, he disappeared into the depths of the bathroom. Presently from under the bathroom door a stream of water flooded into the ward.

A bedmaker now appeared. She put on great airs with the rest of her fraternity, because her husband took part in film crowd scenes. She thought it was because he was so handsome. That was where Caliban should have been by rights, I thought, until I discovered that Caliban *was* her husband, the handsome one...

When this lady came and leant over me, there was a meaning to the visit. She had, by her presence, staked a claim to my breakfast, which was usually untouched. When Caliban heard her enter, he appeared at the back veranda door with his enamelled cup in one hand and a tin plate in the other. She gave him a share. They always disagreed about the sugar.

Sometimes two bedmakers arrived at the same time, each with a cleaner trailing behind. On these occasions, caused by some duplication of Sister's orders, there was a considerable amount of unpleasantness, with disparaging and detailed references made to the family trees of the opposing parties.

The number of expressions of abuse of which these good people were capable was staggering.

The fault was mine, said a visiting local doctor, because I remembered the days of the old-time servants, and told the bedmaker to come after my breakfast time for what was left. He continued that courtesy and gratitude were packed up and carried away when the colonials went.

The situation became worse because they soon found out that my food was never touched and if my husband called one of them for any work, at least four came pelting along to the door with cups and plates. That they were required for some chore was the last thing that crossed their minds.

It was the woman orderly's job to dust my room. It used

to take her half an hour in which time, for all the improvement, she might have gone over the whole building. Every now and again she proceeded to the middle of the room and shook the duster. This was the only vigorous activity she undertook. All the while she carried on a conversation in very smashed-up English.

'You giving me tea--me likin' tea--me good--with all babas--lady giving me tea--giving me varm clothes-- Taking me work home--good--plenty--plenty good--'

She tried to persuade me to take her back home with me. She discovered in me a long-lost mother, who could take her to England and out in the car. She kept saying, 'Wanting go England.'

When I asked about Caliban, the 'film' husband, she confided in me that he had taken another wife; that she and number two fought all day. She showed me several white scars which had been deep scratches received at the nails of the other. This determined who was to give the orders. The fact that she had a son still enabled her to claim first place. The other woman had no children but – and here she called the second wife some shocking names – she was only twenty.

'Is she beautiful?' I asked, to tease her.

'She makes him think she is,' she replied and I thought that was much of the trouble.

I used to wonder while she was dusting, hanging round waiting for the kettle to boil, where she would fit in if she went to England.

Then the probationers went on strike. One missed them only with relief. Listening to their multiple grievances had become almost as bad as the pain, for which I was still waiting for some effective treatment.

These young trouble-makers were out to cause disruption. Several foreign nurses, very nice, educated girls, refused to join the others. These non-strikers found on returning from doing double duty – their own and the others' as well, that the strikers had torn their best clothes, which had been taken from their luggage and strewn all over the floor. Their family photographs had been taken from the frames and torn up as well. Notes were left pinned up in their rooms, to say that if they continued to work they would be 'caught and beaten'. No notice was taken by authority over this.

These girls continued to work, but the others intimidated them to such an extent that they had to go to the Matron to complain.

The Matron had been trained in England and, in a British hospital, would have been capable of good work. As it was, she had very little say in any matter, and instead of using her influence and ordering the probationers back to work, all she was empowered to do was to take the nurses who had not struck, and allow them to sleep in her room for their own safety.

Whether the irreparable damage done to Matron's new car and the poisoning of her beautiful dog had anything to do with the strikers was never determined, because no enquiries were made.

One by one Matron's responsibilities were eroded, and when the nurses grumbled about the food – which was much better and more than the patients received – the ordering of meals was taken from her too. Advertisements for another matron were frequently put in the local paper, mentioning the hospital: but there were never any replies.

Once, when the nurses complained about the food to the superintendent, he sympathised with them against the Matron and the probationers were given a 'chicken supper', about which they told all the patients with great glee. This they affirmed was showing the Matron what they thought of her, and they promised to have repetitions of the supper. 'Hee! Hee! Hee!'

One day there was extra commotion. There was always a fuss going on about one thing or another, but this sounded something special. Knots of nursing attendants, patients and their relatives talked excitedly in the veranda. Orders flew back and forth. Sister was in full action. 'Sheets--Special sheets! (ours were torn, stained and of the coarsest material)--blankets! (the temperature was 101F)--chairs!' The orders were continuous.

We learned from a man who was racing about with potted plants that a high government official had arrived as a patient. He was in the next but one ward to me. From that moment on, all ways led to Number Four. His food, passing on trays with special china, glass and napery, made our mouths water. Was there a world where such delicacies existed?

How hungry we were! We heard of jellies and souffles and roast chickens. We tried to sit up in our beds just to catch sight of the laden trays passing. Had we been able, I feel there were some patients even capable of helping themselves, if they could have got away with it. There was iced water in huge cut-glass jugs, while, if any of us ordinary patients wanted this necessity, our relatives had to queue up at the refrigerator.

The scent of delicately-fried fish came to our hungry nostrils. Every doctor was in attendance, half-running to be at the side of the great man. Till all hours of the night and early morning the agitated footsteps passed. Doctors in twos and threes discussed the important man's ailment.

A shocked foreigner who was visiting a friend in the next ward said that these people had licked the boots of the former colonial power for so long that they were now licking each other's boots. He was arrested for defaming the State . . .

The poor official could never have had a moment's rest. Meanwhile the other Special Ward patients received their medicine – if at all – when and if anyone remembered them. Their relatives called more and more hopelessly for nurses who were always somewhere else.

It appeared that nothing, even death itself, was to interfere with this idol worship.

It was understandable that staff were anxious to make a

good impression on government officials at that time, because letters were appearing in the local papers against the hospital, the food, the deaths and the treatments. There was simply nothing left to say against the place.

Doctors famous in their own specializations made errand boys of themselves, and grinned as they did it. Parleys as to the treatment of the official went on almost all night in the doctors' rooms. Cars drove up, backfired and sounded horns. There was no sleep for anybody.

I used to call for morphia, the only thing which I could have to lessen the pain and shut out the noise.

The probationers, who knew all about the private discussions of the doctors, said that as two patients had died under anaesthetic in one week, the majority were against an operation for our distinguished guest.

Meanwhile, Patient Number One, as we established ones called the official, had a relapse. This caused his daughter (who was staying there) to have continuous hysterics, and her powerful screams could not have helped her father.

Feet and more feet passed and repassed. The ambulance came and the patient was taken for an X-ray. A private nurse was called in. Extra special food was shouted for. All the rest of us were capable of swallowing was iced water, and there was none for us. I stuffed cotton wool into my ears and swallowed aspirin. My back blistered against the discomfort of a plaster cast: the sovereign remedy for any intractable ailment hereabouts.

Nights were worse than ever. Who these visitors were who drove up in such confoundedly high spirits at about 2 a.m., I never discovered, but they carried on the liveliest conversation with the nurses who were supposed to be on night duty, until far into the early morning. Their farewells were repeated endlessly, before at last they dragged themselves away.

I will say there was plenty of attention from the

probationers when people were dying. Even death itself came with noise and clatter.

Unbelievably, stray dogs often came into the grounds, actually entered the wards and carried off any eatables they could find. Outside, these loathsome animals fought for possession of the scraps.

Nobody took any notice of them. Braying donkeys found their way in. Frightened, thin cats crept into the wards through the night, desperately dashing at moths and rats, overturning glasses of precious water – thus robbing us of the only comfort there was. One heard glasses breaking on the cement floors, and feline marauders being chased by patients' relatives.

We paid heavily for broken glasses, though some could not afford the charges, and therefore could not have water except in old tin cans.

Rats scurried gleefully in the bathroom, seeming to play 'last across' up and down the walls, and over the white-washed canvas which was the ward ceiling, while the 'on duty' nurse and night watchman held a snoring competition on comfortable mattresses in the veranda.

Their morning alarm was our early tea being brought. They never missed that.

The probationers were always sleepy in the mornings, and whispered constantly among themselves. They said they had had a 'good time' the night before. They had had visitors; who were not allowed after the gates were shut at nights.

They used to boast of how they managed to get out and visit and have fun. There always used to be at least three of these friends' cars drawn up in the shadows, and Matron made herself more unpopular than ever by flashing her torch on the occupants. That seemed all the authority she was allowed. Later not even that...

But perhaps the greatest nuisance to contend with was the constant universal throat clearing and spitting. It went on from 5 a.m. until midnight.

An Afghan woman who was just as affronted as I was by all the spitting told me a tale to explain how this practice originated in India. They say, when Afghanistan's Mahmud of Ghazni conquered India, he was so disgusted at the worship of idols by the Hindus that he vowed to make them eat these false gods. He had some of these stone effigies ground into powder, and mixed with lentils, which were supplied to the Hindus for food. When the Hindus discovered that they had eaten their precious idols, the story goes, they tried to spit them up again, and have been spitting ever since.

Whatever the truth of the matter, spitting did seem a universal habit in the Sub-continent. The upper classes, as well as those one might excuse, take the greatest delight in nose and throat clearing. It is a shock to see a bejewelled delicate-looking woman, well-dressed and made up, emit such a nasal sound before expectorating as would cause a Thames bargeman to look embarrassed.

It is useless to tell these expectorators that they are spreading infection, or that such behaviour is unsanitary. They cannot grasp what you mean. A girl of about thirteen, who was the friend of a patient, told me, when the undesirability of spitting was mentioned to her, that she would not feel properly clean if she did not spit. I used to have a noisy tap turned on in my bathroom to try to drown the ghastly nasal and throaty sound, without much result.

There was a pump at the back near my ward. Here the cleaners cast their clouts and washed themselves. If you did not care to see that sort of thing, it was your own fault.

I used to think often of the young doctor who came to work at the hospital. After he had been there three months, he said it was a 'blooming circus' and left.

One day the news went round that the Head of State, no less, was coming to inspect the hospital. Every cleaner was rounded up. Sister must have had one of the times of her life – there was scrubbing, and clean curtains hung at each ward door. The plants were trotted out all down the veranda. The bedmakers flicked dusters over the woodwork of the windows. Water – clean this time – was sloshed everywhere.

As the time of the visit approached, the noise became greater, if that was possible. Nurses, doctors and even the cleaners donned their best and cleanest. The place was a beehive, and we now scarcely recognised our surroundings. Few patients had any attention whatsoever, but the surface of everything shone. The big chief, whom I had met when we were both somewhat younger, must have been delighted by the scene. He used to be a clever man. I wonder . . .

Within half an hour of his going, the plants were swept away, ('send them to the market – see what they will fetch') old clothes were fashionable again, and our hearts sank to their familiar depth.

At that hospital I lost sixty pounds in weight, and a lot of faith in human beings. As the taxi passed out of the main gate, I thought that one could not be too careful about the use of adjectives. It was true that that ward was 'special', but we should first have been told in what way it was special.

I had plenty of time to analyse what was wrong with that hospital, and what would be needed to put it right. It is all too common to put the blame on 'the Third World' and leave it at that.

The facts are otherwise. What was wrong with the place was wrong planning, wrong recruitment, wrong administration, wrong training.

And this situation, given the laxity and lack of forethought, could have happened anywhere on earth. Plenty of people in the 'First World' are dying through neglect, inefficiency and incompetence: indeed at the moment the symptoms seem to be spreading. Both the diagnosis and the cure are surely quite obvious.

9

Through the Khyber Pass

The Afghan Consul came to see us off on the mail-bus from Peshawar. In these sensitive parts, it is never certain whether such an association is a plus or a minus. Our friend's presence was balanced, perhaps, by that of the C.I.D. man (locally known by Pakistanis and Pashtuns alike as 'that dog') taking photographs of as many travellers as possible.

I had persuaded my husband to take the Khyber road, and the mail-bus, out of nostalgia. We had travelled that way when first married, over forty years before.

My neighbour on the bus was a tall, lean and grey-eyed frontiersman. He was armed, as such as he usually are, with a modern rifle and cartridge-belt. Made in Darra Adam-Khel, within Pakistan territory, these Pashtun weapons actually out-perform those of Western factories.

No central government – including Britain's at the very height of its power pioneering the bombing of civilians from the 1920s onwards – has ever succeeded in holding sway over that road or the free lands which lie beyond it.

My neighbour now kept turning in his seat. In answer to my enquiring glance, he said that the 'Indian C.I.D. dog' (everyone south of their country is an Indian to the Pashtuns) was now cycling behind us.

I replied that it did not matter, now that we were on our way to *Bala-i-Watan* – the Highlands of the Homeland: Afghanistan. But the Khan was not listening, and he had now turned round in his seat and was facing the cyclist.

His whole countenance was a solid mask of hate and anger.

He shouted to the driver to stop. We were now some miles out of Peshawar, where the road is boulder-strewn and lonely. The surroundings looked as though imprinted at the beginning of the world, before anything had taken shape.

The Pashtun glared at the driver. Suddenly the bus slowed down, and the frontiersman, clasping his rifle at the ready, sprang to the ground shouting: 'Death to the dog!'

I could only shout: 'For God's sake do not kill!' The voice was a croak, not at all like my own.

I saw the Khan loading his rifle. The Pakistani had turned his cycle around, but was too nervous to mount. He was shaking so much, and jerking so convulsively, that it almost looked like a joke, as he looked backward towards the bus.

The hillman fired two shots in the air. The policeman, probably thinking he must be hit – Pashtuns never miss unless intentionally – fell in a heap on the ground. His cycle sprawled nearby, wheels spinning.

Again and again the hillman raised his rifle towards the squirming figure, took a long aim, and fired just over his head. My mouth was dry as cork, my hands were clenched. I suppose it was fear. Everybody else, Afghans all, watched the spectacle with evident enjoyment.

The policeman was calling for mercy and putting the palms of his hands together, teeth chattering and whimpering like a terrified child.

'What mercy canst thou expect from me, father of swine?' shouted the Khan. 'Well do I know thy hog-pound, the police station. Go back to thy dirt; lest one of these bullets find a home in thy treacherous heart.

'If I find thee here after I have counted fifteen, thou shalt be carrion for yonder birds which are even now seeking a meal. What is left of thee will be but a pollution on yonder rocks.' Here the Khan pointed over the precipice.

By now the Pakistani was in a pitiful state. His teeth were chattering. He strove to moisten his lips. His face was soaking wet with sweat. Now the hillman began to count. His voice was steady and determined. '*Yow . . . Dwa . . . Dray . . .*'

I prayed that the Pakistani, who looked like a Punjabi, understood at least the numbers in Pashtu, and that it was an ultimatum.

With a convulsive effort, the policeman raised himself. Fear possessed him to such an extent that he seemed scarcely conscious of anything save that he must get away. '*Salor . . . Pindzah . . .* Ten more to go!'

The Afghan driver, a matter-of-fact man less affected than some of us, called that he was moving off, but the hillman replied, 'Go if thou must, brother, my work is here.' The policeman mounted the cycle, but fell, trembling like a jelly, to the ground.

My husband and the driver tried to persuade the hillman that the 'Hindi' was not worth a shot, and that the Khan's life was valuable. He was deaf to all words. What had caused the Khan to have taken this attitude was known only to himself – perhaps, I thought, that bombing raid at Shabqadr . . .

I tried to turn away as the policeman strove to mount his cycle once more. 'Ready,' yelled the Khan in a voice of doom, while he trained his eye along the gun barrel. It was impossible to close my eyes, or remove my gaze. My entire body was ice-cold, as if frozen to the seat.

After all, it was all of four decades since I had been trapped under fire in a mountain castle in this area, as I have recounted in *My Khyber Marriage*. I was rather out of training, as it were.

The C.I.D. officer had now managed to mount the cycle, but he was crying with great sobs, and the bicycle wobbled. The Khan laughed. It was the type of laugh one imagines a madman would give just before or just after he committed murder.

The sight of that unprotected and terrified creature summoning all his power to escape a death to be administered within seconds could never be forgotten. We heard his trembling highly-pitched voice calling upon the mercy of Allah.

Where we were was a wilderness of rocks, not a green leaf was to be seen – great gaunt rocks rose on all sides. There could scarcely have been a better place, I thought, for a murder.

'Go, Indian suppurating offal,' the Khan shouted, louder and louder. 'Today I have spared thee for the sake of these travellers. We shall meet again, and if I hang for thee, the gates of Paradise will open for me.'

But the words could not have reached the policeman, who had now regained such wits as he had and was pedalling like a fury, back towards Peshawar and civilisation...

For half a minute the gun remained trained on the corner of the road; then the Khan returned to the bus. We would not reach Torkham, the guard post, for some time.

I reckoned that the likelihood was that the policeman would be able to communicate with his headquarters, and our bus might easily be overtaken. Failing that, we were almost sure to be detained at the frontier. I kept thinking I both saw and heard the pursuit. We were all accessories, I supposed.

The hillman was now humming to himself. Every now and again he turned round, apparently uneasy for the same cause. His gun was in his hands ready for action.

'Of such bullying cowards are the southlands made,' he informed everybody. 'They are a people born to be ruled; made to lick the feet of conquerors. Power to them is a weapon with which to murder the defenceless. If that coward had been armed either he or I would have fed the vultures this day.

'Do not we all know them and their vile ways? All the while they try to make up some lying story that will land us in their jails. One of my cousins was in prison in Peshawar.

'No harm did he do. The police took him while he slept. It is said that this government does its evil works because they take orders from some foreign power. Of a surety it is from Satan! Watch their end, my brothers! Allah, the One, sees all. Those vile lentil-eating ones have forgotten the words of Sheikh Saadi: "Beware the heart-cry of the oppressed!"'

For a long time the Khan sat still. His rifle was still in his hands. The knuckles of his hands shone white through the sunburn. His left hand cupped over both gun and the finger on which was a turquoise ring.

As the bus bumped along the twisting road, the surroundings might have been a stage prepared for a tragedy. Immense high rugged rocks walled the inner side of the road, stretching up and up. On the outside, the edge of the road was the top of a precipice and stones flew from under the bus and over the edge.

A puncture is a nuisance anywhere. In the Khyber, just at that moment, under the fear we were all silently feeling, it was a disaster. My nerves were on edge, and the other travellers appeared no less uneasy.

The frontiersman had just finished singing in a low tone the old epic song-poem of Pashtunistan, which depicts the deeds of bravery in Frontier battles:

> I am a lion, there is nobody stronger than me,
> Neither in Hind, Sind, nor in Takhar, Kabul or Zabul.
> There is nobody stronger than me.
> The arrows of my skill will strike the enemy like lightning
> I gallop into the thick of the battle: I chase those who flee;

For the routed
There is nobody stronger than me.
The firmament revolves around my victories,
Under the hooves of my steed, the earth trembles
    and the mountains shake.

The men's hands clutched their knives and guns when
the tyre-burst rang through the hills, then, satisfied as to
the cause, they got out and walked about. Now, thought I,
this will give the pursuers time to catch up on us.

The driver got down to the job in hand, with the energy
and indifference of all of his kind. The Khan and I
remained in the bus.

As I sat there, I remembered the times when I lived
among these people, shared their lives, their hopes and
fears.

People do not really behave, in frontier territory, like
those pretty-boys in spotless or artistically-dirtied Holly-
wood wardrobe clothes.

The hero does not grin on one side of his mouth, with
the gesture of the advertisements for a famous toothpaste.
He lives within himself, and nobody else matters. Neither
does he stalk about followed by the admiring glances of
those around him. His face and his expression are completely lifeless. His eyes may wander to where he expects
trouble to come, but there is no crooked leer; he scarcely
breathes.

Again we started off. Night fell before we reached the
frontier at Torkham. Here, thought I, we shall be stopped
for enquiry, and the thought of perhaps returning to
Peshawar for the same reason was devastating. Surely by
now the Pakistani policeman had reported the Khan's
behaviour and we should all be kept for questioning?

While the authorities went through our baggage and
examined our passports, I for one suffered the agonies
imagination reserves for those who fear. Every time one of

those in control came down the pathway from the offices above the road, my heart thudded.

But the Pakistanis were unusually polite. We did not know until we reached Kabul that they had put a bayonet through a parcel of books and ruined some valuable ones.

Once through the barrier we felt safe. We were now on Afghan soil, in our own cultural area, Central Asia. There was nothing to fear.

The Khan had wished peace upon us and strode away towards his turreted fort among the rocks. We all watched him out of sight.

Once across the frontier a fellow-passenger told us the reason for the Khan's anger against the Pakistanis, as we bumped over the rocky road.

I shall call the clansman Juma Khan. This is what the other frontiersman who travelled with us related:

Juma Khan is the only son of his father, an important man in his clan. Juma had six sisters, and Feroza was their friend. It was natural that Juma should hear much of the girl, and he fell in love with what he heard.

When Juma came to see Feroza's brothers, the girl, like all her sex, was inquisitive enough to have a peep at him from behind a curtain, and she fell in love with him.

Etiquette is strict on the Frontier, and there were no clandestine meetings between the two. None, however, can take away the dreams of the young, which is fortunate.

But Juma's sister, Hamida, who was very fond of her brother, managed to cause an accidental meeting between the two and the heart of the girl and the heart of the boy spoke each to the other of their love.

When they parted, both hearts began to call to each other; then they became silent with the weight of the separation. The depression was remarked upon by members of their families, and Juma's father decided that it was time he was married.

The more the talk of a proposed bride, the more silent and sad Juma became. Now as iron sharpens iron, so does love engender love.

The sadness of Juma was reflected in his sister, Hamida, who loved both her brother and Feroza. Hamida could do nothing but watch how Fate was playing with those two, and hope was removed from all their hearts.

But as Allah is the Arranger of all, He had opened a small window to allow the sun to shine in upon their darkness; that small window was the sister of Juma, herself.

Now the father of Juma was known to be a strong man, feared by enemies, and respected by friends, which is as should be.

Yet the father was but frail when the daughter asked anything of him, as are all men where women they love are concerned.

Unknown to anybody, Hamida had hinted to her father that her friend Feroza was a gifted girl who could shoot better than any of their friends, and ride even as well as the young men, and was beautiful as a rosebud.

Meanwhile Juma's mother was busily discussing this and that suitable girl, all with more to recommend them, to her way of thinking, than Feroza.

Hamida's opportunity came when her father asked her whether she knew the reason for the depression of her brother. Bit by bit, the story was related.

There were times when the father's expression caused Hamida to stammer and halt, but to her the most wonderful thing she had ever known was the affection between Juma and Feroza, and she determined to make a fight for its realization. One has power to do such things when one's emotions are deeply stirred.

Before the story was finished Hamida's father held up his hand for silence. 'This must be discussed with your mother,' he said, and left the room.

Hamida spent a bad hour while the discussion was in progress. She walked up and down the room with fast beating heart. She knew that her mother had built castles in her mind about her future daughter-in-law.

When her father returned, one look told her that the answer was no. 'Your mother does not agree, she has plans that Juma should be betrothed to Aziza.'

Hamida felt anger rise in her heart, and it all came to her lips when she repeated the name:

'Aziza! Aziza who is fond of nothing but clothes and paying visits to show them off! Aziza who is as old as my eldest sister, years older than Juma! She is so stuck-up nobody likes her. She says she will marry only for money!

'You know, my father, that the women of her clan bully their husbands. My mother knows that too. It was Aziza who killed her brother's doves because she was jealous of his going to India. Besides, no girl we know wants to be married to the brothers of Aziza. Feroza is beautiful and gifted and she and Juma love each other.'

Hamida's father listened, then left the room again to speak to his wife. There was another hour to wait, and when her father returned he kissed Hamida's brow, and said he had explained about the selfishness of Aziza, which had not been known to his wife, who had shown great surprise. These things were not reported to her because it is not for daughters to speak against others to their mothers.

In any case there would be much discussion yet before any arrangements were made. One thing had been achieved; the mother had put off the sending of family representatives to propose for a bride for Juma.

Juma was out in the courtyard target-shooting, and the heart of Hamida ached for the unhappiness of him and her friend.

That afternoon an uncle of Juma called at their home. He was on his way to the fort where Feroza's family lived, and Hamida proposed to Juma that he send some message from his heart to the heart of Feroza.

Juma thought long about this, and then said that as he might not be allowed to marry her, he did not want to do anything which might make her unhappy. Suppose, he said, he was forced to marry another girl, Feroza would never forget how badly he had behaved. Rather, he said, let his heart break than that he should cause the same to happen to the heart of Feroza.

'I can look at this in Feroza's way,' replied Hamida. 'You both know that you love each other, and love is love. You are not engaged yet. If you make up your mind to marry Feroza, you will. Feroza would rather the Khyber hills were ablaze from end to end than she marry anybody else! Those were the words she used, and that is what she said.'

As Juma listened, a deep red flush rose to his brow. 'It shall be as she says, and I shall be the one to set the hills alight rather than marry anybody else. May Allah hear my vow!

'What message would it be right to send, something she would understand?'

Quickly Hamida removed a ring from her finger. 'Send this; a message of such importance might fall into other hands. I will give the small packet to our uncle. Feroza as you know, my brother, means turquoise, and this turquoise ring will speak to Feroza, for love is a true thing.'

Juma was excited and afraid at the same time. Hamida went away to parcel up the love-token. In a minute, she raced back; 'What do you think! I am to go, too, with our mother! I will give it to Feroza myself!'

'Tell Feroza to remember what we said to each other when we parted,' said Juma. 'Am I not to know any secrets?' replied Hamida, throwing her arms around her brother. Then in a half-daze at the unexpectedness of events, Juma found himself alone.

On her return, Hamida reported to Juma that their mother had been very charming to Feroza, who had blushed so many times, that their mother referred to this on the way back and said that Feroza was not only well-behaved but modest and gifted, things which she had not noticed before.

Hamida reported that she had given the ring to Feroza who had kissed it and put it on, saying in a 'shaking voice' that she would wear it till she died.

Everybody now seemed happy, and the long, intricate arrangements for the frontier marriage were put in hand.

Presents were exchanged, and feasts were given by both clans. It was said everywhere that there was no girl on the whole frontier to compare with Feroza.

Her eyes were 'the blue-grey of the far hills before a storm', except when she laughed: then they sparkled like sun upon a stream. She was a happy girl and laughed often. Her face was oval and she had deep dimples which played all the time when she smiled. There were 'home-grown' roses in her cheeks. Tall she was – almost as tall as Juma – and slim. She was a bringer of sunshine into any house where she was, and kept everybody happy.

She was a good cook, and Juma's mother was glad of her help. She embroidered her own garments, and those of her sisters-in-law.

The next year a son was born to them. Juma never wanted anybody to forget that the boy belonged to him and Feroza. He invited every friend of both families to a tremendous feast.

Even the old men, who were fond of boasting of the old days – of dozens of roasted whole sheep and the like, vowed they had never seen anything to compare with it, and hoped that the 'performance' would be repeated every year.

The tiny child was carried round for every guest to admire. It looked quite ordinary to those who were fathers, but to Juma it was his and Feroza's and that made it look different to him.

Here the narrator, who had been at the feast, stopped to laugh loudly again and again. He said he was remembering Juma, crack shot in a clan of marksmen, walking round the gathering on tiptoe, asking practically every guest whether they had ever seen so big a child for its age, or one with a better eye or trigger-finger for the hitting of a target? The child was a few days old at the time.

By the time the boy was four years old, he had two brothers. Juma spent hours a day playing with them. The eldest could shoot when he was six and, because he resembled Feroza, was the favourite of his father. Of a truth happiness is one of the wonders of the world.

Theirs was a happy home, and the envy of all the young people. It became good luck to wish that a newly-married couple would be 'as happy as Juma and Feroza'.

'Feroza looked after the boys herself. They were never given into the care of servants. If she could not take them to a party, she did not go. Nor did Juma. Of such little things, my brothers,' said the narrator, 'is love composed, not only for the time being, but for always. When Feroza was ill, Juma never left her side, and if he had any ailment, the skies were black to Feroza.'

Then Juma heard that the Pakistanis had imprisoned his cousin. When the news reached them, the families were expecting the return of the boy. He was to have been married that week, and preparations had been made for the entertainment. Many guests had already arrived just as Fate stepped from her black chariot into their midst.

The report had it that the young man had been accused of robbery, an hour after his arrival in Peshawar. He had been tired after the journey and had gone to sleep at once. The Pakistani police arrested him 'in his sleep'. The police were armed with machine-guns and were said to be looking for a robber.

A year passed and there was no sign of either trial or the release of the cousin. The father of the boy was seriously ill and asked constantly for his son.

Juma talked it over with Feroza and they both agreed that Juma should go to Peshawar, where the boy was imprisoned, to investigate.

It was a poor thing, Juma said, that a man should die, while his son was imprisoned, and innocent.

The next day Juma left. He said that he knew he would not be welcome in Peshawar, as he did not agree with the ways of the police there.

In Peshawar the police were adamant. The youth, they said, had been caught red-handed. Juma told them that his information was that he was asleep when arrested, and he said he had witnesses to prove that.

The police replied that perhaps the witnesses might change their minds if sent for to the police station, and who would take the word of a clansman in Peshawar, against the evidence of the police?

Juma said he knew then that he had lost, but he asked the police to be allowed to give a message to the boy from his father who was dying. The policeman laughed and all the others with him joined in and said that was an old excuse, and if the father had been dying he was probably dead by now: so why worry?

When Juma heard what the police said and their laughter, his eyes swam with blood. He was angry that these miserable dwarves doubted his word, and that other hands than those of the son should lower the father into his grave: the father who would go on calling for his son until Allah had stopped his mortal breath.

Juma forgot where he was and struck the speaker to the ground.

At once he was surrounded, but he fought until there were ten men trying to lay hold of him. It took them all finally to overcome Juma. He was thrown into a dirty, verminous cell. The air stank, and he was unable to eat the abominable, chilli-hot food, infidel food, which the people thereabouts love.

At nights he lay awake and thought of Feroza and the boys. He said the thought kept him from becoming a madman. He remembered the dying man who said he would try to breathe until he saw his son again, and at this thought, Juma beat upon the door with his clenched fists, until he burned with fever, and sank upon the filthy floor.

How long had he been there? He had no idea of time. A guard told him it was a week since he came. He had not come, he yelled, he had been taken by force. That was a killing offence where he came from, although, he said, it was common practice in Pakistan.

That night a new guard came. This man unlocked Juma's cell and called loudly, 'Get up off the floor,' but suddenly he approached the prisoner and whispered in Pashtu, 'When you get out, go to a certain house; there you will find Ahmad Khan – the son of the dying clansman. Take the Smugglers' route. Allah be with you!' The guard made great pretence of banging the door and locking it, but Juma knew instinctively it was not locked.

Juma could think of nothing but his good fortune. Suppose though that this were a trap? The thought was momentary, because the guard had made a certain sign which all clansmen understand and honour. Of a truth he was free. Every breath a frontiersman draws must be that, free.

While the prisoners were eating, the guards were usually absent. Within an hour Juma was entering the arranged house. He embraced his cousin whom he scarcely recognized, so weak did the boy look. It was obvious that he had been beaten, but all he said was that he had not been able to eat the food in prison.

When Juma doubted whether the boy was able to undertake the rigours of the Smugglers' route, the boy said it would be easy after the experience of the Pakistanis, and that now he was so dirty the Pakistanis would take him for one of themselves.

The two lost no time in getting away. The pace was slow, and as the journey proceeded Juma carried the boy on his back through the rivers and over the rough parts of the road.

Eventually they reached their homeland. As they were arriving there was a sound of aircraft. 'There are those sons of Satan,' said Juma. But the words were lost in the sound of an exploding bomb. Both men lay flat on the ground, as other bombs burst.

For a time the planes circled round then made off. Juma hoisted the boy on his shoulders and hurried to his village. Soon they heard screams, and saw that the target had been their homes.

Juma's fort was rubble, the walls were in ruins, and smoke hung over all. His heart rose to his mouth as he thought of Feroza and the boys. And as soon as he approached he began to call loudly the name of his wife and sons.

'Feroza! Hamid! Abdul Ghaffar!' There was no reply. He continued to shout, until he was hoarse. He could not find a way through the rubble. He threw himself on the ground and clawed at the mass. Every now and again he heard the screaming of women. Everywhere there was confusion.

He ran to where some villagers had congregated. No,

they had not seen either the mother or the boys. They had troubles of their own.

Wherever he went, he saw chaos. People were frantically trying to remove the rubbish to reach those who were trapped underneath. Mothers were carrying children and calling to them when it was obvious the children were beyond help. Others were staggering about covered in blood.

Presently some of his friends came and began to clear away the rubble which had been his home. He told them not to trouble, because Feroza and the boys would be at their grandmother's home. They did not reply but carried on. His family, thank God, would be safe! It was natural – when he did not return when they expected him, Feroza would go home. The house did not matter! That was a material thing!

The men told him that the father of the boy he had brought home had been killed. He asked them to go to the help of the others. He said his wife and sons would be safe at her mother's. Houses did not matter.

'Juma Khan.' Later he heard his name spoken by one of the men who was clearing the litter.

'Come,' said the man.

He would go. They did not know that he cared nothing about the destruction of his house! It was now dark and their movements were hampered.

He saw when he turned the corner that the men were pulling something from the rubble. He threw himself on the ground beside it. First the men carefully uncovered a hand. On it was a turquoise ring.

Juma covered his face with his hands. Great sobs shook his body. He would not look. It must be a dream. Since he had had the message from the guard everything had seemed like a dream. He would wake up in the Pakistani prison . . .

He tore his hands from his face, and saw the body of a child being removed. Like one turned to stone he

144

watched the other two bodies being taken out. Then he tried to wipe the mud and blood from their faces. All the time he talked to them. They would be all right, he kept saying. They were only hurt. 'Feroza,' he called, 'Light of my eyes! Hamid! Abdul Ghaffar! Juma!'

He placed his head upon the bodies of his slain family. Feroza's hand, on which was the turquoise ring, was the only thing not touched by the horror which had struck them. Holding the hand tenderly, he removed the ring and put it upon his own hand. 'This I shall wear until I die,' he said.

There were many people round him. The women and men alike were stricken at the loss Juma had sustained. The hand of God, for reasons they could not comprehend, was heavy upon him.

Tears fell from every eye. The men led Juma away. He did not seem to realise what had happened. Love had so long driven the chariot of him and Feroza that he was stunned. From that day, hate and revenge occupied the heart where love had dwelt, and these two emotions are as powerful as love.

When the story was finished the telling had been so graphic that we might have seen the film of the story. All this had Juma relived when he had seen the Pakistani policeman following the bus.

Now, the narrator said, he lived alone, speaking to few. The perfect love story of Feroza and Juma would be handed down from generation to generation for all time in the Frontier folklore.

This, I reflected, is the kind of fact which lies behind what is called in the printed reports of international law 'The Pacification Policy of the Administering Power'.

10

Kabul

The city of Kabul, about 7,500 feet above sea-level, is built on the banks of the Kabul river. It nestles at the foot of the range of Paghman mountains in my husband's ancestral patrimony, in the Hindu Kush ranges: called by Ptolemy and other ancient geographers *Aryana*.

Although the place has always been there, the people have changed somewhat from time to time, what with conquests; so 'Afghan' is a cultural expression, originally applied only to the Pashtuns, ten million of whom live in today's Afghanistan and Pakistan.

In literature, 'Afghan' is first used by Persians, meaning (in Arabic) 'Turbulent Ones'.

'Kabul' is said to mean 'Sheep-fold', and its ancient name, Kubha, appears in those most venerable Hindu scriptures, the Vedas. It is believed to date as far back as 2000 B.C.

This is what guide-books tell you, but the place really has to be experienced to be believed. It is an unique area of Central Asia and the country whose capital it is, marks the ethnic and historical – as well as the psychological – division between the Middle and the Far East. The contrast with the Indian subcontinent, for example, is tremendous. And Afghans, as if to emphasise their identity with the Middle East, claim that their capital was founded by none other than Cain, son of Adam . . .

Here we have a place first named (by the Persians) *Bam-i-Dunya* – The Roof of the World. It is a modern

146

capital city yet full of pack-animals, though some of its transport now includes buses and trucks as well as camels.

Afghanistan has no railways and when one was mooted, it is said, the talk went around the wild Pashtun southland: 'good – high-grade steel rails can be ripped up for Darra rifle-barrels'.

I was once treated with some contempt by an American diplomat on the subject of railways. He had been posted to Afghanistan, and was proposing, as we talked in Geneva at an international conference, to 'get to know the country by train.'

'But, Ambassador,' I protested, 'there *are* no railways in Afghanistan!' He muttered something about the British always trying to make the Americans believe wild stories, 'There are railroads *everywhere!*'

Before the vicious Soviet occupation, the *Shahr-i-Nau* – the new city – was rather different from the quarter which was reduced almost to rubble by bombs and missiles in the nineteen-eighties. The houses which survive in that quarter are up-to-date, built in beautiful gardens. In those prewar days, many more houses were in the process of construction, and the city was spreading farther and farther out.

In spite of the fact that glass had to be brought from far-away India and was very expensive, most houses had sunrooms and many even had 'picture windows'.

Those of us who remember the beautiful city before the Soviet invasion must weep all the harder at its fate. During the winter months, it is true, there was no green to be seen, but as soon as *Nauroz* – the Afghan New Year, celebrated on March 21st – came, which it did with startling suddenness, every garden sprang into life, and within a week or so, as if by magic, roses of all kinds and colours dripped over the walls.

The workers were never too busy to pluck the flowers as they passed along the roads, and often put them behind their ears.

One of the earliest blossoms to be seen was *arghavan* – lilac – rather deeper in shade than the Western variety. About the same time an especially beautiful tulip appeared, its petals as thin as tissue paper. It was a pale pink shade, centred with black and delicately touched with pale green stripes on the outside.

There was also a deliciously-scented mauve flower, shaped like a convolvulus, which made a bold splash of colour in the bazars, where it was sold for about three *afghanis* – sixpence – for a huge bunch. When the cook was doing the shopping, he often bought a bunch for his employer, which she found placed near her favourite seat.

Among the roses, there was an especially beautiful cream rambler, the flowers of which were about three inches in diameter. This rose made a fairyland of any garden; it resembled the English Christmas rose. Usually it climbed, if trained, on supports such as are used for vines, but it was capable of using walls or trees or anything adjacent for its ascent. It was pleasant to take tea or simply sit in the shade of these arbours.

White and coloured irises were everywhere; and surely Kabul might have been called the home of roses. Hollyhocks, nasturtiums, sweet peas and most of the flowers we know in Europe grew well and plentifully.

I sometimes recalled, in Kabul, the terrible loss of face that the profusion of British-type flowers among the Afghans had once caused us in Edinburgh, a generation before. My husband's landlady at his student digs was a keen gardener.

She asked him to send to his father for seeds of some Afghan flowers. When they arrived, she planted them, only to feel intensely betrayed, let alone become a local laughing-stock, when the result was – a riot of nasturtiums and some impossibly English-looking hollyhocks . . .

In spring, the trees along both sides of the roads burst into leaf. The birds, thousands of them sparrows, trim, clean and busy, chirruped everywhere. The sparrows made nests in every cranny in the garden wall, and magpies and hoopoes nested in the high trees. Magpies, which had a high sense of the pictorial in their colour scheme, flew about the gardens. Their voices were unmelodious, but fortunately they were not noisy birds. Although 'magpie' colours are considered to be black and white, the lower part of the magpie's back feathers are a shiny dark blue, and near the tail they are a shimmering green.

Pigeon-sized hoopoes – the bird which was supposed to have taken affectionate messages from Solomon to Bilkis, the Queen of Sheba – were scarce, but the most beautiful of all. Their head and back feathers are a warm beige-brown. Half-way down their backs the feathers are striped, chevron-like in white and black. Upon their heads there is a slim cockade of red feathers.

The hoopoes, birds of good omen – one of them was the organiser of birds setting out to find their king in Attar's epic poem – are seldom seen alone, and are extremely shy. Many people in Kabul, even in those days, had never seen them. It is said that there is a stone in the hoopoe's nest, which, if one is able to possess it, is the 'philosopher's stone'. It transmutes base metals into gold, and gives eternal life. But the hoopoe's nest is not by any means easy to find and the more philosophically-minded say that this rareness is exactly what the legend is pointing towards.

The mynah is another fascinating and energetic little bird, found in abundance. About the size of a blackbird, dark, sooty grey in colour with yellow legs, they have white feathers in their wings, which look like fans as they fly.

They have a song of a few sweet notes, which they constantly repeat. It is easy to teach them to speak. Naturally in Kabul they spoke in Dari-Persian, but in India they were often voluble in both Hindustani and English. They are also very shy, but once tamed they make amusing pets. Their feathers were considered very lucky, kept in the house.

Another favourite bird pet was the partridge, a fat brownish red and grey striped bird. Small boys could be seen by the riverside or at the water channels by the roadside with cages containing these attractive birds.

In the early morning these partridges gave a call, which they repeated and repeated – for some time. They did the same again at night. For some reason or other these birds' cages never seemed to be big enough for the birds inside them. There were also many small birds which resembled canaries and which sang equally well. Swallows, much larger than the British variety, sang well, too.

The British Embassy in (or, rather, just outside) Kabul has immense grounds absolutely full of every kind of bird. This imposing building was designed to be one of the great houses in Asia to show the power of Britain's empire in colonial days. George ('Slay-the-native') Curzon, who was, among other things, Viceroy of India, himself approved of it. If the Afghans could not be subdued or suborned, they could surely be overawed . . .

And yet, there are two sides to every coin. There is a story told in Kabul about that garden and my husband. During the nineteen-thirties, the Sirdar was with the Afghan Delegation to the League of Nations Disarmament Conference in Geneva. An Afghan talking about disarmament might be considered joke enough – but there is more to follow.

The League – precursor to the United Nations – was then considered virtually the club of those countries, mostly colonial ones, which dominated the planet, both politically and financially.

Afghanistan, as an independent State, was an early Member, though viewed with unease because part of most Western Powers' policy was to prevent dependent (or emergent) territories from becoming less dependent or from emerging.

Ikbal Ali Shah was a real fly in the ointment. He had escaped from the magic circle. His father, though an Afghan, was an Indian Nawab as well. This gave my husband 'clout' in India, where the British certainly did not want him to have it.

On top of it all, the British Foreign Secretary, Anthony Eden, (later knighted and British Prime Minister) was supposed to be a Persian scholar, and widely advertised as such in gossip columns and so on. At that time, though it is inconceivable today, such putative expertise was thought by many British people to mean that its possessor was able in some almost magical way to control 'native peoples'.

Alas, though Eden had apparently studied Persian, he knew very little, as befitted a man of his class. Worse, the Sirdar, in good faith and himself a renowned Persian classical scholar, had tried to speak to Eden in that language in the presence of Eastern dignitaries in Geneva!

Eden's fury at Nasser, twenty years later, attributed to the Egyptian's calling him 'that jack-rabbit!' because of his slightly comical prominent teeth, had one precedent at least: 'Get that man, Shah!' he is reported to have shouted to some Foreign Office minions.

The Afghan Foreign Minister, from whom I first heard the tale, nearly choked on his soup as he recounted it at his Kabul home.

By the time the F.O. people had worked out what to do, the 'getting' of Shah had been refined in the mill of diplomatic usage and cunning. The F.O. heard that the Afghan side was to propose the *agrément* – the acceptability of the Sirdar as Minister at their London Legation, and word went out to the British Minister to Kabul, Lt. Colonel Sir Kerr Frazer-Tytler, to scupper the appointment.

Even the Japanese with their judo did not excel the British in their heyday in the ability to use the opponent's strength against himself: indeed, this was one of the features of the British which most intrigued many orientals.

So Frazer-Tytler, under those very trees at the British

Embassy, among those entrancing song-birds, flanked by those so-English flowers, was ready. He stalked up to the Afghan Minister for Foreign Affairs at the Garden Party celebrating the British Monarch's birthday which was held a few days later.

He said something like this: 'In congratulating Your Excellency on this most auspicious occasion, may I say how pleased London is to hear that Ikbal Ali Shah may be your next man at 31, Princes' Gate! I look forward to seeing him myself when I return home. Quite one of *our* best men, you know . . .'

Thus he put the boot in. Two birds with one stone: Eden's opponent blocked, and a far-too intelligent man, with far too many international contacts, removed from the field.

A major diplomatic post would suit a lesser man, with a career still to make: or a retired or even an exiled politician; but not the most celebrated contemporary sage and personality of the Islamic world. Besides, the Afghans would certainly not appoint a man whom the British liked.

It was not only, as Mrs Thatcher would one day actually remind her countrymen before the television cameras, that Britain had had the worst of it during the Afghan wars. Kabul was bitter about the large parts of the country lopped off Afghanistan during Britain's Imperial days.

The Afghan Foreign Minister smiled, and thanked the British Ambassador for his sentiments of friendship. Immediately after the party he started the search for, and soon found, the 'British spy' in his ministry. Then he contacted my husband, and told him the story. 'Of course, you must go to London,' he said. 'We think that they are rattled . . .'

But the proposed Minister Plenipotentiary, by a twist of this tale, did not want to go. He had already once been offered a knighthood by the British, and refused.

The ploy of giving smallish titles to their subjects was frequently resorted to by Western colonial Powers. The honours were intended to make 'natives' think that their leaders had defected to the paramount Power. It was said that this was the device used by London to neutralise Trades Union leaders when they were 'kicked upstairs' to the House of Lords.

Certainly the acceptance of such distinctions, notably by Indians, Arabs and Africans, had the effect of reducing their importance by placing them on a low rung on the ladder of precedence. The effect may, indeed, have been to prevent the emergence of generations of mature political figures in the dependent territories.

A knighthood, to a man of my husband's rank, in any case, was a ridiculously small honour and he took the suggestion, when mooted, as an affront. Further, knights came under the authority of the British Sovereign...

On the other hand, how could he refuse the call of his country? Afghanistan was a neutral country, but already the British and Germans were shaping up for their second trial of strength in a quarter of a century.

The gossip reached Berlin. Before long, the Foreign Minister told me, the German Minister to the Kabul Court was seeking an interview. 'The Sirdar, as an unbiased and cultured representative of your State, which is also known anciently as Aryana, Land of the Aryans, would be welcome in Germany as your representative. It is felt in Berlin that such a posting would be more fitting than his presence among the British mongrels.'

Hardly diplomatic language, but it must be remembered that, at that time, the Nazis actually had an expedition in Afghan Nuristan (formerly Kafiristan) seeking their Aryan-blood collaterals there, where legend placed their roots. Fanaticism was rife.

Even the Italians put in their bid. They were anxious in the inter-war years to expand beyond Libya into the Middle East, and needed local champions. Mussolini's personal representative, Commendatore Luigi Villari, was the channel for this message:

'Il Duce, Protector of Islam, is greatly conscious of Your rank and most distinguished pedigree. He recalls that Your ancestor, the great Shapur, Sassanian Emperor of Persia, captured the Roman Emperor Valerian in A.D. 260.

'Accordingly, if You were to come to Rome, even to reside here, You would be treated with Royal and Imperian [sic] honours. Peace should always reign between the Romans and Your family and Islam, as it has by imperial command for almost a millenium and a half.

'Your own lineal ancestor, Emperor Nushirwan the Just, who acceded in A.D. 531, signed the Treaty of Perpetual Peace with the Roman Emperor Justinian...'

We can see from this vignette, the two European dictators competing for influence in the East, both with supposedly historical bases. Hitler's approach was more fanciful and less accurate, yet Il Duce's was undoubtedly imaginative. He had, too, had someone do the homework. Both, certainly at this distance, seem rather grandiose.

Although such details very seldom emerge, this kind of transaction, certainly this type of approach, is the almost-daily fare in certain circles. Diplomats thrive on it, leaking bits and pieces in exchange for yet other fragments, for their despatches home. Journalists also get some inkling, but I have very seldom read in the newspapers anything to compare with such startling tales as appear in diplomatic messages.

Gardens seem always to have played a part in the hearts and histories of the Afghans: tales set in them, stories about them, and accounts of the Afghan love of gardens, are very numerous.

The Mogul Emperor Babur, founder of the dynasty in India, had previously assumed the title of *Padshah* – king, in Kabul. He loved the place, and from the imperial pomp of his Delhi palace he wrote frequently and wistfully in his diary about the gardens of Kabul.

His love of the area was so great that he had his tomb built there; and the beautiful Babur's Garden in Kabul marks the simple resting-place of that mighty descendant of Genghiz Khan and Tamerlane, whose descent is also linked with that of my husband's family.

There were fountains in most gardens, and small summer-houses like Greek temples. These havens were as much used in the winter as in the summer, because there is always sunshine in Kabul, however cold the day.

Trees grew high and luxuriantly everywhere. Acacias were common, and in the evenings their scent filled the gardens. Some of these acacias grew to immense heights and during the month of May were in full bloom. The blossoms hung, not unlike laburnum, in great luxuriance and it was pleasant to sit beneath and look through them to the sapphire-blue sky.

Most gardens had apples, pears, plums, apricots, quinces, cherries and mulberries. *Jalghosa* – pine kernel, and pistachios grew wild, while decorative *bul-buls*, nightingales, filled our whole district with exquisite song. Most of these birds were migrant and by the end of summer, when their young were well grown, they left for the plains.

During the fruit season, one was invited to 'help eat the fruit', in much the same way as invitations to tea are given. The etiquette, not by any means observed, was that all fruit must be eaten on the premises. The younger people had competitions as to who could eat the most.

I have a feeling that this idea of making guests overeat – and everybody does – is an aspect of the humour of the Afghans, who are so hospitable that the more the guests eat the happier the hosts. Fortunately every host has a chance to exercise his prerogative in this way, and certainly some of the guests have an envied ability to respond.

The English word 'hospitality' is translated by its

equivalent in Eastern languages, but the meaning in actuality is completely different. Hospitality, in the East, means simply putting everything you have at the disposal of a guest; and not, of course, charging. The notion of someone staying at an hotel and being charged and yet being called a 'guest' is completely incomprehensible.

I have seen Afghans, returned from Europe and America, still shaking their heads over those beguiling advertisements by commercial firms in Western magazines, inviting people to come and experience 'hospitality' – for payment...

There was always much fun at the fruit feasts. The young people climbed the trees while others stood underneath holding a huge sheet on to which the fruit was thrown or shaken.

Some of the boys helped themselves to the best specimens, and when the delivery from the tree suffered delay in consequence, others climbed up to investigate.

There were large public parks which were popular with the city people. The palace of King Zahir Shah, later displaced by his cousin Daoud, was the ancient *Arg* – fort. This is situated in the centre of Kabul, in a magnificent park, in which there are many beautiful flower-beds and trees.

Before the Russian invasion there were up-to-date shops, with merchandise from England, especially woollens, which were highly priced but considered the best.

There were also goods from America, Switzerland, Russia, Sweden, and Japan. The prices of these foreign goods were high, but only so if the intricacies of the camel-back road through the Khyber, through which they had to be transported, is forgotten.

The old part of the city, with its narrow streets, high buildings and little open-fronted booths, was colourful and interesting.

Here, as is the way in all cities, one found the real people. The booth-keepers were courteous and quiet-voiced.

They did not call out their wares nor encourage passers-by to purchase.

They sat quietly, turbaned or fur-hatted, inside their tidily-arranged open mini-shops, dispensing sugarless green tea in attractive cups without handles – which is the correct way to serve that beverage.

Quietly they exchanged views on the prices of this and that, and the latest gossip. If the owner of a booth was called away, a friend would always 'keep shop' for him until he returned.

The little open-fronted stalls were set out in a clean and orderly fashion. The fruit shops were piled high with melons – the best thirst-quenchers in the summer heat – pomegranates, grapes, and dried fruits.

Large, good melons sold for next to nothing. If one was not sure of the inside of a melon coming up to the expectation of the outside, the *mewa farosh* – fruit-seller, would cut a little square out, so that you could taste it for yourself.

If you decided against buying, another would be tried in the same way. Even if you were still dissatisfied, you were perfectly at liberty to go to the shop next door – the shops selling one kind of article are usually together.

Nothing disagreeable was ever said to a customer – the Afghan traders were too diplomatic for that. They knew there was always *farda*, which means tomorrow.

Grapes in huge quantities presented a pleasing picture. Each of the sixty-four different kinds in Afghanistan has a special name and fortunately a different season. The price was about fourpence per kilo. Large long-shaped ones, called *ab josh*, are slightly acid, and very palatable.

There are also the smallest kind, called *kishmishi* – sultanas to you and me – seedless, which seemed to be the most popular of all. Many of the office workers made a lunch from a bunch of these and *nan* (bread). To get the full flavour and maximum enjoyment of this simple meal, one must be away up in the hills, surrounded by wild grandeur, with perhaps a sapphire lake twinkling in the sun, and a cool breeze coming from the mountains. Then this repast is a feast.

One reason for the amazing good health and toughness of the people must be that there are such quantities of fruit and vegetables, fresh in summer and autumn and dried in winter, that the poorest have always been well fed and eaten a balanced diet.

Grapes and melons were a godsend to me on long and dusty journeys by road. I made one such weary trip to Balkh, in the north, destroyed by Genghiz Khan in 1220. Once the holy city of Zoroaster, it was conquered by Alexander the Great in 330 B.C. He used it as his head-quarters for the invasions of Turkestan and India. Another was to Herat in the west, also captured by Alexander.

The huge melons arriving in the cities in netting sacks on donkey-back made a vivid splash of colour on the grey roads.

Farther along the Kabul bazar there were the booths with coarse hand-knitted socks, caps and gloves. The wool was a natural colour, or grey-brown, and the black pattern which resembled a Fair-Isle was attractive.

There was also the famous *kakma*, a soft beautiful cloth made from camel hair and very expensive.

Another booth would sparkle in the sunshine with caps in gold and silver sequins. Some of the work was executed in pure gold thread, and of course never tarnished. These gold-embroidered caps fit onto the top of the head, and the turban is wound round so that only the top of the gold cap is seen.

Foreign women often bought these for evening wear when they went back to their own countries. The caps were exported in great quantities to India, where men, women and children wore them. Nearly all the foreigners wore the lambskin hats – which fit comfortably and are handsome headgear.

The correct name for this beautiful skin from Turkestan is *karakul*. 'Persian lamb', as it is often called, is a misnomer. I had early learnt, too, that 'Afghan hounds' are called 'Arabian hunters' in Afghanistan itself. And that the rugs I and most other people, including experts, kept calling 'Bokhara' had nothing to do with that city – apart from being sold there – and were usually made in Afghanistan.

At one time, there were a great number of Japanese small goods to be seen in the bazars: a predominance of combs, looking-glasses, sunglasses and the like. There were also a great many cups and saucers (but never, somehow, tea plates) marked on the backs 'Made in Occupied Japan'.

Then came the Japanese economic revolution, and Kabul became the centre for goods of high quality, often destined for Pakistan, which lacked foreign currency and relied to a great extent upon Pashtun smugglers from Afghanistan. After the Soviet invasion, those goods were still flooding in, though supplemented by pitifully inferior quality merchandise from the Soviet Union and North Korea.

Set out in front of one shop you could see the winter comforts, *Bokharis* – stoves and ovens – which are in use to this day. Nearby there was a shop with tall piles of pink, yellow, and green coloured *qandi*, (hence our English word 'candy') cones of Afghan-made sugar.

Afghanistan is not hot enough to grow sugar cane with any success, though beet-sugar was produced. Much sugar was imported from the Soviet Union, and sold in paper containers. The price was high. Nearby were stacks of rubber boots and galoshes, which diminished when the first rains appeared. While the weather was still hot, and nobody bought galoshes or rubber boots, the merchant offered other items of a more saleable nature, until the rains came, when his laggardly gumboot stock would disappear like dew before the sun.

The Uzbek traders from the north did good business in Kabul. They were intelligent, clean and hard-working. They found a ready sale for the silk *chapans* – coats, either made plain or padded. These coats are what the Western people adopted, centuries ago, and turned into what are now called dressing-gowns.

The silk is made in the north of Afghanistan, on the Afghan silk farms. The quality is good and the material fairly thick. The colours are mostly subdued, and some materials are in two colours, giving a shot effect.

From this the Uzbek merchants make the long chapans. These are loose-fitting with what in the West would be called Magyar-type sleeves. Down the inside of the fronts, two-inch wide strips of silk are sewn in a different colour. This is the only decoration.

If an order was given for a coat, it was made ready in one day. These chapans are very hard wearing and are still eagerly bought by the foreign community for wear as dressing-gowns or housecoats. Many women took them, when they returned to their own countries, for evening wear. The shot colours looked particularly well under electric light. The price of these garments made to order was, in the nineteen-fifties, about $2. Good examples are sold in Europe and the United States nowadays for as much as $1,000 each.

There was also a great selection of very wide scarves and turbans, both in cotton and silk. The former are unique when made into frocks, and the latter attractive as blouses. The background is plain green, blue or another colour. The ends are striped in bright, contrasting colours.

There were also booths which stocked second-hand clothes. As many of the garments were of foreign make, and both cut and material of good quality, they sold well to the poorer people. Outside it was fun to see a male assistant putting on the coats and jackets for the benefit of prospective buyers. It was more amusing still to see him 'modelling' a woman's coat, with fur collar and cuffs and perhaps a flared hem.

In the bazars, knowledge of fashion and feminine garments was sketchy in the extreme, because most clothes were made to order. It was not a rare sight to see a boy wearing a woollen beret in the side of which was a small brooch. He had no idea that, at that time, this was women's garb.

The wheel has turned full circle; today the Paris couture houses regularly turn out model clothes whose appearance is even more bizarre, though triumphantly displayed, often to applause, on the catwalk...

Other shops concentrated on 'antiques'; and not always antiques in the accepted sense. Certainly some of them were old, but not worthy of a collection unless it were to be one of useless junk. The foreign community was responsible for this 'antiques' craze, particularly the Americans. Many of them were good bargainers but just as many bought newish, roughly-made Afghan jewellery at three times the price an Afghan peasant woman would pay.

As a result, even a battered aluminium kettle rose in the world to become an antique. Dirty old sticks of red sealing-wax fell into the antique lists; and a few common American plates were highly priced. Some of these shops were worth a visit, because the miscellaneous assortments were often representative of the Victorian age at its least tasteful.

More recently, a newspaper report of so many dead in a certain quarter of Kabul from a rocket attack, took me back to afternoons spent in one of those shops there ... Here is a collection of what used to be called 'motor' hats, in navy and brown, with which young mothers of our generation no doubt horrified our grandmothers. The veils are still holding on desperately, and one hat is still jabbed by a fourteen-inch hatpin. Nearby there is a pair of shoes from those times, with high-shaped heels, and a very pointed patent toe.

There is a dusty packet of pink and blue dance programmes, to which the dangling pencils still cling. I pick
them up. They have done their duty somewhere in a past
as grey as they themselves now are. I open the top one.
From away across the years the name of Annie Brown
stares at me.

All around the loaded donkeys crush past the camels,
squeezing through the narrow streets, and there are loud
cries of *khabardar!* – watch out!, from the drivers. The
dance-programme is a miniature romance. I see the name
of a persistent partner five times inscribed. The name is
Harold Simms. For the first two dances he wrote his full
name, for the third Harold S., for the other two simply
Harold. The friendship had developed quickly. Did Annie
become Mrs Simms? The car horn of an impatient driver
breaks into my reverie and I put the cards back. The
shopkeeper assures me that they are cheap.

My eye wanders to a once-brown deerstalker hat. That
is real old vintage, and I see again the Highland ghillies of
my own family who seem to have been born in this type of
headgear. I see their lithe strong figures stealing up from
the hillside . . .

'Khabardar!' . . . How and from where came that tiny
pair of white kid boots with the many buttons, and not one
missing? Those old bootmakers could make footwear to
last in those days.

Hanging up on a nail in the wall are some long night-
shirts, which perhaps forty years ago were considered
natty attire for grandfathers. I wonder whether the stock-
ing night-cap completed the ensemble. Possibly it did,
because when this headgear was in fashion, no whiskered
gentleman considered himself properly attired for slum-
ber without it. I pick up the cap – the tassel swings
around. The tassel was no doubt considered immensely
chic.

Who, I wonder, flew over the ice upon those tiny knife-
edged skates with the long laced boots attached? Or wore

the long voluminous lace-trimmed petticoat? Or the one with the many yards of deep hand-crochetted lace? What age would the baby now be who wore those flannel petti-coats, scalloped and embroidered: ninety?

The long silk pelisse is beautiful, probably the only antique in the collection.

An argument about the right of way has taken place near a string of Hazara coolies who, loaded far beyond what might be considered humane, have entered into a discussion with a camel driver. The camels sweep the surroundings with withering glances. The donkey driver wins.

It is said that an Afghan donkey-man has the most complete and shattering vocabulary of abuse and swear-words known to man. Fortunately I cannot understand any of them. But the spell is broken. I close the Victorian album of reminiscence, and pass on.

Across the road, outside the butcher's shop, a boy of about twelve is expertly chopping meat on a huge block of wood. While he squats on the ground, he dexterously applies two choppers, one in each hand, to the meat.

Not quickly but thoroughly, he reduces the piece to mince, which is required for *koftas*, meat balls; then the boy adds salt. Now he produces a small box which looks like a joiner's plane, in the top of which a blade is fixed. Taking up an onion, he rubs it backwards and forwards across the blade. The shreds fall onto the mince. The meat is now turned over and over to mix in the onion, and the boy turns to the next customer.

The owner of the shop sits within, entertaining a few friends. He does no work, but gives advice to the assist-ants; while the guests advise would-be purchasers to make up their minds what to buy.

There are sweetmeat-sellers who sit cross-legged in the sun, beside the river, which is never very far away in Kabul. The sweets consist of highly-coloured drops. There is a cream-coloured toffee which, when home-made, is delicious; another sugary confection thickly mixed with walnuts, and several other ordinary-looking sweets.

Kabul is a paradise for dressmakers: men who can copy any garment and who make it by eye, without having to measure you. It is a heaven of Afghan rugs, of gold-thread embroidery, and of silk scarves and turbans. For a woman, these are the raw materials for fairytale garments.

The rice merchants sell lentils, large split-peas and garlic, as well as sugar, packets of tea, matches and perhaps other dry goods like candles. The rice is of a particular type, the grains long and thin.

The Afghan cooks have a way of making *pulao* which persuades the partaker thereof that another helping won't do him any harm. There are many types of pulao; there is also *chilau*, which means that the rice remains white. Brown pulao in which there is plenty of fat, *roghan*, is one of the most popular. It is far from easy to make. Each grain of rice remains separate; much eastern-type food consumed to cries of delight in the West would be considered a disaster by the good cooks of Kabul.

Thin, crisply fried onions are sprinkled over the dish, as well as shredded almonds and fat sultanas which have been fried for a minute or so in butter. Underneath the mound of rice there may be jointed chicken. In mutton pulao, the chicken will be replaced by pieces of mutton.

One of our cooks, who had been taken to Europe by an Afghan diplomatic family, expressed amazement at what he had found: or, rather, not found. 'Khanoum, can you believe me? In the West, talking to chefs there, I discovered that they did not know about Twelve-Onion Tasting!'

I expressed surprise, and begged him to continue. 'Well, you know that we shred onions very thin, and then add them, a little at a time, to a stew – sometimes a few every five minutes for an hour?' I nodded; though I did not really know about this.

'Well, the test of a good cook, or a good eater, is if, after the cooking, he can tell exactly how many doses of onions there are in the *salan* – stew; and how long it has been cooked; and how much onion it contains. This art is unknown among the infidels!'

There is also turkey pulao; but whatever the meat, the rice always tastes better than with any other! Tender pieces of mutton cooked on skewers, spiced meat balls, and *salan* (which is best described as vegetable or meat-and-vegetable stew) are also eaten with the pulao, or alone.

Accompaniments to these dishes are mango chutney or pickles: one of the most delicious being pickled lime. There is a particular kind of sour orange called *malta* which never becomes sweet. It is squeezed over the pulao if a contrast is preferred.

Whole chickens stuffed and served with thick brown (Twelve-tasting) onion sauce and plain boiled rice make a good meal. Roasted grouse, goose, partridge and snipe are also popular. Most hostesses have their own family recipes for these and other dishes. One thing one must remember in Afghanistan is that guests are expected to eat large helpings, and more than one.

One must not forget,however, to leave a corner for the dried fruit and nuts, and the various fruits in syrup. A refusal only offends. Last of all, comes the green tea.

Whether the tea is green, black or the rarer pink (made by the Mongols with clotted cream), in Kabul be sure to turn your cup upside down when you have reached capacity; otherwise you will find that every time the cup is empty it is refilled. There is no use saying 'no more thank you' – that is taken as modesty and means that you are enjoying yourself and that the tea-pouring is to continue. It is often quite impossible to register anything, even relish, after the second cup following a good pulao, if one has been able to find room for that much.

Pulao occupies a special place in every Afghan's heart;

there are said to be as many kinds as there are cooks. But the tale of the miraculous discovery of the dish is rather less well-known, and I give it here:

When the Mongols, under Genghiz Khan, invaded the area, they knew nothing of rice: there was none in Mongolia. Mongols subsisted on a diet of meat and milk from their herds.

After taking the city of Bokhara, however, they sacked the place and carried off everything portable as part of their loot. One group was camped in their yurts just outside the city when one of their fellows, out foraging for salt, struggled up, carrying a sack of – rice.

The meat was already roasting. A lamb was suspended above a camp-fire with Mongol shields below, to catch the drips of fat for basting. The soldiers had meat, some herbs, and butter, and asked their friend if he had brought the salt.

'This seems to be it,' he said, and took out handfuls and threw them into the gravy.

The rice soon cooked in the juice, and was tasted and pronounced delicious: presumably the Mongols eventually got salt for it from somewhere. And rice, lamb, herbs and butter, together with an onion or two and some dried fruit, remains the basic recipe for all pulaos.

11

The Wood-Seller of Kabul

Every morning, by six o'clock, all the little booths in the bazar are open, and the wood-seller, the *Chob-Farosh*, is always first. Indeed, before five o'clock he is already swinging the great axe which looks mismatched beside his tiny frame.

He hastens to get the wood chopped, because he knows the ways of his lazy customers – mostly servants from the nearby houses – who delay until the last moment. Then they come all in a crowd, each expecting to be waited on immediately. They never learn decorum or patience.

He, on the other hand, is a man of decision, of a certain dignity and status, and of method; nothing so low as an employee: he is a man in business on his own account.

He has the confidence of one who knows the proper order of things. There are, it is true, people with well-paid jobs: they sometimes pass his shop. Expensively dressed, laughing together, well-fed, they have their own servants to buy their wood. But they work for masters: in the words of the great poet Khushal, 'dogs with golden collars' – slaves.

His shop is no bigger than a smallish one-car garage. In it are the stacked wood and a low seat for himself: a perch he has very little time to use. There are no 'fittings' in the minute shop, unless a little tin kettle, a small charcoal burner, a teapot and a tiny tin of tea, could be so called.

The floor is earthen; the walls are the same. There is no electric light; but the summer is nearly seven months long, and in the winter all he needs is a modest oil lamp.

The Chob-Farosh is a little grey gnome of a man. He seems to be very old; frail and ancient, until he begins to wield his axe: then there is no denying he is a master of the art of chopping wood. It is indeed an art, because the logs are big and tough, and the heavy axe does not look too sharp. I have never, in years, seen it sharpened.

There is something attractive in watching the exercise of his art: the deft, even strokes which, with determination and power, eventually reduce the huge logs to pieces which will fit into the cooking stoves of the town.

When I felt impelled to say to him that he has the right knack, he quietly placed his axe, head on the ground, straightened himself taut, and said '*Khanoum* – Lady, I am one of the old ones.'

He smiled a little, as though he would like to add, if he were the type to belittle others, that the young ones had not inherited the same degree of skill.

Undoubtedly he is poor, but he is always clean, both in person and dress. His wide cotton trousers, of blue, or green or white, have seen far better days, but they are spotless. He has no cause to be ashamed of the patches, although they do not see eye-to-eye with the main colour.

His waistcoat, patched too, is more the container of the inner pocket for the day's takings than an article of apparel. It is securely buttoned, however hot the day.

His jacket might once have been blue, or perhaps green. Now it is faded beyond any likelihood of fading any more. It, too, is patched. His shirt is fastened up to the neck, although sometimes, lacking a button, he has to command the services of a safety pin for this accomplishment.

He is not much of a hand at tying a turban and it is obvious he does not wear one to add anything to his appearance. Whether grey, or blue or white, varying by the day, this headgear is tied rather lower upon the brow than is usual. The ends appear to get in his way during working hours, and he disposes of them by tying them on the top of his head or at the back of his neck. If he needs to wipe his nose, he releases them for the purpose, and reties them as before.

He does not, I think, wash at home. Soon after his early tea, when the rush of customers slackens, he will roll up his sleeves, push the low-tied turban back a little, but only a little, on his brow, and, taking his kettle, repair to the *jui* – the open water-channel – which flows in front of his booth. Here he fills his kettle from the sometimes far from clean jui, and begins his ablutions.

He takes a long time to gargle: too long for some of those within earshot. He is thorough and particular over this part of the proceedings. Then he cups a hand and pours water into it. This is carried to one side of the face, which is well and truly rubbed, and the movement repeated several times. The other hand washes the other side of his face in a like manner.

When this is adequately completed, and he is not easily satisfied, he squats like a tailor beside the small stream. He now washes his beard, which is beyond the power of one hand to deal with. Deftly he laves water over it, including his ears in the same action, rather in the manner of a cat.

He shakes the water from beard and hands. He never uses soap, nor has he the refinement of a towel: the sun soon does the needful. Now he produces a short, thick *miswaq*, a toothstick, from a pocket, and carefully, thoroughly, cleans his teeth.

This over, he thrusts one foot into the jui, sitting perfectly balanced on the other. He scrubs the foot well, making a loud hissing sound the while. When this is finished, he exchanges feet.

Then he puts on his wooden sandals. These do not look comfortable, and a novice would surely be obliged to learn to walk in them all over again. Although they are like any other sandals so far as the strap over the instep and the thong over the great toe are concerned, the soles are different. There is the usual wooden sole, flat as a board, but underneath heels and toes, there are thick, square, four-inch-deep blocks of wood. He struts about on them, winter or summer.

In winter they protect his feet from the snow and the puddles made by the thaw, and in the summer his feet are well above the thick dust, or the mud when the water-cart has been along the streets. One guesses they have an extra value to this careful little man: that of being practically impossible to wear out.

He makes a penny, or two, on the side, by selling country-grown tobacco. He places the wide, shallow basket which contains it at an angle in the front of the shop; this helps to emphasise the presence of the tobacco, because the leaves, the wood, and the basket are all much of a colour.

As soon as the wood for the morning rush is prepared, the pile neatly stacked, and all the small untidy chips gathered, the little grey man takes the chips and makes up the fire in his charcoal stove. Over this he boils the kettle for his tea.

If there are few early customers, he is able to finish the drink, sipping it as if tasting ambrosia, more or less in peace. But, more usually, no sooner has he filled his little handle-less blue bowl than customers appear. Often there are as many as a dozen; all clamouring, as usual, to be served at once.

The wood-seller takes no notice of their anxiety. Neither does he hurry. His calling is not one to hurry over. Merchants have dignity; it is only servants, mere employees, slaves in fact, with someone breathing down their necks, who hurry.

Abdul-Alim, Wood-Merchant, a man in business on his own account, has been here, in this little shop, for nearly forty years. Customers may bring him money, but they are still of a lesser rank; he is Mister and You: they are always only Thou:

'*As Salamu'alaikum, Agha Chob-Farosh*: Peace on you, Mr Wood-Seller.'

'*Wa'laik as Salam*: And on thee peace.'

'Permission to state: my master told me to hurry, I have to get the fire going.'

'Haste, my child, is from the Devil . . .'

The weighing is a methodical affair, and the customers must wait. The weighing apparatus might be called somewhat unusual, even unique, anywhere else. It is quite ordinary and correct in our bazars. It consists of two large flat tins, one for the wood, the other for the weights. The tin pans are attached, by much-knotted ropes, to a horizontal stick. A loop of cord from this is held in the hand, to balance while the weighing is accomplished.

It is, above all, the weights which make for the peculiarity of the apparatus. These consist of bolts of all sizes, and round stones. Each represents a certain weight, which has been officially guaranteed. When, say, twelve kilos are required, two bolts will be held together by an immense nail, which is screwed in to ensure the holding together of the bolts. The weight of the nail is taken into consideration.

The stones represent as little as a quarter of a kilo; larger ones may weigh many times as much.

I have often bought wood from our Chob-Farosh, weighed out with this contraption, taken it home and put it on my perfectly accurate scales – and found the weight always true.

The weighing-out of the wood is of never-ending interest to idle passers-by.

Heads are thrust forward and mouths stay agape as a piece of wood is added or removed, or a particular weight added or subtracted, just as though the onlookers were seeing all this for the very first time.

The little man does not enter into easy conversation, either for social reasons or because they might well lead to argument. Sometimes he is moved to interfere when disagreements arise among his customers. He is usually a pacifist, but during controversies his voice assumes the tone of an insulted dictator. He seldom has to repeat his words.

Having dispensed with the early customers, he has a good look at the money they have handed over. He is careful over this. When he is sure it is correct, after much mental addition – though he always counted it just as carefully when he first made each sale – he puts it away, deep in the inner pocket. Again he tidies up the wood which is left on the pile, and only then does he return to the low seat beside the kettle.

The tea in his bowl is now cold, but he pours it back into the teapot, which he sets over the remains of the fire, fanning the smouldering charcoal into life. His mind never seems far away from his work.

Except for the times when he quells rising trouble, his whole life is taken up with his own affairs. As he fills and refills the tea bowl, his eyes keep wandering to the wood ranged around the walls, and his bright eyes seem to be measuring the quantity needed for the day.

Sometimes, when there is a noisy, stand-up fight near his booth, perhaps even with the glint of raised knives, he will emerge, pause for a few moments taking in the scene, like a general contemplating attack, and then cross the road, into the middle of the fray.

This is proof of bravery indeed: because the combatants always tower more than head and shoulders above him, since they are usually of a clan which is infamous for hot blood and a fight to the finish, and because they do not like interference from outsiders.

All this the little wood-seller knows, but to him these youngsters – or oldsters – are really not very different in their own way from the untidy chips of wood which he resents and clears away. These people are on, or almost on, his territory. It is his natural social duty to deal with such situations. After all, if everyone let everything slide ... He shudders at the very thought. Then his eyes go back to the wood-pile.

From the shouting he learns that the quarrel is about the division of money which the head man of their group was given for porterage work the team had done. Most often the wood-seller manages to settle the argument. At times, when tempers are beyond adjudication, he quickly realises his mediation is useless, and just as quickly returns to his chopping. The contestants do not exist for him any more.

On the days when the countrymen bring the wood they supply to him – four days a week – they arrive at 4 A.M. Those mornings he is waiting for them by the time the donkeys draw up in front of the booth.

He will examine the cargo carefully, looking more particularly at that which is more hidden. If he is satisfied with the quality, the logs are unloaded, weighed with his ramshackle scales, and paid for, slowly, with proper gravity.

The weighing is a long job, and the donkeys, tied up under a nearby tree, have time to eat the grass their owner has brought for them, and have a rest. That is, if the wood is up to specification, and that has only one meaning to the wood-seller. It must be right, because he sells only the thick, solid, good-burning variety. If the man has brought the thin, dry-as-paper kind, which fills the air with a pleasant fragrance rather like incense (but is no good for cooking) he will have none of it.

The Chob-Farosh neither wrangles nor vituperates. If the offered wood is unsuitable, he will shoot a single phrase at the man who brought it, and turn his back resolutely upon him. It will be no use for the other to plead his cause. The wood-seller is not listening, and the other man, knowing it, hastens anxiously away elsewhere.

The wood-seller does not encourage idle conversations attempted by passers-by. He will curtly exchange greetings with them. There is no chair for the convenience of casual visitors placed outside his booth, unlike most other shops. There is always a shortage of kindling in Kabul. Commerce, in the wood-selling business, takes precedence over chit-chat, social life, the superficialities prized elsewhere.

He has no desire to entertain anybody. Very, very occasionally, a countryman calls upon him, some old friend whom he is genuinely pleased to see. Then the secret is revealed: he is addressed as *Abdul-Alim* – Slave of the All-Wise, with surprising intimacy. We may now know his name, but he must, for us, remain, with proper formality, *Agha* – Mr Chob-Farosh.

The two will sit upon the wooden frame criss-crossed with rope, outside the booth, brought out for the purpose from the back of the shop, and the water-pipe will be passed between them.

One cannot visualise him anywhere else when he is not in his little domain. One does not even like to imagine him in some other small dwelling, grey like himself, with the rather terrible little old wife who comes, now and again, to the shop for money.

Like him, she is old; one can see that, even although she is enveloped in a veil. She does not seem to have either his desire or the ability to keep herself neat and tidy; nor has she his dignity and longing for peace.

From the moment of her coming, it is evident that he is not pleased at the intrusion. His voice, usually quiet, is not subdued when he replies to her. Hers is far from low when she speaks to him. There is a quality about it which irritates the husband. For a time he listens to her, as the pitch rises to the highest notes she can command, which is high indeed. He tries several times, unsuccessfully, to stop the flow of her demands.

Where, he yells, between her threats, is he to get all the

money she wants? She shouts back that he is a wood-seller, isn't he, and is that not a means of getting money?

She says, with a nasty laugh, that perhaps he sits in the bazar to watch the water in the jui flow past. This she voices from surprisingly powerful lungs.

Is not the selling of wood the means by which she is entitled to the insufficiency of housekeeping money which he so grudgingly gives her? And has she not a stomach like himself? That she would like to know!

Do stomachs not demand food, irrespective of the kind of husbands their owners have? That, too, she would be glad to know. Irrespective, she repeats, of unprintable husbands with unprintably greedy habits! Can he deny that she needs food, even as those passing donkeys need it?

He replies, with blazing eyes, that the donkeys are of use, and deserve to eat. Upon this deprecating reference, the old woman appeals to the now-numerous onlookers, who have laughed loudly and encouragingly at her sallies.

'Have a look,' she invites them, 'at the meanest man that Allah ever set upon two feet! There is no need to look too hard,' she adds, 'because he is so old and ugly he would be instantly recognised in the black of a moonless midnight.'

This causes much laughter, and the old man, whose wrath has been rising, thrusts a shaking finger in front of her veiled face, and asks the audience to listen, just listen, that is all he asks, to the daughter of lies, deceit and every kind of extravagance! His agate eyes blaze and his ragged grey goat's beard wags in keeping with the finger.

'Treat women kindly, for they are of a gentler make,' intones a passing Mulla, trying to make peace.

The Chob-Farosh, now calm as any saint, turns innocent eyes upon him, 'Sir, I tried that for thirty years. The remedy is not written in books, but is the one which really cures the patient.'

The Mulla strides away, pettily angry at the lack of respect for his own vain dignity – amid some laughter from the crowd. They know who has the upper hand in this frequent contest, for they have seen it all before.

As the old woman shrieks now-incoherent sentences, her hand, covered by the folds of her grubby robe, looks like the wing of some bedraggled bird darting about within a measured distance.

The wood-seller has made his point. He turns his back on the old wife, and carefully and slowly extracts some money from the secret security of the inner pocket. He bends his head over the coins, as though taking a sorrowful farewell of them.

'There is no need to be so slow,' cries the old woman, 'because in forty years you have never given me even the smallest coin too much.' Again the onlookers chuckle with delight. As the husband hands over the money, he drops it into the hand which looks like a claw. She grasps it and counts it twice. She raises her voice to complain at the smallness of the sum.

He warns her, with head and beard and finger aquiver, turban bobbing up and down, that one day, before long, she will be responsible for his ruin, daughter of impossibility that she is. There will be no more money from anywhere, and what is she going to do then? He will be dead, cold and inert, unable to chop or to sell, she will stand in this very place, hand outstretched, begging from the Believers, may Allah make them more generous to her than she, in speech and action, has ever been to him . . .

She is quieter now, but one feels it is only because she has the money clutched in her hand, and her silence has nothing to do with a problematic future.

As she arranges her veil in preparation for going, he warns her to spend the cash carefully, remembering all the time it is the sweat of his brow, and that the law of life is that that which we do not appreciate is taken from us. With this profound remark he retreats into the shop, and the old woman cackles a laugh in his direction, bending her steps towards the food shops of the bazar.

176

Some of the onlookers, men and women alike, gaze admiringly after her, others purse their lips and give their heads a half shake, as though thankful that their lot is different.

When Abdul-Alim thinks she is safely on her way, he emerges from his shop, walks into the middle of the road, and looks carefully into the distance, as though only the assurance of his own eyes is sufficient proof that she has really gone. 'There is no god but God,' he says piously, 'and Mohammad, upon whom be peace and blessings, is his Slave and his Messenger.'

He nibbles from his small store of bread, onion, raisins and cheese, raising his hands in thanks for the bounty.

He says his prayers the prescribed five times daily, washing himself before he spreads the clean piece of sacking on the ground in front of his shop. There, as he faces Holy Mecca, he again thanks Allah for vouchsafing him bread and tea and the other delicacies – and the privilege of the strength to earn the same.

In the afternoons, when it is hot, he lies down for an hour as the echo of the gun which signals midday dies away. His string-bed could not be called comfortable, but it is a solace, a real rest – after the rigours of swinging an axe for nearly seven hours. There is no mattress of any kind, or any covering except the turban-ends which he places over his face, to deter the attentions of the flies.

There will be no customers during the hot hours and even if there were, he is on the spot. A rest before the evening rush.

After the day is finished, punctually at seven – he has no clock or watch, but he 'reads the sun', he closes the double door of his booth, making sure, with a long look up and down the road, that no laggard customer is approaching.

When he has turned the key in its massive, rusty padlock, he gives a final look around to make sure there is no untidiness in front for which he might be held responsible. The market's Superintendent is strict. Only then does he set off for the home over which his wife has all control.

One hopes, as the erect little figure disappears into the distance, that the lady has relented. That it was rhetoric, affectionate, stylised and acceptable grumbling, not unknown in business circles, when she threatened to send him supperless to bed, and that there is something nice for his evening meal. He has earned it.

12

We Take a House

Hotel life is all right anywhere, for a time. After that there appears an unimaginative, repetitive quality about the meals which, sooner than later, irritates the sensibilities: mine, at any rate.

It always seems that the gap between the expectation and the event is wider than it need be, because at first the management invariably assures us of something which we would never have dreamed of demanding from it: that it exists for no other reason but to serve us, to our entire satisfaction.

The ambience of the *Hotel de Kabul* certainly spoke that message, but the first few meals there gave us little encouragement to think that it would succeed.

The *Hotel de Kabul* was pretty much like any other hotel anywhere, East or West. And it had its good points. It was a Government Hotel. It was built and equipped by the Royal Afghan Government, no less.

Thus much trouble and considerable expense was undertaken by the authorities so that visitors from abroad, accustomed to international standards of living and food, might be comfortably catered for.

The hotel was well-built and well-furnished; the rooms were large, and there was a satisfying supply of large private bathrooms. There were more than a sufficiency of the beautiful, expensive Afghan-made carpets, which cost a lot even in the land of their origin. There were comfortable beds and chairs, and plenty of wardrobes.

Altogether the Royal Afghan Government had expended

much effort to make their hotel better in every way than many Western hotels in which we had had the discomfort of staying.

Doubtless the government thought that the place would be run as they intended; but the management fell down badly on several scores, heating and food among them. It was not that the charges were even moderate. The wood and coal to feed the stove which heated one's room was a major expense. The amount was entered, perhaps with an eye to the unfitness of things, as an extra to our bill. That we could bear.

What we could not understand at first was why the beautiful, well-furnished and spacious lounge was unheated. It therefore remained unused. Later the reason became obvious. While each guest paid for the heating of his or her bedroom, the management was expected to meet the cost of heating the lounge.

For most of the time we sat in our bedrooms. That we bore, as did the other guests. Even the fact that we had to see our friends and any other callers either in the icy blasts just inside the main door or else, like the tenants of bed-sitters, in one of our heat-paid rooms.

Still we did not grumble, after all, travellers must be made of sterner stuff. What we were unable to tolerate in the end was the food. The breakfast started the inauspicious day with a cereal. There was about a tablespoon-ful of some grain faintly resembling that which was a joy to us in London, Cairo, Mecca, Khartoum, Beirut, Basra, Cyprus, and even in unlikely Bahrain. The tea was never more than lukewarm.

We never could discover whose job it was to make the tea. He always seemed to be absent when we were particularly displeased with his efforts.

There were times when, roused at the thought of our ever-mounting dollar liability on the hotel meter, we demanded better fare. We were tired of sending away meal after meal untouched. Food which even hunger failed to flog us into eating.

Twice, during our three months' stay there, other guests, of the most reasonable natures as ever entered any hotel, were driven to adopt the measure of asking us to put our names to a petition to the government itself. This plea set forth in agonising detail the entire situation: the cold, the hunger, the untouched meals; and finally demanded the immediate reorganising of the kitchen.

The names included a number of nationalities. French, Italian, German, Japanese, Austrian, and one which was illegible, perhaps from weakness due to privation.

The manager of the Kabul hotel was a rare type of comptroller, because he never appeared, not even when message after message was sent, and even after two petitions. If anything could be said to be noticeable after our complaints, it was that the food became even less in quantity, and still more unpalatable in quality.

It appeared that if we were not going to put up with the food as it was, he was showing how much worse he could make it.

Why not go elsewhere? There was nowhere else to go. Had there been, the manager of the Kabul hotel might have found himself without a job. Therefore, although you did not like the slovenly and incompetent ways of the management, what were you to do about it? We never discovered whose idea it was that foreigners – the chief clients – should live mainly upon hard, half-cooked beans, soapy potatoes, and meat of mysterious appearance and origin.

We were now finished with the place. We made up our minds to take any house which appeared fairly suitable, thus saving ourselves the ritzy prices, and the hunger and inattention which was all we obtained in exchange.

During our walks around the capital, we had noticed many attractive houses in the *Shahr-i-Nau*, the new city. These houses were large, with good walled gardens. There were also many trees, which would be beautiful in spring, and shady and decorative in summer.

We lost no time in making our way to the first house on whose gate was the sign *TO LET*: incongrously, yet somehow encouragingly, in English. Here we knocked. There was no reply. We repeated the knock, somewhat louder than before.

A passer-by, who had been driving a much-overloaded donkey, immediately joined us. We exchanged no word, the object of our desire easily enough understood. The man was evidently no stranger, because he called out loudly the name of Amir Ali.

Soon more than a dozen people of all kinds and calling gathered, including a man with two camels, which wore the superior look of their kind, and a small boy with a hamper on his head, out of which a child of about three years just managed to keep from rolling off.

Each one added his quota of knocking and shouting. We knew none of them, nor do I think they knew each other. However they differed in looks and occupations, they were agreed that that door was going to open, if they had anything to do with it.

Yet even though the stout door itself showed signs of giving admittance, the much invoked Amir Ali did not.

The noise was now considerable, enough to sound almost like the beginning of a minor revolution. The crowd of interested passers-by had grown considerably. It was obvious that the latest comers had no idea what was afoot. This was becoming a *tamasha* – an event.

There were loud references to fire and murder, and another enquiry as to whether there might be a body. Presently those well up in front held up hands, as a sign that silence might reveal the next development. Had they heard something from within?

There was now a great rattling of chains on the other side of the door, and bolts were shot back. A small door within the immense portal opened, and a tall and heavily-bearded man, evidently a watchman, appeared.

The crowd surged forward as we enquired whether the house was vacant and to be let. The rustling words, 'Is it empty? Is it still to let?' rushed back to the outer edge of the crowd. Hereabouts it is as well to ask first, because it is not uncommon for the place to have been occupied for a year, and the notice left, especially if the lettering on the notice is regarded as pleasing – calligraphy perhaps.

Amir Ali was not pleased to see any of us. He was not fully awake. He cleared this throat and we repeated our questions. The house was both vacant and to let, he said, and shut his mouth with a distinct snapping sound.

The crowd wanted more than this, and one wag at once proposed that he go back and send out a man instead. This caused quite a ripple of laughter. We asked whether we might see over the place. He pondered some time over the question, as though he had never been faced with such a demand.

'Wake up brother,' said the camel leader. 'Is there a bathroom, such as a Europoi one, in the house?' The watchman stretched his hands above his head, and yawned before he asked who actually wanted to see the house. We said we did, but by now there were hints from the crowd about vulgarity to important people, *buzurg-waran* – the great, and the lack of common decent manners now fast developing in the watchman class.

At the reference to important people, Amir Ali woke more fully, and opened the double door. A number of the onlookers entered at the same time as ourselves.

The watchman did not know whether they were with us, and we knew Kabul well enough not to dismiss them as disinterested. For all we knew they were servants of the owner, or friends of the owner's servants.

The watchman asked us whether we had come from a certain Sirdar. We said we had not. One of the onlookers said it was not necessary to come from anybody to see an empty house; and in any case the speaker did not think that the house nor anybody belonging to it, so far as he had seen, were what we required.

Everything which we or any of the others said took Amir Ali some time to assimilate. He appeared to have a troublesome ear, and each time he was addressed he preceded any reply by attending forcefully to the site of the irritation with his little finger.

Perhaps to gain some time, the watchman now yelled, 'For the love of Allah!' rather loudly. A quick-witted onlooker at once replied with a piercing, 'He who loves, works!' A particularly loud-voiced member of the audience now said that as we would not want to sleep in the garden, Ali had better open the inner door of the house. Veiled hints were made regarding the wrath of the afore-mentioned Sirdar, who would find out about the reception given to prospective tenants.

This had the effect of bringing forth the first sign of alertness we had seen in the man, and he retired hurriedly to the rear of the house. Presently the front door was fully opened, and we and the full complement of well-wishers entered.

It is quite in order in Kabul for interested and even merely inquisitive people to join in with a house-hunting party. Sometimes one or all of them know of other more suitable places, and are always willing to accompany anyone looking for a house.

This is not done for gain; most of the attendees would be insulted if offered any money. It was fortunate, they would say, that they happened to be passing at the time of one's trouble, and what better word is there for house-hunting than that?

They know the history of most houses. If there are scorpions because of the proximity of old houses, they know. If there is not a twenty-four hour water service – in some districts the water is cut off for several hours each

day – they know too. If the roofs are not completely snow-
and rain-resistant, they will tell you.

They know what the rent should be and generally try to
make sure that the price does not soar because of the
status of the inquirer, or merely because he is rich or a
khariji, a foreigner. If the foundations are not to be trusted,
they can tell to a week just how long they may be expected
to continue to do their job.

Little incidents for or against this house and that are
related between times, and hoary wisdom which seems
applicable to one's present position is quoted.

When, for example, the watchman complained that the
last tenant had been a hard man, an onlooker, who had
said nothing until then, remarked that the tyrant always
complains of the man he has wronged. Another warned
that it was better not to talk with a foot in the air, a
proverb the Afghans are fond of quoting when they speak
of one who is not so secure as he thinks he is.

The crowd invariably feels it a duty to recommend a
suitable tradesman for the new tenant, which involves a
certain amount of discussion of the merits of various
candidates. So and so, they will say, was correct for the
last tenant but for oneself, of a truth it must be Hafiz Jan, a
man of even greater character and integrity.

By the time the inspection is over, we realise we would
never have known the weakness of the first or the second
house and that, but for the advice, we would have taken
upon sight that big old mansion, which we did not know to
be rat-infested.

The rats rather nullified the attractions of the huge,
ancient vine and the rose garden; for, as one of the crowd
said, a thing such as a rat is like the one small stone which
can shatter an entire house of glass.

One wondered, sometimes, why these wise and witty
helpers bother. It is not that they were people of independent means, or that they are not otherwise unemployed.

Sociologists I have questioned tend to believe that the

motivation is due to the fact that what to some people is a private matter may be a public occasion to the members of other cultures.

Whatever moves them to help the househunters, I, for one, hope it may long continue to be part of the life of Kabul.

The difference in taking a house in London came to my mind. Although it would seem to be simpler than finding a place in Kabul, my experiences proved that appearances are deceptive.

First there was the enticing advertisement in the newspaper, followed by the simple telephone message from the dulcet-voiced house-agent. But most of my readers will know, from experience, what nonsense then ensues.

The only way out for me, from the false smiles, the false claims, the pressures, is to mutter that it is advisable for my husband to see it first. This is still looked upon as acceptable in England, although it often means nothing at all.

Yes, some day again in the West I am going to miss the Afghan well-wishers, those who are bent upon my getting the kind of house I want. Or even, as it may be, the house which they themselves would want, irrespective of the importance of either owner or previous tenants, and completely oblivious to the adjectives applied to the property.

The garden of that first house we looked at in Kabul was at the time covered with snow, so that, as one spokesman remarked, we would have to take that as we would take a purchase which had been wrapped up in paper, *kaghaz-pech*, at the time of buying. Was that wise?

As there was more than one sign that any snow or water that landed on the roof might prefer to come through the ceiling, we turned the place down, in our minds. The watchman said that at that time of the year such leaks were quite a usual occurrence, and the best talker of the party said he could well believe that this was so, at any rate in this house, because those whose job it was to sweep the snow from the roof obviously slept instead.

There was no bath, but there was a shower, to partake of which one stood upon a slatted wooden raft-like affair, which took up a good part of the floor. It gave one a feeling, far from pleasant and even from relatively afar, that it might well slide when the floor was wet, and that unless one had qualified for the Cresta Run, there would be not a few contretemps upon the sloping floor.

'There is no bath,' I said. 'No bath ... NO BATH ...' The word resonated in the crisp air as the crowd took up the refrain. Without this greatest necessity, one ventured, the whole matter resolved itself into a decided negative.

The watchman said that those who were not going to take the house ought to allow the person who was, to make decisive statements. He seemed now to have been driven to defend himself from the others.

The spokesman replied that everybody there present was of the opinion that the Khanoum ought to be protected and they were prepared to continue the good work. Also, he quoted some Persian philosopher as saying that the sound of clapping does not arise from a single hand. 'Though we are firm as the fingers of a single hand!'

Another said that he had been told that in Europe there was a bathroom for every member of the household and that in this indescribable structure not only was there not a bath for perhaps six people, but there was not even a bath for one.

Supposing, for illustration's sake, he continued, twenty people were living in the house: that would mean not one bath among twenty! Or fifty, even.

Everybody agreed with this apparent mathematician that the thought was insupportable, and there were many cries of *Wai! Wai! Astaghfirullah!* and *Ai Khuda!* meaning: Alas! Heaven help us! O God! etc., at the frightful thought of twenty people looking for somewhere to bathe, in this very house, perhaps all at once.

The watchman said it was true there was no bath. It might be, he continued, that he was correct in stating that a bath was a necessity, which would lead to the Khanoum having one put in properly, and not just anyhow; which would have been the method employed by the critics in the crowd, and such as were no doubt to be found in houses where there actually were baths.

Here the mathematician blew out both cheeks, drew his lips tightly against his teeth, and caused a long hissing breath to be taken in. At the same time, he made a cartoon of his eyes. If all this was to be, then the expense was going to be *bisyar* – much.

An onlooker gallantly remarked that a man in his position should be told, if he did not already know, that people such as the Khanoum had baths in their houses because the price of installing them was no more to the Khanoum than the equivalent of a piece of *nan* – bread, would cost him for one meal.

Comments now became even more general. One opined that, in spite of the undoubted quality of the society in which he found himself, and for which he was making allowances, the rent was high. That was what he thought, at any rate. Another said that people were allowed to think, because we were after all in a free country, thanks to Allah, but that fools should not speak.

Although I had long decided against this house, there was some difficulty in getting out of the crowded place, especially with the atmosphere becoming as heated as that of a debating society. Someone was asking where the owner lived, and I took this as my cue. It was a good idea, I agreed, to see the owner.

The watchman told us that the owner was in Jalalabad. He hinted that as the owner was a rich man, the seemingly high rent was related to *his* status. Rich people were like that, he said. They had, and the more there was to the having, the more they sought to add to it. In the south it was warmer: why should the owner stay here when he had rents to give him wealth?

If we cared to put ourselves to the inconvenience of returning in a week, he thought we might have the pleasure of speaking to the Sirdar Sa'ib himself.

The crowd began to move, and presently we found ourselves outside. Some of the sightseers melted away, reluctantly, walking backwards as though unwilling to lose sight of us before anything had been arranged.

All promised to let us know of any likely house of which they heard, and which they would make it their business to track down. They did not ask where we were stopping. Everybody in Kabul somehow seems to know where everybody else lives.

The houses are seldom numbered. The names of the occupants are scarcely ever upon the doors. If the man who built the house or was the first to live in it was one Sirdar Ali Khan, the place is known for ever after as the house of this gentleman. He may not have lived there for many years, he may have made the last journey of all, but this matters not. The house took and keeps his name.

One house which we eventually occupied had been the headquarters of a Western firm. These people had long since moved elsewhere, yet our house continued to be known under the cognomen of that firm.

Foreigners find this rather difficult to follow, especially when they hire a *gari* – that much overworked horse-drawn taxi of Kabul – and give their own directions.

It is useless to say the house required is near this embassy or that, because the driver feels that if you are not going to that particular embassy why mention it at all? The house you want may be next door to the embassy you mention, but after all, that house is known to every gari-driver in Kabul as the residence of Mr Amir Aga Khan, therefore why not say so?

It is possible you have never heard of the gentleman, in fact it is a hundred to one against, but that seems hardly credible. This is because foreigners are all educated, and educated people know everything, and what is known to an uneducated Afghan gari driver is surely a matter of small knowledge to the educated. If you have said that you do not know, clearly there is a deep and disingenuous reason for your ignorance and it must be feigned.

I am inclined to think there is a good deal of extra-sensory perception in the composition of the gari drivers. Otherwise how on earth do they track down, from the puzzle of far-flung mansions in the Shahr-i-Nau, the house required?

It is easy to imagine the zest with which those who had accompanied us related the morning's 'adventures' to their companions later over green tea in the cafes of their choice.

Every detail would be woven into a tale consisting of this question and that reply. There would be moments of suitable breath-taking suspense at crucial turns in the story. Who we were would be known; where we came from; and a shrewd idea of our income arrived at, not least because of the extravagance of the idea of a Europoi bathroom and a sun parlour. Not to mention that we were proposing to install twenty, even fifty, people in a house only large enough for, say, ten and wanted a large bath-room for them all to immerse themselves in.

Also discussed would be the fact that we could afford to put up at the Kabul hotel, which was definitely Europoi, and where people kept their own servants as well as keeping busy the ones belonging to the hotel.

By the time the fourth cup of green tea was finished, our importance would have soared to such heights that our power would be likened to that of the Indian Maharajahs, who, it was invariably said, had the power of life and death over all their subjects.

After several of these parties had accompanied us, there were many offers of houses at all prices, houses both for sale and to let, houses in which as many bathrooms as we required were promised. Had we been going to occupy the bathrooms, sitting, sleeping, cooking and even washing in them, such eccentricity could hardly have aroused greater local interest. The word had gone out that 'bath' was the key word, and it became thus established.

If we asked first about the garden or the water system, the belief seemed to be that we were indulging in some type of personal humour, or approaching the matter of bathrooms obliquely, at which assumed gambit it was polite to smile a little, thereby indicating that the joke or cunning was understood.

One man, we were told, was frantically and hopefully converting half of his double drawing-room into a luxury bathroom. Later when this was completed, we saw the house, and realised he had ruined one of the finest views in Kabul. There may have been a tenant for this place willing to sacrifice the artistic for the ablutionary. I do hope there was.

Another house we visited was even more difficult to enter, although the accompanying well-wishers were fewer. After we had politely knocked twice, the onlookers took command and banged properly upon the stout door.

Finally, after one who limped had frequently enough applied his walking-stick, the door was opened. A man introduced himself as a servant from the next house. There was nobody, he said, in the house where we had knocked.

The nephew of the owner lived a short distance away, and had the key. Where, we asked was the owner? The owner, he replied, was in Paris, a place located in *Europa*, 'they say,' where he had taken his stomach, for attention.

This announcement gave me a momentary picture of the poor man trudging along, in no condition to do so, bearing in some suitable container a most important part of his anatomy.

It was but 10.30 a.m. and we proposed visiting the nephew. Upon hearing that we were to return to the house, the crowd lowered itself upon its heels, to await developments. We climbed into the gari.

The sun was not long enough risen to warm the air, and the nag had the speed of a racehorse. As we had not the local ability to find houses by instinct, we were glad of the offer of the servant who had opened the door. On arrival we found the nephew was not yet up, but he sent a servant with a polite greeting and asking us to wait a few moments.

Presently he came out, still tying his dressing-gown cord. He was scarcely awake. He was a handsome and intelligent young man. We asked for the key of his uncle's house. He said he would dress speedily and accompany us. He said it in such a way as to imply that the idea of our being burdened by the weight of the key was not to be considered.

The Afghans are a quiet-voiced and polite people, and their beautiful *dari* (court) Persian, lends itself more to polite expression than any other. The young man dressed quickly, apologised a great deal for having kept us waiting, and in no time we were conveyed, by the mad racing-gari, back to the house.

The crowd rose smartly from its heels as we approached, and with a great roar of welcome wished peace upon us.

Even at that early hour, entrepreneurs with such necessities as koftas and chewing-gum had arrived and were doing a brisk trade.

The door opened into a large and beautiful garden, and it required no thought-reader to know that here my husband saw the chance of establishing in grand style his hobby, which is rose-growing. This means that somebody else does all the work, while he shows people round the garden and takes the credit. He would, I knew, have the house on the strength of the garden alone.

As usual, we were shown the bathroom first, and I do not wonder. That place stood as the prototype of all that is correct, artistic and desirable in such a room. The bath itself was sunken, and of grey and pink alabaster.

It made one think of the plumage of doves and the anger of the thundercloud, of the pink of the first faint hue of sunrise and the colour of wild roses along a country hedgerow. All the other appointments took their cue from the bath.

The beauty of Afghan alabaster is a thing apart. I have seen nothing like it elsewhere. It looks like the most delicate interweaving of applied colours, and yet it is natural. When you look at it, nature seems to say, 'Behold, Human, the refinement of colouring, and the blending thereof. Would you ever have guessed that an artist, even like myself, could have produced such warmth in the marriage of greys and pinks? I have made this for you to admire. Now get a palette and try to imitate me!'

Felicitously, I was ready to vindicate the assertions of the audience and take the house on the recommendation of the bathroom. One could never feel an ordinary human being in that room. Imagination might easily be aroused to thoughts of being a sea queen, or a sea goddess, but never merely a vulnerable, perturbable, frail human.

The rent was high, but the rooms were large and in good condition. Everything was right, and our names seemed written upon it, as the Afghan saying has it.

We both agreed to take it, and congratulated ourselves upon our good fortune. I remarked that there was also a twenty-four hour water service, which my husband replied would be excellent for the roses.

The bathroom was not to him what it was to me. We returned in triumph to the hotel, where we found a number of the morning's followers awaiting us with fantastic descriptions of gigantic houses at Lilliputian rents. We left a servant to deal with them, and proceeded to work out furniture details for the new abode.

A few days later we were well into the preliminaries of the moving, when a young man was announced. He turned out to be another nephew of the landlord, and said that some relative was returning immediately by air from Paris. She had previously made that house her head-quarters, and might want it – only for a short time – again.

He was asked to express the pleasure of the owner that we had not had time to be inconvenienced. Would we wait until she came, and until her wishes were known? We agreed to wait.

Next we heard that she had broken her journey at Karachi; again that the plane was held up by weather, and there was nothing else to do but wait. Besides, we consoled one another, it is a relief, after the hustle and hassles of Western countries, to reach a spot where time is the servant it ought to be, and not the master.

Then news came to us that as the lady was not well, she might stay a week in Karachi. Now a week can be a very long time in Kabul. It is sometimes three weeks and has been known to be five or six. It is not, however, as long as 'soon' which may even stretch to years.

While all this was in progress, we looked at other houses, just in case. The dreams of humans are difficult to liquidate; my heart was in that pink and grey bathroom, my husband's in the prospective rose garden. We became impossibly choosy.

Eventually, after ten long days of patient and, I hope, polite inquiry as to the return or otherwise of the lady, she seemed to vanish from the picture, and we were informed that there had been a slight error in the amount of the rent. As is usually the case, in such circumstances, the sum was more than originally mentioned.

We had been too stupid to realise that the lady from Paris and Pakistan could have been vanished long before by a judicious offer to pay a higher rent. Relieved that the opportunity to live there was still open to us, we agreed to the new terms and made light of the incident.

Still we were no nearer occupation. Every visitor was looked upon as someone who might bring the news, good or bad, that we really could now move in. If someone whom we did not know called when we were out, we became nervous and testy until his identity was revealed.

Between the anxiety of the house so near and yet so far, and the unpleasantness of being perpetually hungry, we were driven to set forth to pastures new, in search of another house.

There were no European restaurants in Kabul, so that the Kabul Hotel had, unfortunately, no opposition there. As we set out, the snow was deep and the wind chill. Long lines of hard-worked Hazara coolies were toiling past, bent almost double under the weight of firewood.

Walking is a pleasant exercise, but only when all steps are in a forward direction. That day we took one forward and two back – that was if we managed to keep our feet. The snow was deep and the wind icy-toothed. Kabul looked well in its mantle of white, and the surrounding hills glistened and sparkled, like an iced cake, ready for a giant's feast. It was one of those days when there is a thrill in being alive.

There was nothing for it but to take a gari. It was better than walking, though not safer. Both the horse and the driver of the one we hailed were high-spirited. The horse had considerable difficulty in keeping its feet, and simply loathed the snow and the ice underneath it.

There was no rough-shoeing in Kabul, because this spoilt the roads. It was up to the horses to keep their feet as best they might, which was not well. Every now and again the animal's hind feet slid together, upon which the gari driver gave vent to the cry of his kind, beginning on the lowest note of which he was capable, and rising, quickly, to the highest.

When the horse hears this, he knows to expect something unpleasant, and the one we had, after a few anxious moments, regained his balance. This it celebrated by flinging its back feet with entire abandon, whack! against the gari. These vehicles have to be strong (the life of a car is only five years on the Kabul roads) but the trap we had that morning rattled as no trap should if it intends to keep together for another week.

Suddenly, giving a loud snort, he took to his hooves and bolted, as though saying, 'If you want to go this way, I am willing to take you, but it will be at my own pace. Observe my speed.' One usually lashes a horse, if at all, to make it go. This driver whipped his to make it stop.

This appeared to have no effect until, without warning or slowing down, it planted its two front feet in the snow so abruptly that our heads hit the roof of the gari. For the hundredth time that morning we were almost thrown to the ground.

The driver jumped to the ground and held on, leaving nothing to chance, until we got out. We were nowhere near where we wanted to go, but at least we were safe upon the ground.

Surprisingly, we saw a HOUSE TO LET sign nearby, and were admitted by a slatternly woman servant, wearing the usual *burqa*, that all-enveloping garment known to amazed westerners as a 'shuttlecock', and shaped rather like one. She had arranged the head part of this so as to leave but one eye uncovered.

This member was particularly black and round, and inquisitive. As soon as we were within the gate, she told us she did not know where either the watchman or the owner were. Several dirty children immediately surrounded her.

They fixed us with the type of unbelieving stare one would give to creatures from one of the more distant planets. They seemed all about the same age, and there appeared scarcely enough time on the part of Nature to have made one before the other appeared upon the scene.

An interested and inquisitive passer-by told us that he knew where the occupant of the house we were really seeking was. We all got into another gari, and set forth. The man accompanying us assured us that the house we were to see was a good one. There was, he said, an

American staying in it, but he was returning home in a few days.

If the other horse was quick, this one was just as slow. Every now and again, like a happy terrier, it skipped with its left hind leg. Its loud whinnying was disturbing.

The journey took three times as long as it should, but at least we arrived safely. We thanked the man, wishing the customary peace upon him, but his appetite for house-viewing was sufficiently whetted, and he remained with us. Business, he said, was in any case not brisk.

The American was out, but fortunately the landlord was there. He was a charming man, and said he would be delighted to have us as tenants. The bath looked all right, but we were told that the 'water arrangements were not quite in full working order'.

That sentence, lightly spoken, has a multitude of interpretations in Kabul. It may even mean that all the water required for the bathroom has to be carried by the *sakao* – watercarrier, and one does not want the bath to be filled with cold water which has to be pailed out and then boiled as required.

Presently we were assured that the man who attended to these affairs was finishing a job, and that his very next port of call was this very bathroom.

The house was attractive, and we went upstairs by an outside staircase, to see the upper veranda and the servants' rooms. Here the American had kept dogs. He had either been careless about the state in which they lived, or had left them in charge of a servant who was.

Somebody had tried to grow tomatoes, and had put them, just anyhow, into one of the rooms, after which they had remained forgotten. They lay about, higgledy-piggledy over the floor, in the most unpleasant stages of decay. The whole place was nauseating in the extreme.

The landlord assured us that everything would be cleaned up to our entire satisfaction, although it was difficult, as things were, to visualise the metamorphosis. Yet we were willing to believe his statement.

The *pièce de résistance*, he told us, was the roof. That was one hundred per cent leakproof. One hundred per cent. It was his own invention, which he even used in the house he occupied himself. He told us this with considerable pride and emphasis. Never, we were assured, never, would we ever see so much as one fugitive drop of water coming through that roof.

That was certainly something, because we had seen the pools of water in the houses of friends and realised that, during the few months when the rain pelts down, practically everything in a house is liable to be soaked. This impermeability, he told us, was a definite promise. He knew what he was talking about, he said.

We talked over everything on the way back to the hotel, and the nearer we got to it, the firmer our minds were made up that we had better take a chance when it presented itself.

Each was aware that the other was in mourning. One for the wonder-bathroom; the other for the rose-garden which would never be. At least not where it had been planned.

That afternoon the agreement was signed, and the next day we sent over a good deal of our baggage.

The American sold us cutlery and china. These items were very highly-priced in Kabul and, considering the roads from Pakistan, for whose ups and downs there are no adjectives to describe, it was a wonder that any glass or china ever arrived intact.

The American had these desirable things for disposal, and all American-made. The only stipulation was that the purchaser bought the whole lot. The list pronounced that the knife handles were bone. In England we call it plastic. The cutlery was said to be silver-plate, which is known in England as E.P.N.S., used by way of flattery, because everybody knows it is nickel, or even brass.

The plates were emblazoned; there is no other word (unless it be 'blazing') to describe the larger-than-life red 'roses' which covered them, together with reminders of how great a person Mom was.

Without seeing it properly, we bought the lot at a price that I feel entirely covered the initial purchase, the hire of same while in Kabul as well as the shipping from America.

The American was leaving Kabul because he was demoralised. I asked him why, since foreigners generally loved the Afghans. He said:

'I asked some professor guy at the university here why people in so many Third World countries disliked us. Know what he said? He said, "Because you are so dislikeable".'

Such candour must, I was sure, have been learnt by the Afghan academic at some foreign university. Unless this particular American had, perhaps, sold him some of his household goods . . .

The china, if overpriced and appalling in design as well as embellishment, was not quite useless. It saved better things in a country where cups, plates and all the rest of their family have a way of slipping through the fingers, just like that, preferably onto a marble floor.

The five teacups had been carefully riveted in more than five places each: perfect germ-traps. These the servants fell heir to.

That night it snowed and snowed. In the morning the city was blanketed deeply in the glory of purest white. From the flat roofs opposite the hotel, the servants were sweeping immense loads of snow, which hurtled down splosh! into the streets below. Most of the passers-by knew from past experience that the middle of the road was the safest place to walk. But from the window we saw several pedestrians receive more than their share of the sweepings.

There was no vituperation, because it is impossible to

argue with a person one cannot see, and if one did start an argument, the man with the great broom has the last word. Better not to annoy roof snow-sweepers!

The sun was shining brightly and outside looked so inviting that we put on parkas and rubber boots, and gave orders for a gari to be brought. It would be a good opportunity to visit the new house and crow over its hundred per cent ceilings. The snow was melting fast.

Imagine our surprise to find the floor of every room flooded and water pouring through the ceilings apparently without let or hindrance. And we were moving in that day! We sent for the landlord, whose son came.

We asked how this could have taken place when we were assured the roof was leak-proof. The young man returned to report to his father while we wandered about in the ice-cold, damp rooms and thought of that agreement. By and by the boy returned to say the roof would be put right. And '*awli* – now'.

That, in Kabul-speak, means somewhere between 'a week' and 'soon'.

We returned dejectedly to the hotel and typed a first class lawyers' letter saying that we were 'surprised' the way lawyers do – only we *really* were – and that we considered the agreement 'null and void'.

Our servant was to await a reply. He returned with a letter in which the owner said, quite simply, that he understood our point of view, and that if we did not want the house, he also understood. There was nothing left but to reclaim our baggage and start again from scratch.

Now there restarted a spate of reports of houses to be let. The room boy who brought the meals, obviously well-coached, gave fascinating descriptions of houses with gardens, sunrooms and bathrooms.

The man who attended to the *bokharis*, the stoves, revealed himself a poet so far as description of properties went. Rooms, gardens, fruit trees were well-nigh indescribable, so good were they. And as to the size of the bathrooms . . .

The dining-room waiter knew of a number of the same, and we felt we could scarcely wait to see these so-desirable residences, all offering the prospect of escape from the awful food we were being served.

Alas for the reality! None was suitable. Many of the places were of the meanest order. Had we entered them, it would have been necessary to wade through mud and slush. Once a house is built in Kabul, the owner seems to forget all about everything in connection with it except the rent. The tenants may do the repairs, and some do. Many others do not.

But the spice of house-hunting for the Kabuli servants and shopkeepers lies in the gossip attached to the undertaking. As there are no house agents, and few landlords advertise their property, it is natural to enquire from servants and shopkeepers, who know everybody's business, and act as local newspapers.

These tradespeople enter the house-hunt with as much energy as the knights of old must have entered the lists. Soon they know every particular about the house-hunter.

These particulars may either be prodigiously improved upon, or just the opposite, depending upon the amount one's servants spend on purchases in the bazar, the number and social position of the friends one entertains, and the quantity of food produced for parties.

There are few shops in Kabul in which the goods have a fixed price. When foreigners who know none of the language are in the habit of buying goods without bargaining, the temptation often proves too great for the trader. The women in Kabul are keen shoppers, and will argue in order to have the price lowered by one *Afghani* – a fraction of a penny.

This explains why house-rents are both imaginative and impossible, and known to be subject to bargaining.

Eventually, quite by accident, we got a house by

ourselves. The day we left the hotel really was a red-letter day. The other guests envied us, and gave us a half-joyful, half-miserable send-off party. We almost felt like taking them along: but that would have much more than fulfilled the popular prediction of twenty to a bathroom, so we had to promise to visit them, like captives left behind.

The house had been occupied by a foreign family who had left it in good order.

But there was no escape, even though we were settled, from the well-wishers, who kept hearing of other houses. Life was a little dull for a time, after so much coming and going, in the company of those crowds we shall see no more.

And reputations, like the names of houses, do stick. I last looked for a house a quarter of a century ago. But only yesterday a woman came up to me: 'I hear you are looking for a house – with a good bathroom, of course.'

13

Ashpaz-Lore

When my 'elevenses' were brought there was a halt in the kitchen. The cook, the *Ashpaz* named Hashim, was somewhat highly strung, and cooking, to him, was the only job worth doing. He did his work well but, being an artist at it, he demanded that everybody around should have the same interests. He was intolerant of talking, when he was not the chief speaker. He was equally impatient of the others moving slowly about, because he did not understand slowness. He could do so many things at once that he was frankly puzzled by those who could not.

He could talk upon different subjects to two or three people, and keep up a running commentary on what he was doing – like the juggler who dexterously keeps all those coloured balls in the air.

He was usually the chief speaker, although not by any means an easily-understood one. Yet one never heard any of the listeners ask for a repetition of a sentence. The speed of the conversation made it untranslatable. He really had an astonishing gift for quick talking.

There were times when he brought along his three small boys, whose ages ran from three to six years. Although they remained the whole day and they played either in the garage or near the kitchen, no childish scream or cry ever percolated to the house. It was obvious that father's dictatorship was recognised at home as well.

He was fond of animals, and sometimes brought a chicken or a cat from somewhere outside. These pets had to conform to his ruling and not make a nuisance of themselves. Once, by way of relaxation, cook rounded up the staff and put them to work in the garden.

The gardener had not started the work because the spring had scarcely arrived. Each servant was armed with a garden implement. They weeded, hoed, pruned and cut grass. By teatime a great mound of rubble had been collected from all corners, and disposed of by throwing it over the wall. The idea here is that once off the premises all responsibility is shed. I felt guilty about this but nothing untoward ever seemed to happen.

That afternoon the chicken discovered, as chickens will, that it might scrape to its heart's content, and find interesting things. Next day we had it for lunch. It had scraped up some of the newly planted seeds, and death was the penalty passed by Hashim.

I did not recognise the poor chicken in the pulao until too late. It and I had got on well together, I reflected, and it had even seemed to trust me when it came quite near to be fed.

Our Ashpaz had many peculiarities, and when orders for the day were being given, he was always anxious to know how many guests we were having. The more there were the better he entered into the spirit. He turned out countless dishes from a small kitchen, which was notable for the absence of up-to-date gadgets.

He could cater, with the help of one efficient assistant and two boys who sounded more trouble than they were worth, for three hundred people. Indeed, when Khruschev and Bulganin, the Soviet leaders, visited Kabul, Hashim cooked for more than three hundred, at a feast we gave for them.

Though up to then apolitical, he was heard to mutter that that 'would show them what food was really like'. With the U.S.S.R. across our northern border, across the Oxus River, we knew, fifty years before anyone else, it seemed, that the great collectivist experiment had failed. Russians, such as diplomats, would spend days buying up the simplest things in the Kabul bazars, to take home, their eyes wide like children's . . .

Hashim would roast and stuff turkey, make a dozen different kinds of pastries, sweet and savoury, Turkish, Italian, French and Afghan.

He would make delicious meat balls, salads, cakes and cakelets, all within an amazingly short time, and all done to perfection. The making of so much is within the scope of any cook, but our Ashpaz performed the miracle with a tin oven over a charcoal fire and an old fashioned Eastern fireplace, consisting of a mud-baked object resembling a great square box, in the top of which there were four-inch apertures into which burning charcoal was put. The popular belief was that we had at least four cooks, and I am small-minded enough to have been flattered.

The trouble was that Kabul was a party-giving city. Not small affairs, but quite elaborate. Quite a number of people wanted to borrow Hashim. At first we loaned him to anybody who asked.

He would serve our breakfast, then, having obtained permission, he would cycle off to where the party was being held. There he worked like a machine until 6.30 p.m. when he hurried back in time to prepare our dinner.

As time went on, he became so popular a 'borrow' that difficulties arose, and I was obliged to make a rule that he was definitely not available, owing to the work he was expected to do for us. Yet he had never grumbled about those extra engagements.

If it happened that he was left on his own, it was to be noticed that his weak point was table work; although he insisted upon organising the settings. A soup spoon to his way of thinking was as good for puddings as the ones he put down for the soup. He appeared to have an idea that everybody was left-handed. These trifles were entertaining and it gave me a chance to be amused, thinking how shocked he would be if he knew his deviation from our customs.

If a new kitchen assistant was needed, he engaged him himself. He trained him too. The most unlikely material was shaped and polished with rapidity. If staff problems arose, he dealt with them.

If by any chance there was an altercation and it got out of his control, he brought the aggrieved party before me. Upon these occasions he was the chief speaker. All the time he kept a dominant eye upon the other, while he related at top speed and word perfect, every syllable which had passed on each side since the start of the problem.

If the victim showed any sign of interrupting, the look was intensified, and the words died before they were framed. Nothing was hidden at these 'carpet examinations'. Hashim would report exactly what he said. If he had hit the other, he would show you where and how. He would also tell you the effect it had had. All this with much histrionic effect.

He relived the whole affair, honestly and squarely so far as we could determine, and then he awaited your judgment. He must have been the kind of witness, lawyer, plaintiff and accused, that judges the world over pray for.

Nearly always, Hashim would ask that the *contretemps* be considered past and forgotten. He harboured no ill-will but he would have every detail clarified. Once the situation was presented, the axe was buried, and the domestic wheels revolved smoothly again.

The *dobizan* – washerwoman, came once a week. She arrived in time for breakfast, which she had in the kitchen. Over this meal which to her was *nan* – the flat pancake-like bread, and tea, there was a free exchange of bazar gossip.

Dobizan was a great talker and, judging by the frequent ill-suppressed laughter, an amusing one. After they had had a round of the water-pipe, she would begin her day's work by calling loudly for pails of water to be carried by one of the servants. No one liked the job but she always won, in the end.

She liked her work and liked others to see the result of her labours, in full view. Thus she preferred to hang the clothes to dry on the trees and over the bushes at the front of the house. Although she ought to have learned by now that this was not allowed, she was willing to take a chance. She preferred to use a china wash-basin for steeping clothes. She liked to spread the handkerchiefs to dry on the lawn. She proved a difficult student where other people's susceptibilities were concerned. The garden, she said, was a good place, and she 'wanted a good place'.

Each wash-day she carried the clothes to the front of the house. Hashim would soon sense what was taking place, appear like a hurricane, and give out a torrent of words, sounding from a distance like a sports-event announcer. They would both talk together. Then she would retire quietly, defeated, until he was out of sight.

There would be calls upon Allah to witness this and that, and the breakfast-time camaraderie completely forgotten. The wrath of the one and the curses of Satan flew through the air, when she would demand that he tell her how rope drying is better than grass drying? Why a rope, when ropes are expensive? What do cooks know about washing clothes? and much more.

Then there would be silence about it until next wash-day, as with an angry gesture, she flung her white lawn scarf-veil across her mouth, and glared towards Hashim's kitchen with her penetrating eyes.

During the Muslim fast of Ramadan, she was a quitter. She submitted to rope-drying without the fatigue of argument. There was no laughter. No water-pipe. No bazar gossip. After the day's work, she looked worn and wilted, and there were still two and a half hours of the fast before the gun went, releasing the faithful. It is a long time between the signal gun sounds at 3.15 a.m., announcing dawn, until sunset at 7.15 p.m. Sixteen hours. Smokers say they miss their pipes and cigarettes most. Dobizan always said she was used to hunger and thirst, but missed her water-pipe. Washing, she said, was 'smoke-thirsty work'.

Thirst troubled her, but not the heat. On the warmest day, Dobizan would continue to wear her once-white thick woollen cardigan. There were two large pockets in this garment. These were always filled to capacity, but what they contained was hidden from inquisitive eyes by a giant safety-pin, fixed fast across the centre of each.

She did not trouble with the official veil; her Hazara clanswomen do not wear them. She was short and stout, and looked rather like a bundle of clothes herself. Her face was still round, at perhaps fifty years old, but crinkled.

Her calling might be a humble one, but she had expensive tastes. When ironing time came, she preferred to use the most costly of my travelling rugs, rather than the oldish blanket provided, to iron upon. She had a poor opinion of starch, and used it only for lingerie. It certainly gave these garments an original look.

She liked the electric iron, and used it carefully. Hashim and she disagreed over it because Dobizan thought it was important enough to be kept in the store-cupboard. Hashim would not have this.

There were numerous other arguments, during which time Hashim would allow her to speak, then he had his say. It was generally enough even for Dobizan. When there was a longish lull, it could be taken that the washerwoman had gone for another week.

One year our dog was stolen. This kind of thing often happened in Kabul. Knowing how much we thought of it, Hashim assured us that if he ever saw it he would bring it back. 'Please do so,' I said.

Days passed and there was no sign of the dog. Finally we came to the conclusion that some of the traffic, more speedy than careful, had been the cause.

We considered the matter closed. One morning some weeks later, I was awakened by what sounded like a number of large dogs fighting. Looking from the window I saw the garden was crowded with numerous ill-assorted and hostile dogs.

The cook was summoned and looking very pleased said it was no trouble – he had seen the dogs running here and there when he went to the bazar and though it was not easy, he had managed to lure them all into the garden. Which one did we want? There are many dogs in Kabul whose parentage is a mere guess. When foreigners left the country they very often turned their one-time pets out to fend for themselves. Regrettably, this was most common among the British community, because – unlike other countries – there was a six-month quarantine law in Britain, and the owners refused to pay for the upkeep of the pet while in quarantine in the U.K.

In time, of course, the dogs mixed with others of equal misfortune, became half-wild and grew to a great size. At night when the traffic ceased they haunted the roads, barking and fighting. It was a cruel sentence indeed, after their years of loyalty.

Hashim could not understand why we did not choose a dog from the ones he had brought. The animals, for their part, finding themselves in an enclosed space, took an extreme dislike to each other and were by now making a frightful row. It was not an easy job to get them to leave.

Hashim, since that day, continually bore reports of dogs, 'so high', and 'so big'. Description, as he said, was better than presentation...

China and cutlery were expensive in Kabul, and it was amusing sometimes to see one's own plates upon other people's tables; until one gave a party and found that the servants had borrowed other people's, for no matter how much or how many one had of these things, there was always a time when there were more guests than cups and plates. So there was no feeling superior.

Borrowing was understood. These adjustments

functioned in a quite natural way, and nobody remarked upon them.

Tinned foods were scarce, but they were always popular. The finding of any one of them, in some remote corner, was a red letter day, notwithstanding that the manufacturers would have been horrified at the grubbiness of the tins.

In certain places, where there were resident foreigners who regularly received parcels from home, tins formed a large part of these gifts. Sometimes the tins mysteriously disappeared. The mystery was not a baffling one, especially when by some extraordinary coincidence the same kind of can would appear in one of the bazar shops.

Sometimes the faith we had in those who may have been instrumental in the tins' disappearance, was greater than the desire to have one's doubts confirmed by questioning. After all, there were a number of people receiving these things from abroad, and it might only have been coincidental. After all, one tin is like another, and anyway the grocer was a polite man, as well as a diplomatic tradesman.

Sometimes stranger things happened, such as when three neighbouring servants became ill at the same time. The symptoms pointed to poisoning: high temperatures and swollen faces. When they first felt ill they had told Hashim and then helped themselves to all my aspirin. They had taken six each of these. That had no effect.

Neither had the after-dinner mints. Each had then had two gargling tablets, which they stated were nicely-coloured pink, and which they chewed. Still no relief. The pink 'medicine powder' from the box in the bathroom had been difficult to swallow, they said. Considering it was medicated tooth-powder, that was understandable. As a last resort they had mixed the 'medicine powder' from the glass bowl in the dressing-room. This was face powder.

I was more afraid of the 'medicine' to which they had

helped themselves than of their ailment. Questioning them, they had no idea as to the cause of the illness.

The doctor is not usually called in such cases until everybody's advice has been taken. After all, a pious incantation requires some time to take effect, and the *tawiz* – charm, tied round the wrist will be helpful. It cost five afghanis, a few pence, and is guaranteed for all time.

The doctor, they will tell you, is but a human being. Allah is above all. Besides, why does he cost so much, when amulets are cheap? And why, if he costs so much, does he work at hospitals where treatment is free? As none of the patients improved, the doctor came. He pronounced that they were suffering from poisoning. After much questioning he arrived at the conclusion that a tin of fish was the cause.

The empty tin was produced and the inside was greeny-black. This tin of fish had been given by the servants of a neighbour, who owed a few afghanis to the cook, and here was a way of repaying with a whole tin of food; thus saving the money. The giver of the tin was produced.

He said that his employer often threw out tins of food. He usually gave them away to his friends who thought he had been given them, and this made them think very highly of his importance. The employer said that he threw out the tins which had been too long in the pantry.

The woman servant who had been poisoned said she did not know the food was fish, and when she noticed it tasted bitter, she added sugar and this improved it greatly.

When asked how she did not recognise it as fish, she said it had neither head nor tail and how was she to guess that Europoi fish had neither? She said she had often helped in Europoi people's houses in Kabul, and had eaten food after their parties. Some of the soups were quite good, but she found they were improved by the addition of the 'glass' puddings. The 'glass' puddings, she explained, melted in the soup.

211

Afghan servants are very fond of foreign medicines, and have no idea what the different ones are for. Any bottle, to them, is medicine, and any medicine must be a cure for everything. They have a pain, and therefore need medicine. Medicine, they feel, can also be taken as a precaution, so as to come into effect, as it were, if ill-health strikes. Many women used to go to the clinic where the U.N. dispensed medical care and, after thorough examination, were given medicine by the women doctors. The preparation was to be taken like all medicines, a little at a time. They were given enough to last ten days. Within three days they would be back, saying that the medicine was finished. Everyone in the family had been dosed.

The clinic book in which everything was entered would be examined, and found to contradict the women's claims that a full ten days had elapsed since their last visit. They could not understand how the secretary remembered the exact day.

When they visited the clinic about the birth of expected infants, they would always estimate the birth would take place within a week, when usually it was months away. The doctors had great patience with them, especially as none of the women doctors knew Persian or any other local language, and every question had to be answered to a secretary who acted as interpreter.

These servants would swallow anti-insect powder without hesitation, and it was always safer to keep all medicines out of the way, lest the cure prove worse than the ailment.

Aspirin is the tablet 'which makes pain go where it came from', and because most foreigners carry this and pet cures of their own, most are looked upon as being doctors.

It is possible to become famous as a medical man in an afternoon, through curing the headache of some hotel servant.

The others then find that they have caught the headache

infection, and by the next afternoon, at least three relatives of these who were 'miraculously cured' by the 'doctor Khanoum' are waiting, suffering from all the ailments under the sun.

If there is no medicine, they say a touch of the hand will be enough.

Some of them have had chronic diseases for years, and claim to be completely cured before nightfall. After all, has it not been said, in a not dissimilar culture, 'By faith ye shall be saved'?

14

A Rug is Needed...

An Afghan visitor will never say, 'I came to see you about such and such a thing'. Your health comes first; the success of your garden; the show of flowers; the promise of fruit; the weather; your hobby; all the latest news of the town. Only after preliminaries may private problems be broached.

These subjects will be discussed over many cups of straw-coloured green tea, taken either plain or cardamom-flavoured.

Then, when the cup is turned upside down on the saucer, there is still the ceremony of fruit-eating. Whichever fruits are in season will be brought. If it be the dried fruit season, almonds, shelled walnuts, and *kishmish* – incomparably delicious sultanas, will be served, as well as cakes and biscuits.

The Afghans, being good hosts, know the wisdom of discussion between people happily regaled with food, and say, 'a hungry man makes a bad bargain'.

Perhaps the fashion of giving tea to all customers before business preliminaries were broached had the same basis.

Now that I had a house, I was a recognised and recognisable – indeed well-known by repute – customer of the Kabul bazar.

When such a personage approached a shop, a servant appeared from the back premises with delicate porcelain teacups and a huge pot of tea. Today, this ceremony has been abbreviated to an extent that the old-timers not twenty years ago would have called barbaric: the visitor is actually asked whether he will take tea!

During the tea-drinking there is a pleasant and informative conversation. One might sit cross-legged on a cushion or if that appeared too much of a gymnastic feat – which it can be – a chair is provided.

By the time the cup was inverted in the old days, such was the skill as well as the hospitality of the owner; all had been indirectly discussed about the article required.

There was a feeling of well-being about those transactions. The price did not matter so much, because the merchant had extended hospitality. One had 'eaten his salt'. He was a friend.

Today his son is equally polite, but the full tea ceremony is only for very close friends. It is a pity: certainly it took time: but in those days there was time to take. Nowadays the customers are freer, on account of the absence of hospitality, to compare prices and choose here and there.

It seems impossible, considering the stream of shoppers in the West, that time to dispense tea there would be possible. Certainly, when in London or New York I am offered, by a gesture into some corner, some imitation beverage in a plastic cup; I feel appalled. An Afghan would, I am sure, feel insulted.

On the other hand, there are few Western comforts supplied in the East for the shoppers. And yet there are three kinds of shopping: the first kind is part-social, when you visit the bazar with servants as an outing to 'beat the feet and eat the air'. The second kind is when servants do the bulk of the fetching and carrying, so that there is not the same necessity for the employers to go to the shops. The third is when the merchant visits you, bringing goods for your inspection.

In Kabul the foreigners generally liked to do their personal shopping, especially the ferreting out of tinned goods. There was a feeling of triumph in having rooted out a box of imported chocolates or – rarest of all finds – a tin of golden syrup or a box of icing sugar. Such articles were considered non-essentials, and during long periods, due to shortage of foreign currency, luxury goods were prohibited from entering the country.

Yet it was an easy matter to buy Russian perfume of powerful intensity at a pound a bottle, smuggled across the Oxus river frontier in the north: or American shoes at five times their value. Quite easy too to acquire plus-luxury goods brought somehow even from Paris, and on sale, though not quite openly, at staggering prices if you knew where to go.

Garments, such as angora jumpers, sold in Kabul like two-pence-a-kilo grapes at ten times their Western price. If that was not luxury, what was it?

Years ago, both French and German teachers and engineers were in the capital in considerable numbers. There was even a school for the German children, and both these nations sent flora- and fauna-hunters to Afghanistan. Then came the Americans, who trained a whole generation of students.

It was amusing to the British there to hear the Afghan students speaking what they called 'Yank'. Of course they had no idea they were not speaking standard English, and were considerably surprised when people guessed that they had either been to America, or been taught by American teachers in Kabul.

Evidently the arrangement suited the Afghans, who paid huge sums to these teachers. And the Americans often got excellent results.

In return, the Americans paid the local servants five times what Afghans paid. The Americans also gave the highest rents for the best houses, and generally kept the gardens in good order; at least so some owners boasted.

There were generally few foreigners in Kabul, with the exception of the personnel at the embassies, a sprinkling of German engineers engaged in the new Afghan electric installation, and the Americans employed by the Afghan State in the enormous Helmand Valley irrigation project.

There were also a few nurses and a woman doctor from Scandinavia attached to the U.N. which maintained a technical advisory mission in Kabul. They entered the homes of the poorest people and administered help and healing, at all hours of the day and night. All were keen shoppers, whether for imported or Afghan goods.

Although the original notice at the Afghan frontier, which gave forth that it was 'absolutely forbidden' to cross into Afghanistan, had been removed, the incoming road through the bleak passes of the Hindu Kush was not by any means easy. Difficult access or not, few people, apart from carpet-dealers and timber merchants, were interested in what the Afghans had to sell.

Then came the hippies, who bought embroidered waistcoats and discovered the rest of the peasant para-phernalia which so captivated Europe and America in the 1960s. This trade boosted the economy, but severely strained the hospitality of the Afghans, who were flooded with some of the lowest social elements from the West, who imagined themselves to be 'special', but were in reality, for the most part, mere drug-addicts.

They hardly noticed the country, whose mountains had all the beauty of the most admired tourist resorts in, say, Switzerland. Before the Soviet invasion, too, things were very quiet.

Many beautiful artefacts, knitted goods, metalwork, ceramics and fruit came from Paghman. Although Kabul is high up, the nearest area considered to be *highlands* is at Paghman, about twenty miles north-east of Kabul – a famous beauty-spot and summer residence during the heat in the capital. Paghman has not recovered from extensive bombing raids by Soviet jets during the occupation.

Before, in summer the gardens were a mass of flowers, making a little paradise of each house. There were no encircling walls and passers-by had the benefit of a flower show in every garden. Here there was a beautiful palace, built on a hill. Paghman was the ancestral fief of the *Sayeds* – descendants of the Prophet, my husband's family, and earlier given by the Emperor Babur to his grandmother.

The *Qila-i-Miran*, the Castle of the Princes of the Family is still there, though ruined, and the gardens are now an astonishingly beautiful public garden. Much of the rest of the place, such as the Arch of Victory and numerous houses, is in ruins.

The snow-covered hills, of course, are still magnificent, making a perfect background for the truly breathtaking valley, dotted with magnificent villas. The river runs through what has often been called some of the grandest and most enchanting scenery in the world.

Shopping in Kabul, with or without Paghman goods, will always be of interest to everyone who has time – and the most unexpected people seem to have it – to look on. To observe a bargain being made, here, can be almost as rewarding as taking part: and many of the humble folk saw so few foreigners that they never lost interest in them.

Sometimes I was followed around by spectators, who usually included a preponderance of small boys. The friends of the shopkeepers who were drinking tea – whatever the hour of the day – mostly supported the interests of the owners but sometimes they would enlist on the customer's without any ill-feeling on the part of their host.

Or, in support of their friend, they would assure you that the goods, perhaps drapery or clothing, are '*fashoni*' – fashionable, and without doubt *Europoi*, which is not only their way of saying European, but was sure, they felt, to appeal to me.

The fact that they had never been to Europe sharpened their imagination, and while they would ask you whether Europoi was wicked, they would agree that the merchandise therefrom is good, although 'expense'.

Another tea-sipper would tell you that he knew at least a dozen shops where double was charged for an inferior article, which looked exactly the same. That, he would say, is where expert advice like his became useful.

Perhaps, after all, nothing was bought; but no feelings were ruffled. 'Some other day,' the shopkeeper would say, 'because we are always at your service.'

The traders small or large, would willingly bring their goods to a prospective buyer's house. Word would go round the bazar that so-and-so was looking for this or that. Everybody in the market would know within a few hours, by some bazar telepathy unknown to those not in business.

Presently, let us say, a carpet merchant arrives. He sends in a message to say that he waits without. You have never heard of him, but you did ask about carpets that morning in the bazar.

You give permission for him to enter. Some few minutes elapse before he arrives in the garden. The cook or some other servant is probably making the most of the occasion by striking a bargain with the merchant. He will be telling him that he – the servant – might have sent the other away without informing the master, and that if the business ends satisfactorily in the sale of any item, the servant will expect to be remembered on the way out.

The arrival is quite a scene. Sometimes as many as six Hazara porters enter – those hardy Mongol highlanders who do most of the carrying on the plains – bent double under their loads. They are admitted, single-file, into the garden.

Their work leaves them with no time for attention to things sartorial. On their heads they wear turbans which look as though they do duty during the hours of sleep as well. All they require of their headgear is that it grips well and stays on. There is a long end left dangling, which finds a place across the nose and mouth in rain, snow or dust storms; or simply on a windy day.

Their much-patched jackets have long since lost all colour; even the patches on the patches are faded. A cord is tied in a workmanlike fashion round the waist to support the frailty of the coat, which even when new could never have fitted the wearers.

I wonder, looking round them, why these men have not thought of the system of exchange, and how much better that very tall man over there, say, would look in the ankle-length jacket of the smaller one.

Their cotton trousers have even less regard for fit. Most Hazara men are tall, and their peg-topped trousers seldom reach more than a poor halfway between knee and ankle. They wear no socks, even in winter, unless they happen to have the coarse hand-knitted Hazara variety. These are worn until they refuse to hang together, when they are tied on, not expertly, but firmly. The highland knitting patterns resemble with uncanny closeness the Scottish Fair Isle work. Some of the stockings are sold without feet, so that cloth feet may be sewn in and easily removed when beyond repair.

Nowhere in the world is it possible to see so much ingenious make-do-and-mend. Even a pipe-cleaner is useful where there are two buttonholes with no hope of closing by themselves.

The porters have all moved in. First the cords which tie the loads well and truly across the chest are undone. Next the carpets are spread out. If the lawn were a drawing-room floor, the merchant could not give more orders about the laying.

While number one is thus employed, the others sit, backs to the wall, easing the burdens from their shoulders. They utter no word. They appear to have learned the value of conserving their strength. Most of the porters are young, fair-skinned and red-cheeked. Their immobile features could be made considerably more presentable. Two look too old for the rigours of load-carrying. Their breathing is laboured. They have perhaps realised the fate all porters thus employed must expect; to work on until they can no longer toil, and then die.

Each in his turn spreads out his wares, under minute directions. Each retires to sit against the wall without his burden. Their expressions have lost their strained look. The carpets are minutely examined; turned over to have the number of stitches to the square inch counted. Folded back at the corners to see whether they are soft or whether there are ends sticking out. The minutest flaw is searched for, while the owner assures you that, by Allah, you know a good carpet when you see it, and that he is willing to swear on the Koran that those carpets will bear even your scrutiny.

Measurements are now taken and the room for which the carpet is intended is measured too. The whole staff and any visitors they may have, undertake the job. Voices are muted but urgent. There is a good deal of argument, because each helper has measured the room using his feet, and it stands to reason that the small boy who runs odd messages finds a few more feet in length and width than the tall cook, who does not seem to be able to disentangle the problem.

Eventually the carpets are carried in and tried. One is too broad and one too long. All are carried out and the measuring begins again. More measurements and foot-shuffling follow, and others are carried in.

The prices usually begin at twice the value of the carpet being sold. It is well known that foreigners often pay without quibbling, because the carpets are really beautiful and half the price of those in Europe. We are not classified as foreigners, so we begin to bargain.

The merchant scents some difficulty and sits down upon his heels. His face expresses some anxiety, it looks as though he has begun to suspect that we know a little too much about carpets.

He does not reply to our bid, but assures us that he

charges so little that he is actually out of pocket over the deal. We seem to have heard this before, elsewhere.

The merchant refuses to lower his prices, and the carpets are repacked, which disappoints the cook. However, the bazar telegraph is still working, and presently there are another lot of coolies, immobile like effigies against the wall.

Before the bundles are undone, we ask the prices. The man says they will suit us. The unpacking time is filled with conversation about trivialities.

The merchant says that he is known for his moderate prices, and his grandfather served my husband's grandfather, and now here he is, serving the third generation! He believes that his great grandfather also served the family. Indeed, since the first appearance of the Family from the bosom of the Blessed and Prophetic in the eighth century A.D., he and we have been bound in a paradise of carpet-buying . . .

By the time the entire family tree has been recited, the mutual cries of 'Those were the days!' and 'I am still in touch with their hereditary Swordbearer, who lives over the Third Mountain!' become more frequent. And I know that we are going to pay every penny of the previous man's prices.

The carpets are examined. I have little say in the matter because the expensive one, which to my way of thinking would be right at half the price quoted, is, the man informs us, the very absolute double, to the centre embellishment, of the one which my husband's grandfather sent to Queen Victoria.

Did she not send back a large picture of herself, sitting on a chair upon which the carpet rested? Is that picture even now not at the shop, to be sent for at a moment's notice?

The involvement of two such important and highly discerning personalities from the past (and especially the name of the Soul-Scattering Khan, the Great Nawab himself) seems to dissolve all doubts. My husband buys the carpet. The merchant supervises the laying of it. For a time there are more helpers standing on it than would be needed if every room were to be carpeted.

When a mealtime comes during these purchasing-arguments, we retire to the dining room, leaving all the porters in their static position. The merchant goes to the kitchen where he is given tea, and no doubt reports about the sale.

The coolies are glad of the rest and more glad of the tea and food which the kitchen-boy carries out to them. Some of them, I notice from behind the curtain, are nodding.

They look like figures roughly carved from driftwood, ranged along the wall.

Lunch is over and the afghani notes are counted into the ready palm of the merchant. Now he has the money safely in his possession – a tremendous lot of slips can happen in Kabul between the idea of purchasing something, and the final handing over of the money – only now does the carpet dealer relax. He smiles broadly as he makes the wad of paper into a tight bundle and deposits it somewhere inside an undergarment.

He assures my husband that it has been a pleasure to do business with such a *sharif* – a noble, and one who knows so much about carpets, into the bargain. I am not so sure, but smile too.

Within fifteen minutes the rest of the carpets are bundled up, and loaded on the semi-circular backs. The cords are securely fastened around brows and waists and, single file, the men leave the garden, which resumes its regular repose.

The carpet-merchant bows low, and kisses the hand of his customer: which must always be done in the case of the People of the House . . .

I join my husband in admiring the blend of colours and the beauty of workmanship of the carpet. The Afghans certainly know how to make them, and the middlemen how to sell them.

Whether the traders are those humble ones who sit quietly by the side of the river displaying their goods, or whether they are the owners of large shops, there is always a feeling that they consider themselves well above the work they are doing.

They are never rushed: never servile nor cringing. To them there is always time. Bellew, (who wrote about them many years ago) said, 'The pride of the Afghans is a marked feature of their national character. They eternally boast of their descent and their prowess in arms and their independence. They despise all other races: and even among themselves, each man considers himself equal to, if not better than, his neighbour.'

15

Son of Ahmad Khan, Pashtun

When Ahmad Khan the Pashtun came to me to seek service, I asked him why he, who belonged to the free tribes of the Khyber region, sought to enslave himself in service.

It was a good question, he said, and the reply was equally good: that poverty and a personal reason had been the causes. Otherwise, I must know, he would never have left the world which his hills encircled. Never, in history, he said, had his clan been conquered; they are the real free people of the world.

I engaged Ahmad, and sometimes I used to wonder what 'personal reason' had a power strong enough to drive a man from a people known to have an intense dislike for service, under any name.

Duty to Ahmad Khan was tiresome. The idea of being obliged to present himself at a certain time each day bordered upon the sordid. If left to himself he would have worked when he felt like it. That occupation would have been none other than the cleaning and re-cleaning of his rifle.

The idea of being a permanent servant, to run here and there when ordered, ('like a dog') was the most repulsive thing of which he could think. He was perfectly honest. Nothing in our house was locked. There was no necessity to do so. Ahmad Khan had the eye of an eagle and the instincts of a first-rate detective. He may have been poor, but he was not a crook. Neither was he going to serve – he said, if such humiliation be his lot – where there was a thief. If there was a dishonest person in any house within a mile, Ahmad Khan knew all about him. Yet, being a man who knows freedom, it is said that he never aided the police in the arrest of anyone.

He was a commanding figure, over six feet five inches; straight and slender as a willow. His eyes had that peculiar mixture of grey and green which one sees so often in the Pashtun clansmen. He gave the impression of being too laconic to be much interested in anything, an ability which might have given him high status in the police service of any country.

He would work well and faithfully for three months or so, then say he must go: he never asked, like the other servants, *whether* he might go. The word was must. If you asked him why he used so strong a phrase, he would place his hand over his heart, and throw a far-flung glance southwards, the direction of his homeland.

If you belong to the highlands yourself you will understand what he meant. You would appreciate that inward loyalty to your own hills, although you might be surrounded by other, higher ones elsewhere. You would know that assuredly there comes a time when the heart remembers. Regret asserts itself, and back you must go.

When I asked him how long he should be gone, he would lower his eyes to the ground. What passed before them none might know, but when he raised them again he would say, 'one moon', or 'two moons', or 'three moons', and at that time he would return.

If he did not arrive on the first day of the new moon, he need not be expected until the next. He always left someone for whom he vouched, as substitute in his absence; someone, he said, who would carry on his traditions. Not just perhaps, but positively. Once I asked his locum why Ahmad Khan had again gone home. He replied that there was work for the son of the father of Ahmad Khan to do.

That time he returned in one moon. We heard his loud, cheerful voice booming long before he came to report.

There was much laughter at his quips. After dinner he came, as he always did, to ask how our health was, and hear all that had befallen in his absence. Had we any cause to feel aggrieved, all he wanted to know was the name of the person involved, and the extent of our displeasure. The details were immaterial: he could arrange satisfaction...

I enquired how his family and his clan fared. 'Better than well, by Allah's mercy,' he replied. I gathered that the improvement was brought about by a certain amount of help from himself. This he had inferred so proudly that the words did not appear as bragging, and naturally I thought he had been able to assist them with his pay, which he had collected after three months.

He unslung his rifle, from which I seldom saw him parted, and proudly pointed to a newly-made notch on the butt. 'Another enemy of my clan gone to *Jehunnam*! Now the oil in his lamp is dried, and he may tell the angel Gabriel why he stole our horses and killed my cousin who was as my brother.' The vendetta still rules in the Free Land. There it is called *badal* – exchange.

Work I knew would be difficult for a time, and I always had doubts as to his ability to fall into the old ways on his return.

He saluted and loped away, with that panther-like tread which probably led to the undoing of the stealer of his father's horses, and was the cause of the notch on the rifle butt.

For the first few days he seemed to mark time restlessly, but everything ran more smoothly now he was back. There was less noise coming from the kitchen quarters. Blinds were drawn punctually to keep out the heat. There was always iced water in the vacuum jug within easy reach. Dainty biscuits and small cakes were served at teatime. There were flowers on my bedside table, always fresh and different every day.

His voice became quieter, and little by little the

227

hillman's pride seemed tamed by the service for which he had no heart. An expression of resignation took the place of the bold look which so denotes the pride of the Pashtun tribesman.

One thing he would not tolerate, and that was being shouted at. Anybody who wanted him, that is any of the servants, had first to find him. One day a new houseboy, not knowing this unwritten law, called him from a distance, loudly. Receiving no reply, the man repeated the shout, with added vehemence.

For a few seconds there was silence. Then the whole district was shaken by a roar from Ahmad Khan. The words used were no doubt forceful in the extreme. There was no reply from the new man, who, it was later reported, rushed into hiding from which Ahmad Khan took him by the collar of his jacket, threatening to throw him a hundred yards if there were ever any repetition. None ever needed another lesson.

Ahmad Khan would do any task asked of him, but he would not be called. He said there was a humiliation about the process which roused him to anger. No hillman, worthy of the name, would bear such disgrace.

He usually wore his own border clothes, which consisted of a pair of white cotton pegtopped trousers, tight at the ankles, a military-looking belted khaki jacket, a white jauntily tied turban, and upon his feet the usual thick-soled leather *chaplis*. When he came at first I gave him the same clothes as the other servants, but he felt uncomfortable in the tight English trousers, and was afraid, he said, to sit down, lest they split. His steps became so mincing, and his expression so comical, as though he did not know what he had done to deserve this, that we asked him to revert to his own more picturesque costume.

He was glad, he said, because when he wore *Europoi* clothes, they made him feel like the Europoi clerks, and clerks made him think of offices, and offices had walls, and walls were prisons. Altogether it was a pretty complicated affair.

He always slept out of doors, even when there was a hard frost or snow on the ground. He felt suffocated in a room. Yet when one of our sons was ill, he sat by his bedside continually for three nights without sleep, and worked as usual during the day. When pay-day came that month, I gave him more than usual, because he had done so much during the illness. He handed the extra money back, saying that a man should never shirk that work which is presented to him, even outside his occupation. He must do it for nothing, because it is the work of Allah, and Allah pays nobody.

In his opinion, he made me understand, it was easier and better to go without the extra remuneration here than some day to answer to the Recording Angel about it.

Ahmad Khan had numerous daughters, and one son. When he spoke of the boy, there was a look in his eyes such as comes when a man speaks of that which is the realisation of a dream. It was an expression that nothing else brought, not even the telling of the stories which accounted for notches on the rifle butt. The boy had been called Khushal Khan, after the poet and hero of the frontier, who had fought the great Mogul emperor Aurangzeb in India.

To this day, the frontiersmen sang the glorious exploits of Khushal Khan, and everyone imagined himself to have lighted his taper at the beacon of the hero. Ahmad Khan would tell how the boy, but ten years of age, could ride an unbroken horse, hit a particular light-coloured stone on the hillside a hundred yards away, find his way home from any distance, repeat more than half of the Holy Koran by heart, quote long passages from the works of old philosophers and write plainly enough for those with the ability to read and understand. Was not this, he would say, with that look in his eyes, a one? Did not the frontier need such youths, who would grow into men, of whom future generations would sing, even as the men of the time sang of that other liberator, Khushal Khan?

It seemed a great deal for a ten-year-old to accomplish, especially as he had never been to school. For as Ahmad Khan said truly, the boy's own clansmen could teach him to shoot straight, the local mullas were gifted enough to teach the Holy Koran and the example of his family taught him how to live as a worthy member of the community, in which his word would be his bond, where any deviation from the truth brought its own judgment. That, said Ahmad Khan, was beyond the power of a mere school to teach. It was the duty of the parents.

Once when Ahmad Khan returned, he brought Khushal. He was a handsome little fellow, cheerful and intelligent. Proudly Ahmad Khan led him in front of me. The boy stood straight as a die. There was an air about him which only the pride of freedom brings. Fair-skinned and blue-eyed, he would have been considered handsome anywhere.

For my benefit he recited poetry, philosophy, and stanzas from the Holy Koran. All this he did without any sign of shyness. Then he showed his prowess with a rifle. His father had three small bottles in his hand. These he threw quickly, one after the other, high into the air. Khushal scarcely had time to take aim, before he shattered them.

Then he hit several apples on a tree in the distant orchard. When I praised him, the boy assured me that it was nothing. He would be honoured, he said, if one day I might see the marksmanship of his clansmen. He hoped eventually to equal their ability, and he would, by Allah's mercy. Ahmad Khan watched proudly. Perhaps, he said, the boy would show me one more thing he could do. He asked Khushal Khan to take a good look at the garden, then tied a handkerchief tightly around his eyes. 'Go now round the flowerbeds, and take care not to step upon one flower or border.' This the boy did, stepping confidently along the paths. He approached a rose tree and, carefully taking a rose-bud, brought it to me, bowing and placing his hand upon his heart. Then he turned and made his way to the garden wall, and cleared its seven feet easily. The next moment he scrambled back.

There was something uncommon about the boy. He was so gifted and simple, and yet there was that pride shining through his eyes all the time. I wished I could engage him, simply to run odd errands, but I could never have had the temerity to propose to his father that his son should become a servant.

I could imagine him saying, 'Your Presence, the boy belongs to the hills, to the free life my clan is willing to die for. He must never know any other.' No, it would be impossible to ask.

Later we saw him kneeling at prayer-time beside his father, and it seemed right and just that an honest man should have such a son.

Before he returned home with a relative, we gave Khushal some illustrated magazines, just a few, because he would have long distances to walk, and he was but a small boy. We also gave him two kites and a rifle. This gun was a thing for which he had longed, he said, for many moons. He was pleased with the papers, and the kites, but he loved the weapon.

He took it in both hands and raising it ran his cheek along its smooth surface. He knelt down and wrapped it carefully in the papers, tying these on with string. The last we saw of him was cradling it as one would carry a small child.

Young as he was, he made a great impression on us and our friends. There were offers of adoption and education in Europe, of good homes and settled sums. Ahmad Khan listened to it all, was silent for a short time, then said, 'The work I do here is for this boy, because I would not have him seek service. Service breaks the spirit of the young, and that is a sin in the eyes of the just. If I do not work enough, I can work more, but not Khushal Khan, he is my

231

Nur-Chashm – the light of my eyes. He will be nobody's slave. He belongs to the Free Lands.'

It is seldom in life that a man without learning has the power to make the educated feel small and ignorant. If such an exceptional case arises one learns anew that the dignity of a man is not measured by money or position. One learns that dignity cannot be lessened by work; that perhaps it even inspires to nobler thoughts than are entertained by someone who has always had everything.

Next year the boy died. The news came to me first, because the bearer of it came when Ahmad Khan was out at the bazar. So far as was possible to understand, Khushal had died of pneumonia, as a complication of bronchitis. Doctors are few and far between in the Frontier.

I went out. The thought of the blow about to fall upon the father seemed too cruel, and like too many of its kind, so inexplicable. I did not want to know when he received it. We had some meals with friends and when we returned Ahmad Khan came to us. He looked like a man walking for the first time after a long illness. The shock had blanched his face. There were lines and hollows where none had been before. He stooped as though bent under a weight. He stood first upon one foot and then another; his cable-strong nerves were gone. He struggled to regain his usual calm. I could think of nothing but the cheerful little boy excited about the rifle.

'Khanoum,' said Ahmad Khan, 'this day, it is the will of Allah that my strength has been sapped. His is the power to give, and also to take back that which he has given. The more appreciated the blessing, the more we in our rebelliousness dislike the retaking, because in our pride we claim that gift as our own. Here have I worked for my son. May Allah be pleased with him. It may be a truth that this has found displeasure in the eyes of Allah, whose forgiveness I ask.'

232

I could think of nobody requiring the forgiveness of Allah less than Ahmad Khan, the honest man.

His voice came again, so quietly as scarcely to be heard. 'And now, Khanoum, there is no need for me to work. The strength has gone from my arm. The joy from my life. I must return to my people. There is no longer a reason for working.'

I said the few consoling useless phrases one utters at these times. Although the going of Ahmad Khan would leave a gap, and the work would never again be done with the same ability, I could not find it in my heart to ask him to stay.

He drew himself up and said that he would see that another came in his place before he went, and that our welfare would always be in his heart.

He said that he wanted to thank me for giving the rifle to his son, because the boy had needed one, and he had not been able to give the high price for one himself. I might like to know that the boy had said that that rifle would protect me if he lived, and I needed his protection, and Ahmad Khan said that I was to consider that he had now taken over the pleasure of that vow.

Any time he would come, if even the highest in the land sought to harm any of my family. They would do so only after Ahmad Khan, Pashtun, had died in our defence.

16

Music, Dance, Sword-Play

On the first day of Spring, during the elaborate celebrations of Independence Day and after the fasting month of Ramadan – there is a great deal of dancing to be seen in the open air.

A suitable field is chosen around which huge Afghan flags wave and a pole is erected in the centre. Round this the men dance in ever-widening circles.

The crowds are enormous. Every inch of the huge temporary stadium is filled. Men and women, young and old, people dressed in Western clothes as well as those from the numerous ethnic groups – Pashtuns, Tajiks, Hazaras, Nuristanis – mix happily, with no concern for class or other status. In spite of this mixing, there are hardly ever any incidents: the crowd is well-mannered.

Urchins sell sweets, green tea and lemonade; fortune-tellers try to read palms and purvey charms, soldiers, police, even village lads in gaudy turbans, are showing off to all and sundry.

A great deal of Afghan dancing evidently derives from warlike exercises. Over the centuries, Afghans have conquered such neighbouring lands as India and Persia, or provided enormous numbers of trained warriors, regarded as the best in the East. Legions of them even fought in the Crusades, and their families still cherish captured banners and weapons taken from 'the Franks' six and seven hundred years ago.

Some of the performers who know the dance well are quite old. These usually take the inner circles, thus making a smaller and easier area for them to cover. The most agile of the young men carry a gun in the right hand, and a sword in the left. At first when the dance begins, the gun is spun around the head, next the blade; then both seem to be wildly mixed up in the whirl of the dance – yet they do not touch.

Surrounding the dancers are about a hundred amazingly expert horsemen. The short, high, proud heads of the horses bespeak their Arab strain: their grandsires carried the Arabian conquerors here in the eighth century.

Now the horses are galloping around the dancers; the riders rise up in the saddle, and, standing in the stirrups, shoot several fusillades into the air. As one man, they take their seats again; only to rise in unison and, with flashing scimitars, describe circles in the air above their heads.

The music of the military and pipe bands is punctuated now and again by a roll of drums that adds to the general thrill of the festivity. The dancers are now executing measured steps. The animals are trotting circumspectly round; as they proceed their steps become more and dainty while the music is slowed down.

Suddenly the rhythm gathers momentum, and the dancers and horses obey the beat. Faster and faster thuds the music, faster and faster the pace of dancers and horses, until the tempo is tremendous; the dancers are whirling like tops, the horses in full gallop with their beautiful tails streaming behind them, and the horsemen are sometimes standing, leaning far out to right then to left, firing into the air, or brandishing their weapons as though dispersing an attacking foe.

Although the movements of dancers, horsemen and mounts are synchronised, and thousands of different steps and movements are made, there is complete unison between each and every participant.

Suddenly, with one tremendous short roll of drums, as harsh as a colossal clap of thunder, the dancers and the horses alike stop dead. There is not so much as the flick of a horse's tail.

For a full half minute there is utter, almost unbearable, silence, until the drums roll again, and off they go once more with a completely new set of movements, with similarly impeccable timing and discipline. During a brief pause, the onlookers shout and clap their approval. Horses, swords and gunplay are immensely popular with them, and as they cheer and clap and call *shabash* – well done, the sound seems to fill the entire arena.

This play and dance goes on until the horses are foam-flecked, the ammunition finished and, one guesses, the dancers are exhausted.

A new set now takes up position and the *Attan* national dance is performed. A hundred dancers, including women, take part. The dress of the women, some of them astonishingly beautiful, is attractive. Their baggy trousers fall in graceful folds to their ankles where they are caught into a tight band. The upper garment is a tunic, high at the neck and elaborately hand-embroidered. The clothes are in all colours, and blend artistically. These dancers are fair-complexioned, some blonde with blue or grey eyes.

The hair of the men is neck-length, and glossy. Some wear curls and flowers behind their ears; strangely, this does not look at all effeminate. Their peg-top trousers are ankle-length. High-necked shirts are embroidered and reach to the knees. Sometimes coloured stones enhance the beauty of the designs on breast and sleeve.

The heads of men and women are uncovered, and both use scarlet scarves to wave during the dance. Sometimes the girls wear coloured scarves around their shoulders and the bright colours add to the gaiety of the dance. The women who take part are not in seclusion: they do not belong to clans which veil their women, which means that these women do not wear the *burqa*. The Koran, of course, does not ordain that women should be veiled, but a Middle Eastern custom, dating – amazingly enough – to early Christian women in Palestine – is believed to be originally responsible for the custom.

The dances take a long time to perform, and there are quite a number of them.

Tent-pegging is both exciting and picturesque, and is a popular game at the *Id-el-fitr* – the Day of the Feast, following upon the fasting month of Ramadan.

Every man who can sit upon a horse, and almost anyone who owns or can borrow one, tries to take part. All players carry the long lances of iron-tipped bamboo for this national game, which attracts tremendous crowds.

For *nazabazi*, as the game is called in Afghanistan, wooden pegs are fixed in the ground, in threes or fours, so that a number of riders may compete at the same time.

While the competitors are gathering, the horses make a fine show. Some of the horsemen pass the time doing tricks. One rider will gallop round without touching the reins, standing upright in the saddle, the ends of his snow-white turban flying behind. Another will gallop his horse while he leans over and touches the ground first on one side then on the other. A third will jump on and off a fast-moving horse. The applause is deafening. The Afghans love horses and are loud in their praise of good horsemanship. '*Shabash! Shabash!*' they yell, until the word is given that the game is about to begin.

Like polo horses, the nazabazi mounts know the game. As they gallop to the start they require no heel encouragement and spurs are not worn: indeed, spurs are regarded as extraordinarily barbaric.

I once saw an internationally-celebrated horseman from one of the embassies in Kabul attempt to mount one of the King's horses, using his own tack, including bit and spurs.

The animal threw him, again and again, until he pronounced it unfit for riding under any circumstances. As soon as the Western devices were removed, however, this highly-trained prize animal was easily ridden and put through its paces by a thirteen-year-old boy!

The riders converge wildly upon the pegs, the successful ones riding away with their spoils carried triumphantly on the end of their lances. There is great applause. '*La ilaha illa 'llah Mahommad rasulu 'llah* – There is no God but Allah and Mahommad is his prophet,' call the pious ones in encouragement.

Excitement grows, riders, horses and spectators all enter into the spirit of the game. The competitors are all known to the crowd, and when a favourite prances on with his lance held high to denote he has succeeded, the onlookers shout his name and the surrounding hills echo and re-echo the words.

Eventually, when the horses are as exhausted as the competitors, which is not soon, the game is declared finished.

Tod – wrestling, is as popular as nazabazi, if not more so. Two groups of young men take up opposing sides on the field. Each is obviously aware of and pleased with his own muscles. Each flexes his arms. Each one is stripped to the waist, and radiates assurance and not a little conceit.

The game begins when a muscular athlete steps into the arena, after a last word of encouragement and advice from the trainer. He is not by any means unconscious of the applause, but in an exaggerated way takes no notice of it. Two young athletes now step in from the opposing side, and the game is on.

The athlete who came first has to avoid being captured by the other two, yet he must make it possible for them to be near enough to receive from him two or three slaps given by the open hand. At this time, while the slaps are being given, the pursuers try to throw the young man to the ground. If this occurs he is defeated, and another takes his place.

The agility required to evade the pursuers and yet to deliver the slaps without being thrown is something to be wondered at. The spectators hold their breath, following every movement with suspense, until the throw, when the applause is really wild.

Sometimes members of the audience take sides and disagree, and there are a number of free-for-all arguments. But on the whole the game is great fun.

The wrestling is followed by hockey and football. One Afghan football player insists on playing in bare feet. This, spectators think, gives the advantage to his side, because he is a perfect wizard at sending the ball, however great the distance, just where he wants to place it.

Between the various events there is much drinking of sherbet; ice cream and various sweetmeats are eaten, as well as quantities of fruits which happen to be in season: mulberries, melons, apples, pomegranates. Everybody seems to know everybody else and there is frequent embracing among friends as the spectators move about. Old friends hold hands while they enquire about each other's welfare and after their 'houses', i.e. families.

Brothers report all that has taken place since their last meeting. Descriptions of this young man and that are relayed to the mothers who may have one or two marriageable daughters not averse to settling down and many romances have their beginning at the *Id-el-fitr*.

The month of fasting is a severe trial on the temper, especially if the lunar month of Ramadan, (pronounced Ramazan in Afghanistan), which each year falls several days earlier than in the preceding year, happens to coincide with the very hot summers of Kabul.

A cannon sounds at dawn – perhaps around 3.15 a.m. – and again at dusk, at around 7.15 p.m. Between these two times, no food may be eaten, nothing drunk, and the faithful must refrain even from smoking.

In some Muslim countries, in Africa and the Gulf, where the temperature rises to over 133 Fahrenheit degrees in the shade, thirst is almost insupportable, and those who have to work as well as fast may collapse from the effects of dehydration.

Small wonder therefore that the feast which follows Ramadan is celebrated with tremendous zest.

Everybody entertains and is entertained. There are pilaus and chilaus: spiced and plain rice dishes; koftas and kebabs and dried fruits, nuts and fresh fruits. As soon as the fasting month is over, or on occasions such as Independence day, and the day on which the Frontier clansmen celebrate the inauguration of Pashtunistan, wild celebrations break out.

The Afghans love music. Singers and players descend upon the towns from the highlands and neighbouring villages. Sometimes the parties are large, sometimes they are small. The usual troupe consists of one or two singers, and the instruments are mostly original. There is the harmonium, too, which probably originated in Europe, and found its way to India via missionaries, arriving in Afghanistan around the beginning of the twentieth century.

The harmonium is portable; and there is little written music. The musicians and singers learn from a teacher or by repetition from parents and grandparents.

Afghan airs have few of the high nasal sounds of other Eastern tunes. To Western ears the music cannot be said to be 'oriental'; rather is it monodic and modal, and consequently quite pleasing to European ears. The bellows of the harmonium are worked by the left hand and the instrument is capable of quite surprising volume.

The *rohab* has six strings, and is played with a *chahbaz* – a plectrum. It has a sweet, haunting note and people in the audience are moved to nodding their heads and looking soulful while their favourite songs are being played.

The *dilruba* looks like a huge violin. Its strings are gently plucked, and great feeling is put into its music. When songs describe the loneliness of a young man for his beloved, or artistically make comparison between the sweetheart and a rosebud, this instrument almost seems to speak, and the emotions are easily aroused.

So animate does it seem, that it almost conveys personal feelings, which have the power of awakening past memories too deeply lodged in the heart to be forgotten, and as the song ends there are tears on most cheeks. Small wonder its name means 'ravisher of the heart'.

The *tambour* is a traditional instrument, seen in many European paintings. Its body is most often fashioned from a dried gourd. It is particularly suited to such old-fashioned Western songs as 'Just a Song at Twilight', or any of the old Scottish airs.

The *santour* is a stringed instrument, rather like a guitar, both in shape and sound.

The *tabla*, a small drum, is perhaps the most remarkable of all the Afghan musical instruments, and a good tabla player has the power to make a success of any ensemble.

The tablas are struck with the fingers and the flattened palms of the hands. Practically any sound may be drawn from them: high or low, flat, *legato*, double-sharp, *tremolando*. A really first-class player is able to make this instrument sound like a harp, a violin, a ukulele, or even the bagpipes.

The skin responds to the slightest touch, clear as a bell: when the palms are applied the volume can rise to a sound as loud and deep as a bassoon. The tabla player usually gets a great deal of attention.

Delicately, as a woman arranging flowers, he draws forth the tune or haunting love song, then follows this with another tune such as 'the gathering of the clans for war'.

Thunder rolls and thousands of feet march with great realism. Then all at once, in what seems to be the very midst of the music, he raises his arms high and seems to be about to destroy the instrument.

Suddenly a *fortissimo* note ends the piece. This unexpected ending is tremendously thrilling, and the entire audience claps and cries 'Shabash! Shabash!' An almost mesmeric influence emanates from the tablas, and it is a long time before the effect of their fascinating witchery dies away.

The *saranda* with flat sound-box has a short handle, and bow. The saranda is an Indian instrument, resembling a ukulele. Its melodies usually begin on soft notes, which gather momentum as the song proceeds to a climax. The singers and players are reliving the story, like minstrels in the days of long ago.

They are oblivious to their surroundings and the audience. They do not 'play to the gallery'. There is no coquettish smiling or seeking for applause during the performance. Only with the end of the music do the performers re-emerge once more into present time and space.

The pure Afghan songs are still sung by the mountain people, and have, fortunately, remained free from the impact of Indian and Western music. The country and hill people sing as they travel to and fro along the roads and mountain paths. Shepherd boys play the flute, its sweet notes travelling on the wind.

Often there is no player to be seen and this gives the music a feeling of other-wordly charm, as though the mountain sprites were amusing themselves.

One day in the countryside, I watched a boy of perhaps eight years lying on a grassy slope in the shade of a tree. His flock of sheep and goats were grazing near and his attention was divided between the animals and his flute. It is likely therefore that he did not see the traveller down on the road beneath.

It was easy at first to mistake him for a girl. His face was oval, his eyes large and grey. Long dark curls nestled low on his neck. The whole picture was of a beautiful pastoral scene, and the notes of his pipe followed me far along the lonely path. How right, it seemed, that the flute should be associated with hills and shepherd-boys.

How right it would be for all flute players to be dressed as simply as these sheep tenders: a flautist in a stiff shirt has no place here. Could I ever stand the sight of one such in England again?

The *damboura* belongs to the music of the tribesmen on the southern Frontier – the North-West to the Indians and the British. It is quite different from other Afghan musical instruments. The damboura is two-stringed, and the playing consists of striking the strings with the fingers of the right hand, giving the dominant and tonic-tones of the song, and keeping time.

The *toula* is a metal or reed flute. The *dohol* is like the tamboura of Afghanistan, except that it is hung around the neck by a strap and resembles a small barrel.

The frontiersmen sing too, on their long journeys. Like the other Afghans, they sing if they are happy; and if they are sad they still sing, except that the songs are of a rather depressing kind, such as when the hero loved in vain and although he had the heart of a lion on the battlefield, yet his heart turned to water when his love was not returned.

The public singers, both grown up and children, have remarkably good voices. They sing without nuances, and have a habit of holding the right hand pressed to the neck.

Like the bagpipes, these Afghan highland songs and instruments sound best in the hills and valleys. Based on a scale of seven notes, Afghan music is said to be a mixture of that of the ancient Persian empire of King Darius, and – farther west – of Chaldea, Phoenicia, Assyria and Greece.

Since the ancient days, instruments have been modernised: today modern European and Indian music, brought by radio into the Afghan home, has been enthusiastically adopted and it is common to hear the latest western song hits being repeated in the bazars and hummed by schoolboys and girls all over the country.

It will be a pity if Afghan music and the beautifully made musical instruments, with their pearl, lapis, and ivory ornamentations, give way entirely to Western influence. There is a tremendous difference between the impersonal radio or television programme and the live presence of singers and dancers with their beautiful instruments and colourful national clothes.

17

New Year

In Afghanistan, the twenty-first of March is considered
the first day of Spring: and celebrated as the traditional
New Year's Day. The snow has melted from the nearer
hills, although the heights of the Paghman ranges and
beyond are still white-crowned, and will be for some
weeks.

It is interesting, if complicated, that three calendars are
used in Afghanistan. The official one is called *Shamsi*, and
conforms to the signs of the zodiac. Then there is the usual
Islamic calendar, in which, for example, the year 1374 fell
in 1955 of the Christian Era. Lastly comes the Gregorian,
as used in the West and by the foreign community in
Afghanistan.

The first day of Spring is a universal holiday. People
come from all over the country to celebrate the day at the
Jashn – Festival. Afghans from far-away Hazara, Pushtuns
from the southland, Baluchis, and all the population of
Kabul join in the celebrations.

The servants have been given new clothes by their
employers. These consist of trousers and a jacket and
either a fur cap or a turban, and a pair of shoes (English
preferably; even discarded ones).

As there were few ready-made clothes in Kabul, there
was much excitement when the servants had their gift-
clothes made for them, and the hours of leave were made
exciting, having them fitted.

All offices were closed and domestic servants given from
mid-day to 6 p.m. off duty. Arrayed in the new finery they

245

appeared early to offer good wishes to their employers. After that, a good deal of subdued tittering came from the kitchen quarters, and for once breakfast was not only at the proper time, but five minutes early.

We hurried through it, conscious that the table boy was hovering just outside the dining-room door ready to clear away the dishes. During the morning we gave them some errands to run, to friends' houses, knowing they wanted to show their new outfits to their friends.

We made arrangements for our lunch to be at twelve o'clock instead of one as usual, so that all would get away except the boy who would finish the clearing-up, and place the tea-tray in the lounge. There would be tea in a thermos ready for 4 p.m.

Beside my lunch plate there lay a huge bunch of *nargis* – narcissi, whose scent filled the room: a gift from the staff. There were several plates, jugs and dishes on the sideboard containing dried mixed fruit, cakes, almonds and raisins, dried mulberries and walnuts, pistachios, oranges, limes and apples. These were gifts from friends and the tradespeople.

At 11.50 luncheon was announced. Excitement ran so high by this time that faces were wreathed in smiles, and there was more dashing about than I had seen since the last holiday. My anxiety turned towards the safety of the china.

At twelve precisely we saw them tip-toeing out of the gate. They had been given their pay in advance, and they had that look which only the sure possession of money gives.

As is the way of the world, the one who was left behind to do the necessary chores was the youngest. He hurried through the work and presently with a speed of which he never before showed himself capable, put the tea-tray in the lounge, replete with all etceteras. Trying to keep excitement out of his voice, he asked whether he had our permission to go. He assured me that everything was done to our satisfaction, as his small brother had been helping. The brother was ten.

There was now nobody left except the gate-keeper, who said he was too old – at forty – for such frivolity. He said he liked peace.

I could think of several ways in which he might indulge his preference other than answering our door, and told him so. He stated that every man has his own opinion as to what constitutes peace.

He confided that there were three women in his house, and this did not make for the harmony for which the heart longed. I told him that that was easy to understand, and he intimated that he was regretful that my knowledge 'extends to such misfortune'.

The first person to call was the grocer. He brought his two sons and a jar of fruit in syrup. It is etiquette to receive the caller and reciprocate the good wishes. This occupies but a few minutes, wishing peace upon them, added business and good health.

Several other tradespeople arrived with gifts, then we rested until teatime, when the sunroom was flooded with the sun's warmth.

Sharp at 6 p.m. the servants reported their return. They were still dazzled by what they had seen. Each one had brought a small offering – a wooden bowl, a Japanese egg-cup, a few sheets of dazzling coloured paper, tinted marbles, artificial flowers of colossal size and unknown species, or a thick tumbler with what looked like streaks of lightning painted on it, and a curiously shaped bottle.

They had seen! What had they not seen? When the question was asked they looked at each other. Then one stammered that time, 'which usually passed as though its wings were broken', had miraculously recovered at the fair from this disability and flown, just like that. The illustration was a sweeping movement of the arm in a wide curve. The others agreed.

Cook said they had returned early while the fun was at

its height, because 'high-spirited horses are not driven by the whip of poverty'. It sounded bad for those wages.

They related how they had had their fortunes told. I asked the shy one what he had been told. His neighbour said: 'He is to have money.' Cook said he was glad to hear that, because he had first claim, owing to a loan the previous week.

Another said that the boy had told him that the sum was in the region of 'heights', and that he would get married when the money came.

As I knew the boy was already unsuitably united to a lady of uncertain temper, I hastily asked him what they had had to eat.

This did not appear to be a popular question. One replied by saying that too much money had gone on sweet things. Jelabies, pink ices, sherbets, and other highly-coloured saccharine enticements.

The small boy wished he had brought home what he had eaten.

They spoke freely about the mountains of coloured balloons, horseback games, and the dancing; I gathered that the last few swings had not agreed with the jelabies they had eaten.

They had met all their relatives, and everybody they had ever known. The small boy, remembering the coins now gone, said that money was a snare which led to other and worse temptations; two of the worst of which were fried fish and jelabies.

We thanked them for their gifts and presented them with some money. This seemed the best way to comfort them, for in front of each stretched a long penniless month, about which they had fortunately not started to think.

Surely no better dinner was served in Kabul that night than the one we had. In it figured stewed pigeons, baked potatoes, asparagus, grilled chops, plump little cheese turn-overs, and more pastries stuffed with walnut marzipan.

These are Turkish delicacies, and the stuffed triangular pastries are fried in butter, then dipped in thick rose-flavoured syrup.

As an alleged grand finale we had stewed apples and whipped cream: but this was followed by dried fruits, fresh fruits and fruits in syrup. The *pièce de résistance* was a large dish of luridly coloured sweets, placed in the centre of the table, and artistically embowered in paper roses of a wild purple hue, together with other cerise and emerald paper flowers – a surprise from the Fair!

For the sake of politeness we asked for the centre-piece to be placed on the sideboard. It was later and diplomatically disposed into the welcoming, although grimy, hands of two depressed-looking children outside driving a donkey. The pair, boys, were mute with surprise and excitement when I told them the things had come from the *Jashn*, of which such as they hear only echoes, as one does of some distant, unattainable Valhalla.

After dinner we shared out the fruit and other gifts of the day, handing them to the cook to dispense. Cook said they would be given to the women relatives who made 'big eyes' when they asked for *shirini* – sweets, to be brought them from the Jashn.

Women used to be allowed to go, but that was stopped after a number of gallants kidnapped their girls from under the very noses of their menfolk, who did not miss them until the round-up at home-going time came. By then, these young Lochinvars and the perhaps not unwilling ladies were well away.

Thus the New Year's Day was rounded off happily for those who came on duty at 5.30 a.m. and were sometimes still at their posts at midnight, with never a grumble, backed by no Trades Union, but happy in the knowledge that their employers treated them as human beings. For them tomorrow would be another ordinary day; but this is one they would remember.

18

Aziza and the Jinns

No road in Afghanistan is ever too far-flung or lonely to lack the long, straggling nomad caravans. Their local name, *Kochi*, may mean 'People of the Mountains', but there is not a valley, either, where they are not to be seen.

There is a continual trekking from the plains to the hills after the winter, and from the hills to the plains when winter is about to set in. The goats, sheep and camels have to be fed, and the only way of doing this is to walk them to pasture. There is a chance on the way of helping the farmers, which puts some money into nomad coffers.

This life makes the nomads a hardy people; only the fittest survive.

When passing their caravans it is noticeable that the women are as tough as the men, and handle the camels or horses with ability. Nomad women do not appear to have any foot trouble; they stride out along the rough roads sure-footed as goats.

They are unveiled; their faces have the look of people who are on a journey of more than ordinary difficulty, but who are used to that. They meet one's gaze with steady eyes; seldom do they exchange greetings.

Some of the women are attractive, their expressions intelligent. The young girls and children have rosy cheeks and bright eyes, but the outdoor life later tans their complexions.

One of the prettiest sights on the mountain roads is that of one or two small children warmly and safely packed in carpet bags, slung on camelback. Sometimes their companions are tiny lambs, which they hold in their arms. As they pass the foreigner the children's eyes become larger, but no smile ever crosses their small, intent faces. They look back as far as they can see.

The parents and elders seem to take good care of them. Even though the women walk long stretches of the roads, children are never to be seen on foot.

When a nomad child is to be born, the caravan halts for an hour or so, then the new member of the tribe is tied on its mother's back, and the journey continues.

All seem to be so healthy, a legacy of the open-air life which they and their forbears have led. Illness to them is something to be ashamed of; they speak of it as others would of a disgrace. For this reason they endure pain long after they ought to have had medical treatment. They look upon doctors as they do upon ailments, something to be avoided: people whom townsfolk frequent.

But a change has slowly come over even the Kochi customs. The nomad women, when passing each other on the roads, have exchanged news, as is their way with their own kind. They have spoken of the wonders which are to be seen in the *Khariji* – foreigners' – hospitals. A woman would say, 'you take your pain and leave it there.' Another said, 'the pain is stopped for all time.'

Another who had had an operation in one of these wonder-houses would proudly show the others the very place 'where the pain came out'.

The day came when one who had heard these things could no longer remain quiet about a pain which had been getting worse and worse. Reluctantly, she remembered the story of Hayya, a Kochi woman of her very own clan, who has actually been in hospital with a similar complaint. But that was Hayya the evil-tongued, and she was unwilling to listen to the full details. And, still more unwillingly, she reported the trouble to her husband.

There was much argument before permission was given by the tribe for one of their members to be submitted to the hands of those who might kill her. How, they reasoned, could they guarantee that the Kharijis would cure her? There was silence when this question was put.

Have they not heard that sometimes people go alive into these hospitals and come out dead? Is it not a truth that some of the same doctors are Christians, drink wine and eat pigs' flesh? They worship the Prophet Jesus as if he were a god, and yet think that they eat his flesh.

Yet, ventured another, the woman who had spoken of the Khariji wonders had got away alive and healed. Jesus, after all, is known throughout the East as a miraculous doctor . . .

Then the oldest member of the tribe spoke: her white hair and experience of life commanded respect. In her opinion, the ailment was getting worse, and without doubt the woman would probably die soon in any case. She was a strong woman and young, and if saved might be expected to give birth to many more children which would increase the tribe's strength. Therefore, every effort should be made towards her recovery.

This arrangement being arrived at, preparations began for the long slow journey through the hills and valleys and over the rough mountain-passes. The pain would be torture for Aziza, during the two or three weeks the journey would certainly take.

The little mounds overlooking the roads, with a stick with rags attached for the purpose of keeping away evil spirits, tell of many similar journeys which had failed.

Before the caravan set off, every formula known to the tribe was tried out. Holy texts sewn up in pieces of cloth were suspended around the neck, or bound over the place where the pain was. Offerings were placed on saints' tombs, and simply everybody's advice was given a good trial.

Yet the pain continued. The demon which had taken possession of the patient, the Kochi elders said, was too cunning for them.

There were always members of the tribe to predict the worst in the presence of the invalid, but the pain overruled their forebodings and, once the decision to go to hospital was made, it was final.

At long last the mountain roads and new-fangled bridges of the towns were negotiated, the traffic contended with, and the hospital reached. First Aziza was taken before a man who appeared to be very inquisitive.

Her husband told him that his wife had only come to have the pain removed, but the man said it was necessary to ask about many things. He said he must know. Now the pair were in the hands of the Kharijis, it was obviously necessary for the Kochis to humour them.

When the doctor had asked many questions and a Khariji woman in white had written something down in a book, the wife was taken away to a room to be washed.

Akram, the husband, was told he might not come. He asked why. He was told that he must obey the hospital rules. What autocrats, he thought. Because they took away pain, they had to twist people's tails first, just to show authority, no doubt.

What, he wondered, had washing to do with the removal of a pain?

He must keep quiet in this strange place though, because his wife was now at the mercy of people he knew nothing about. Like a hostage.

He looked at the white walls. No images of the Prophet Jesus here, which was all to the good, of course. Perhaps Jesus had passed down some knowledge, and these people, white-coated, white-walled, hurrying in and out, looking at boards and papers, wheeling strange carts, were in a sort of *tariqa*, members of a spiritual path...

They were taking a long time to finish the washing. Perhaps these special ablutions, which must be quite a performance and no doubt necessary, would remove the pain.

While the husband was waiting in the discomfort, to

him, of a bench in the whitewashed waiting-room, his wife was having the first thorough wash of her life. She was too frightened to speak, because there was nobody of her tribe there to support her.

All her clothes were removed. The woman in the white clothes told her that the garments were too dirty to be washed. They would have to be burned. This must be a sacrifice the Kharijis make to their heathen gods.

'Where are more clothes to come from?' she asked. The reply was that while she was in hospital clothes would be given her, and more when she left. But she said she could not wear foreign clothes. No, one of the women said, she would be given garments like her own, only clean.

But, she explained, she had worn the clothes the hospital had just taken from her ever since she was married. The foreign woman dressed all in white told her not to worry, because soon the pain would be gone.

Finally, the bath was over and she was in a ward.

She was afraid of the great high bed with its long legs, and said she always lay on the ground. She would probably fall out of a thing like that. She had never been in one of those things before. The ground, she felt, was the safest place; everybody in her tribe knew that. These foreigners, undoubtedly, were even more peculiar than she had imagined, and must have many idols to placate.

While Aziza was refusing to get into the bed, another woman who was called Sister came in, saying the patient must have her hair cut off. Why? 'For good reasons.'

This was too much. The washing was bad; the burning of the clothes worse, the sleeping up in the air, a thing to be avoided; but the cutting of the hair was something that no decent nomad woman worthy of the name would tolerate.

She told them, with rising anger, that her hair was plaited in its bootlace-wide strands for her marriage, and that it must remain thus until the day of her death, never touched in any way during life.

The bed, after all, might have its uses. Aziza, despite

the stabs of pain, mounted it, and dared anybody to approach her. She said she would fight to the last for her hair.

'Even if the Kharijis take the hair of their own kind, they are not to have *mine*,' she shouted. The sister left the room and returned with two foreign men dressed in white coats. These were employed to deal with recalcitrant patients.

They advised her to do as she was told, and not to make trouble. She replied that they, not she, were making trouble.

The man who had questioned her when she arrived walked into the room. She shouted, asking him if the doctors of unprintable ancestry wanted even a woman's hair? He said of course not. He said he was a doctor.

Aziza told him that she wanted her husband, and that she was going back to him. She would bear the pain, she said.

Now thoroughly roused, she aimed a blow at the nurse nearest to her. She saw her husband entering the room. The doctor explained the situation, and told her husband that they were anxious to perform the operation immediately.

The husband told her that nobody wanted to kill her, and that even if they did, nothing could be done about it now she had placed herself in the hands of the foreigners.

She was about to throw herself upon the two white-coated men, to whom she had taken a dislike, when she felt a jab, as of a thorn, and everything became black, and she felt herself falling, falling . . .

When Aziza came to her senses her mouth was parched and her head aching. It took her some time to remember where she was. The pain which had tortured her for so long was much less. She tried to sit up but she felt too weak.

A woman in white who was sitting beside her gave her some water. She drank it out of a glass, instead of taking it from her hands as she usually did. She could not get a good drink from this Khariji contraption. Why was everything so difficult? Did these foreigners not know that the best place to drink is from a stream?

The nurse held the glass to her lips and almost choked her. She was aware that her husband was standing near. The nurse gave her a little white tablet to swallow. She could not swallow it, so she crunched it and took some water. She meant to spit it out but swallowed it in her fright. She suddenly felt terribly tired and fell asleep.

When she awoke the pain was gone, except for a feeling of soreness where it had been. The Khariji woman handed her a cup with a spout from which she drank soup. It tasted good.

They had not killed her! She felt surprised to be alive. She asked if the pain had been taken away. The nurse said yes, and asked if she was not glad? She said she was, but how long would she have to eat and drink in this peculiar way? She would rather go hungry, she said.

The other patients in the ward asked her how she was. She felt weak and homesick for familiar things, as do all those accustomed to far wild places, when they find themselves in the hemmed-in artificiality of a town.

Again she slept, but before unconsciousness came she wondered whether this was death, the thing she had seen happening to members of her tribe. She did not want to die among foreigners. She distrusted their fine ways.

She awoke to find it was night. She could not see the stars, but knew that when night came the foreigners lit up their houses instead of going to bed.

She saw the doctor entering the ward with her husband. The doctor asked her how she was, and she asked him whether she was going to die.

He laughed, and asked why she thought that. She said that this was what people were like when they were dying, lying down and too weak to get up.

'You will be on the road home in a week, as strong as ever,' the doctor replied.

'*Rasti?* – is that true?' she asked, 'yet if what you say be truth, why am I not able to get up now?'

'Because you have had an operation. If you had not had it, you would have been dead in two days.'

This surely was the magic of the foreigners! To know that one should have been dead and yet to find oneself alive! Not only would she be able to show from where the pain was taken but to say that she should be dead as well!

'Where is the thing you said I had?' she asked the doctor. 'You mean the operation?'

'Yes, where is it?'

'It took away the thing which gave you pain and as soon as the wound heals a little you will be able to go. You see, you did not fall out of the bed.'

Aziza said: 'So you'll not be needing my hair for the offering to your spirits. I'll give you a good Kochi rug instead. That will surely placate them. Our rugs are the best in all Afghanistan.'

The doctor did not reply, instead he pointed to the nurse who had brought her medicine. 'This,' he said, 'will make you better more quickly.'

The woman gulped it down. 'Is it magic?' she asked. 'Almost,' the doctor replied, but only the nurse heard him. In a few minutes the patient slept.

'Thank God,' said the nurse to herself, 'for sleeping draughts.'

Three days later the patient discovered for herself that her hair had been cut off. Her shrieks woke all the patients in her own and all the neighbouring wards. Nurses rushed to her bedside.

'Where is my hair, you thieves? Idolators! Sons of noseless mothers!' she shouted. 'Now I am no better than an outcast, without my hair. I will kill every one of you!'

The doctor was called and quiet was restored.

'Your hair will grow again,' he assured the patient. 'We

had to operate, and it was necessary to remove the dirt and other things which were there. The condition of your head was what is called unhygienic.'

Aziza did not understand a word of the explanation. She knew that her treasured hair was gone, cut off by the foreigners. Their excuses were nonsense and sounded it, of course. Her hair had clearly been taken as an offering to some pagan god, and there was the end of it. A stream of untranslatable nomad oaths reverberated against the ceiling.

The doctor allowed the rage to pass. Like others of his calling he had had to deal with all types of humanity, and he was a practising philosopher. Here, he realised was something more terrible, more important, than mere life or death.

He thought of the other Kochi woman who had had a similar ailment and treatment, and the loss of whose hair had been the cause of a burly ambulance-driver being taken to the casualty ward.

'There was another nomad woman who had the same operation two years ago,' the doctor said. 'I think she was of your clan. She also had her hair off, only her head was shaved, and quite bare.'

The patient rather painfully raised herself on to her right elbow.

'Rasti?' she questioned.

'The nurses will tell you it is.'

Having received affirmative replies to all her questions, the patient suddenly began to laugh loudly and hysterically. The doctor and the nurses looked quickly at each other, while a confused outpouring of nomad words tumbled out: punctuated by 'Hayya! Hayya!'

The ward-sister hastened to do whatever it is these wonderful women do at such times. Then calm spread over Aziza's features.

Now, quite quietly, she explained that Hayya, that bitch who had been in that very hospital with the same

258

kind of problem, had never told her or anybody else that she had had the shame of a bare head. And a completely shaven one!

That one had an opinion of herself. She was stuck up, and sometimes thought so much of herself that she would not speak to Aziza. Now Aziza knew that Hayya, daughter of the son of a so-and-so, had been as bald as the under-foot of a camel! Aziza's hair had only been cut, after all, and washed.

Hayya, bald as an egg! Never again, at any time in her life, would Aziza tolerate a word, or so much as a look from that one-time hairless one. 'Hairless', *Sar-Kal*, was the magic word which in future would sew up the mouth of Lady Hayya!

Of a truth the Kharijis had not only taken out the pain, which was of the devil, but had passed on a secret worth the price of twenty camels. Wonderful was life.

She realised, she continued, that the pain was schemed by fate on purpose that she might know of the brazen one's disgrace of the bare head.

When, she asked the doctor, might it be possible for her to get upon her way that she might try out *Sar-Kal*, the magic word?

Later, on the way home to the far hills, she told Akram that, in her opinion, the Khariji gods might not be magic, but she was sure that the doctor and those women in white were genies, *Jinns*, good ones, of course, in a fairly thin disguise...

19

To the Valley of the Giant Buddhas

The Mercedes bus (the *Marsidis-Bins*) started on its journey northward from Kabul, and then westward to Bamian, full to capacity. We were heading for the valley of the giant standing Buddhas, carved into the stone perhaps two thousand years ago.

The truly beautiful valley is situated at the centre of the country, across the caravan-route between the land of the *Hazaras* – the Mongols of Genghiz Khan – and Afghan Turkestan, which abuts the former Soviet Central Asian republics.

To the south is Pakistan, formerly a part of India, from where Buddhism came to this immense, now long-abandoned, monastery complex.

The Arabs failed to conquer it, but the father of the great Turkic emperor Mahmud (contemporary with Omar Khayyam) took control a thousand years ago.

Our trip took a day and a night in the end; and that is a longish trip, when it is along the rocky roads of Afghanistan. I was pleased to learn that this road was an 'improved' one...

My seat was the second from the back, specially booked, because on a long journey it is more fun to sit at the back: this is the best vantage-point.

While the driver was making the last arrangements prior to starting, I took stock of the other passengers.

Just in front of me sat an old man with the beard of a patriarch; beard and turban were both white. Beside me there was a middle-aged man holding a decorative water container; one of those we see in old Persian or Turkish miniature paintings, jugs with squirrel-tail handles, and equally long spouts. It would have fetched quite a sum at Sotheby's in New York or London. All the travellers were well wrapped up, either like weary, semi-reanimated mummies in enveloping fur posteens or in thick blankets, ready for the long, cold journey.

There was no question of really settling down for the hours ahead. The seats allowed only for a bolt-upright position. Upright one was, however, only when the bus was on level ground, which would be seldom. The 'road' revealed itself to be, preponderantly, a natural rocky route, practically untouched by human hand.

The long stops at the far-flung teahouses might also have been diplomatic pauses when the passengers attended to the stiff limbs and bruises collected on the way.

On night journeys the only thing of interest is the passengers. The light is not good enough for reading and even if it were, the jolting swaying and leaping of the vehicle soon causes motion-sickness.

Travelling north, the road to Charikar was bearable, and the driver pointed out places of historical interest, such as where the British Gurkha regiment had been annihilated in the First Anglo-Afghan War.

Presently, as we struck west to approach Bamian via Ghorband, I became aware that water was drip, dripping from the roof. I saw, too, that the drops were coming to rest upon the ample turban of the man in front.

He was not aware of what was taking place, because turbans such as his consist of many yards of cotton material and are bound tightly and thickly around stout skull-caps. The thicknesses were capable of holding a considerable amount of water unperceived.

In the less foreigner-trodden parts of the East, it is a good policy to mind one's own business, because if arguments do arise, they may include everybody within sight and hearing, and the end is never predictable.

Moreover, it is easy to misplace a word and give a wrong impression. Drop! drop! fell the water, while the bus swayed and cavorted around the hairpin bends.

An hour passed and I saw that the victim of the drips in front was beginning to register something. He put his hand to his brow, and then looked back belligerently at my neighbour. In so doing he caught sight of the antique water-container, and accused its owner of spilling it over him. Each raised his voice above the rattle of the bus: one challenging, one denying.

My neighbour said he had been asleep, which I knew to be true because each time he lost consciousness his head rolled against my arm. I had been afraid he would drop the heavy jug on my feet, which were placed upon a small case and practically immovable in the cramped quarters.

The ancient said that of a truth my neighbour had condemned himself, because while he slept how was it possible for him to control the water jug?

By this time interest had been aroused, and sides were being taken. Some said without doubt the water had come from the jug. Others said that it was well known, though perhaps not to idiots, that water did not fall upwards, which would have to be the case if it came from the jug.

Arguments sprang up in various parts of the vehicle, and several passengers of a gentle turn of mind offered to mediate. My neighbour then volunteered the information that he had bought the jug only a few hours ago, and that there was no water in it. He was going to fill it later, he said. Water 'did not just occur in jugs'.

The dripping had now stopped when it would have been of most use, as a toothache does when the dentist's front door is reached.

The driver took no part in the argument; after all, he carved a way through that area with his bus three times weekly, and that gave him problems enough.

The jug was now passed round for all to inspect. The sound of the metal lid banging noisily after each had examined it vied with the sound of small stones which the tyres flung against the sides of the bus.

One minute we were climbing up and up; the next we were trying to hold ourselves back in our seats as we plummeted down into a valley, where stood a teahouse. There we stopped.

Thankfully we got out, lowering ourselves stumbling to the ground; the descent and stumbling passage to the teahouse could hardly be dignified by saying that we alighted and walked.

One side of the ravine was nearly vertical cliff: against and into it was built the teahouse, half underground, which was our goal. Inside, great steaming samovars stood by a roaring fire and, from these, teapots were filled again and again. We drank cup after cup of the green tea; finally we took our seats once more in the bus.

For a change, I sat near the driver and noticed that the victim of the dripping water had exchanged seats with the one who had most vehemently supported the statement that the water came from the jug. The driver looked round at me and volunteered the information that we ought to finish the journey in 'the usual time'. How long was that?

'It depends on the Will of Allah. It took the British Infidel [Indian] armies over a month to reach Bamian from Kabul in the 1840s.'

'Is the road like this all the way?' I enquired as we dashed down an almost perpendicular hill.

'No. This is the easy part.'

'Had you not better put on your brakes?' I said nervously, as the bus careered down and down.

'Brakes?' he queried. 'My brakes have not worked for some hours. But I am an Afghan.' This last assertion is often used hereabouts to finish any conversation, to explain anything. You fill in your own details.

I tried not to scream, and only just overcame the temptation. Surely this would be my last journey, if the roads got any worse with the brakes out of order. 'You should have seen the road before it was improved; this is a Government road,' the driver explained.

Just then the offside headlamp, hitherto lighting up what looked like the jagged edge of a precipice, went out. The road was now a switchback, which gave the impression that a giant was playing with the bus, snatching at it here, and throwing it there: the howling of the wind was exactly like astonishingly magnified maniacal laughter.

'So you want to go out, *Janab-i-Barqi* – Electric Excellency!' shouted the driver, apparently addressing his errant headlamp. Now, cackling to himself, he seemed to have gone slightly mad. The thought of the narrow, stony road and the black depths on the outside edge was broken into by his voice, a total contrast: boastful and carefree.

'See, I am able to drive with my eyes shut.' He demonstrated as we swung round a corner, where the rocks seemed to be so low that we appeared to be hurtling into a cave.

'Here,' he continued, 'here, on this hairpin bend, is the place where only last week a pack-horse went over the precipice; the fall must have been at least a thousand feet.'

A little way further along the road from here we stopped, again at a teahouse and again we lowered ourselves to the ground, stiffer than ever. Our feet were numb and cold, and the same performance of tea-drinking was repeated.

We were offered accommodation, due to the bad weather, at the local Hujra (the guestrooms kept as a free charity for wayfarers), situated near the village mosque. The driver treated the kindly suggestion with scorn. 'Such places are for *unfortunate* travellers,' he insisted. I was glad to hear that, exhausted and bedraggled as we were, we did not fall into that category. Later, perhaps . . .

The only other thing I remember noticing here was an abundance of beautiful porcelain teapots, common in those parts. Many of these came from the factory of an Englishman named Gardner, and were made in the old

Russian Empire, long before Communism. So famous are they that replicas, made in China or Japan, still carry the word 'Girdnar' in Arabic letters.

But tea for once had no appeal to me, although the man who brought it very courteously kept removing the un-touched liquid and bringing a fresh cup.

The rough-and-tumble of the journey had no enduring effect on the other passengers. They might have looked awful, but none spoke of the cold or the rigours we had undergone. Everybody drank many cups. Eventually we embussed again. The others had the benefit of the warmth of the beverage, I still felt queasy. Before getting in I flailed my arms in the old cabby manner, and at last felt some movement of circulation to my frozen fingers.

Occasionally we passed travellers on foot, driving sheep, or mounted on camels – nomads who were making the most of the hours when traffic is less.

All the men we passed had wrapped the long, trailing ends of their turbans across their mouths and noses, against the sharp winds, and perhaps to make sure that no enemy would recognise the muffled traveller.

This is more important than it appears, because clans-men who have blood-feuds with others must often thus pass unrecognised. If their faces were shown up, even at night, by the lights from passing vehicles, there might easily be another notch on a clansman's rifle butt.

We had proceeded neither far nor quickly, the ascent being steep, when a breathless individual raced up behind, calling out that a teapot was missing from the our recent port of call, the café.

The man jumped onto the bus and called to the pas-sengers to give up the pot. Everybody shouted at once that we were honest people and had porcelain teapots aplenty at home. One asked who the man was accusing of theft.

Another said that the café man was a hooligan and must be thrown off the bus. We were now on what was quite possibly called a level road locally, and the driver speeded up, laughing to himself, no doubt because the café-keeper was getting farther and farther away from home, along a pitch-dark road.

The same thought struck the café man, who was now calling for the bus to stop and let him off, in the name of Allah. This request was met with peals of derisive laughter, and jeers about the fate of those who accuse honest people of stealing trifles.

'Now,' said the driver, 'we are to show this noseless son of a disgraced father what speed is,' whereupon the bus leapt and bounded, rattled and slid – even faster than before – for what seemed an eternity. Then the joke seemed over and the driver brought us to a screaming halt. Evidently, he sometimes had brakes and sometimes not...

With loud groans and vituperation, now he was safely out, the café keeper disappeared. Everybody enjoyed the joke, and every now and again the driver continued to laugh to himself.

The night seemed blacker than ever, and the single headlamp we boasted lit up the wild rugged rocks, and made quasi-sunlight on the water through which the bus often splashed. I sat quietly, hoping the driver was tiring of showing off his tricks.

His voice came again, boastful as before.

'There is but one headlamp, which as anybody knows is insufficient. Any moment we may leave the road on the wrong side. *Insha-allah* – God willing, I, Nur-Mahommed, know where I am and what is expected of me.' I wanted to reply that nobody expected acrobatics, but all were interested in safety. That, however, would probably have had an adverse effect on him.

Now Nur-Mahommad extracted a cigarette from a packet and lit it. Most of the time his hands seemed to be off the wheel.

'Here,' he said as he quickly clutched the wheel and guided the errant vehicle back onto the road, 'here, only a few weeks ago, a trailer broke away from a jeep and disappeared over the edge. Here we come to an interesting double corner.' But my eyes were tightly shut and my hands gripped the edges of the narrow seat.

'Brakes,' the driver continued, 'are used too much by drivers. You see by my example that they are seldom necessary.'

'However infrequently you normally use them, what will happen if they are needed on this journey and you have none?' Someone nearer to Nur-Mahommed and with a louder voice than mine, was evidently almost as worried as I was.

'I have got brakes; it is only that they are not in use.'

The reply seemed illogical to some. Heads were shaken, and perhaps the driver thought again: he added, 'Allah is merciful.'

'But you have heard the saying of the Prophet that it is well to tie one's camel securely and only then trust in Allah?' someone cried, above the din.

'*Ya Rabb!* O Lord! Either you trust in God or you do not. If you trust fully then your camel can remain untied.

'The saying means that you should learn to have faith, so that you can then trust, so that your camel will be safe.

'Unbelievers, for instance, do not have true faith, and cannot therefore trust properly. Their camels are consequently always getting lost. Nur-Mahommad will, Allah permitting, take the bus in safety to our destination.'

I began to have the distinct impression, both from the unanswerable reasoning and the pitch of his voice, rising and falling didactically, (to say nothing of his cast-iron faith) that our driver had been a theology student at some time, perhaps at the school for mullas in Paghman.

Sitting there, with the rattletrap vehicle dashing over and along the intricacies of that road, I found myself praying that the other headlight might not fail.

After a time, I looked around me and saw that most of the passengers were in what must have been a most uneasy sleep; their heads rolled and broken snores tore through the clamour of the labouring engine, the howling of the wind and the snatches of song from Nur-Mahommed.

But soon the second man who sat underneath the dripping water, which had begun again, called the driver's attention.

'Stop the bus,' he shouted.

'Brother,' replied the driver, 'the stopping of the bus is in the hands of Allah at the moment. Who am I to come to a standstill, even if that were possible, before we reach the steep hill?'

The driver now broke into an Afghan love-song which deals more than sentimentally with the arched eyebrows, the graceful form and the fawn eyes of his beloved. I could not help thinking that the latter had more chance of being bereaved than married.

The song sounded terrible under the circumstances. It would have sounded pretty bad anyway, since the driver certainly lacked absolute pitch. The bus was keeping the road, but gave no promise of continuing to do so.

As the words deepened in sentiment, and the bus seemed to be going ever-faster in speed, someone suggested that a tarpaulin, which was folded up on the luggage rack, be hung inside from one end of the ceiling to the other, as it was obvious that the water tank on the roof was leaking.

This being decided after a brief discussion and by democratic vote, a number of volunteers, in spite of being thrown about by the lurching Marsidis-Bins, managed to affix the tarpaulin, which now loomed above us, steadily and ominously drooping and filling with water.

Somewhat later on the brakes actually began to function, just as the driver, with a long steep bending hill in view, was calling to the guard – now at his post clinging onto the back of the bus – to creep along as best and as quickly as Allah might permit, and apply himself, brake-like, to a front wheel.

The driver inserted several adjectives when he spoke to the guard, or rather shouted at him, and referred to the incline which we were approaching as *Koh-i-Marg* – Death Hill.

Nobody now looked over-happy, and we must all have been saying prayers for our deliverance when the brakes worked, as if by a miracle. The driver said it was no miracle. It was owing to his faith in Allah, which had never failed him. I believed every word. There could be no other reasonable explanation . . .

Just then muffled shrieks came from the back of the bus, from the rear bumper, where the guard still was. Now the man was repeating the *Kalima* – the Confession of Faith and last prayer of those about to die. This awakened the sleep-snatchers who, hearing the words, and having temporarily forgotten (or, perhaps, remembered) where they were, took up the chant.

Those in the seats near the back heard the guard shout that we were in the river and Allah in his mercy forgive all his sins, see him safely over *Al Sirat* (the bridge over which the dead pass to Paradise) and look after his poor wife and children.

The driver took no notice. We were now climbing the hill but the strangled shouts from the guard continued. 'Of a surety,' said the driver, 'a mad one is behind.'

'Perhaps he has been attacked and wounded,' somebody suggested.

The driver laughed. '*Nay, faqat majnun ast*. No, he is only insane.'

My sympathies were with the guard, outside on the small wooden seat provided. It was now very cold, with a whip of a wind blowing in all directions, not to mention what felt like multiple dislocations, caused by the jolting.

Noses required frequent attention, but how to let go of the protection to which one's icy hands held in order to attend to it? The cries of the guard ceased. Had he dropped off on to the road and rolled over the precipice?

I asked the driver. 'Not that one,' he replied, 'nothing has happened to him.'

'But the calling, the shouting, the Kalima?' I persisted.

'Presently, when we stop, investigations will be made.'

A hen, which was the property of a passenger who slept so quietly that he appeared to have died, broke loose and flapped around the bus. The passengers made grabs at it. Some expert explained that it was best to leave it until it tired. This it refused to do, and while the owner slept through the incident, the hen lurched out of the window, to everybody's relief. Someone advised informing the owner, while another said, 'never wake anybody to bad news'.

I noted that the driver was now singing a song whose refrain was 'If you give only an onion, give it with dignity'. I wasn't sure if this was a learned reference to the hen's disappearance. Perhaps, for instance, there was an un-official superstition that the sacrifice of a bird to the elements might help us to arrive safely . . .

It was clear by now that we were not in the river, the Kalima notwithstanding. When, finally, the bus stopped, it transpired that water from the leaking tank had drenched the guard, who thought the bus had gone off the road into the river, and that the end had come. '*Qiyamat bud*,' he said: 'It was like the day of judgment.'

This admission brought curses down upon the head of the guard, who was soaked to the skin and had enough trouble already in the bitter cold. He remarked that the breath was taken from him when the water poured over him as the bus mounted the hill, but all he received was more abuse. He was told that he deserved to lose his breath permanently for making so much noise, 'and caus-ing us all so much worry,' added one man, to a murmur of assent; which helped to show that Afghan bus-passengers may be kindly people at heart.

The stopping of the bus and the argument with the guard caused the owner of the missing hen to wake up. The driver was accused of slackness of duty. 'As a hen's guard?' he roared, making as if to throttle the other. Again sides were taken as to who was to blame. The replies from the driver in his defence were too quick for me, but the silence which followed from his audience showed that he was as capable with his tongue as he was with his driving and theology.

I remarked that the guard must be frozen in his wet clothes with the wind beating upon him. An old man, who might have been anyone's idea of Noah, remarked that the wind was good, even in the early hours of the morning, for drying clothes, and that he often left his clothes outside to dry in the night. A neighbour asked whether he ever happened to be inside the clothes on such occasions.

After that, conversation dwindled. There was no arrangement made at any of the caravanserais for our convenience. Necessity forced us to discard the ways imposed upon us in civilized towns and, returning to our simplest of beginnings, we became perfectly natural.

Not once do I remember feeling any real inconvenience through the behaviour of any of my fellow travellers: nor did I expect to do so. They argued, but only as a short preliminary to dealing with problems encountered. They were full of humour, kindness and quotations from classical literature.

The natural behaviour of companions on those caravan routes when one is the only woman, is surely unique to that part of the world.

None of them was what an educated person would call educated, so that there were no inhibitions or false modesty displayed, yet there was no feeling of familiarity. Robust in expression when necessary, they were yet truly civilised people.

Many questions might have been asked me, because a Western woman travelling alone in Central Asia is still extremely rare. But nobody ever disturbed my peace if I looked as if I wanted to be alone with my own thoughts.

I asked at a number of caravanserais whether any foreign women had come that way. The replies were that there had been none.

The people in the bus exchanged their kabobs for my provisions in the most friendly manner. The sliced-bread sandwiches intrigued them, each comparing his with that of his neighbour. Finally they folded them in two and ate them. They were good they said, but small. They would be better to be so thick – they placed three fingers together. Then, one speaker said, there would be more than one bite.

They were diplomatic, too. When I mentioned, 'This form of food was invented by, and named after, Lord Sandwich,' one whispered to another: 'Poor things, *becharaha*, in the West! We have had meat or vegetables in bread for thousands of years, and they only discovered it recently...'

Next I handed round my thermos of tea. The thermos they did not understand. But they had seen them in shops. They were intrigued to see boiling tea being poured out, even after a night and a day. What kind of tea was it which kept hot for so long?

I replied it was because of the vacuum in the flask. Was there fire in it? No, I said, there was no fire. How then, they asked, was it still hot without fire? They pursed up their lips and raised their brows over the problem. One ventured to ask whether the flask was a matter of magic?

Realising the thinness of the ice on which I was skating as a foreign woman travelling with a bare face, not caring who looked upon me, and producing hot tea out of a strange receptacle after many hours, I replied steadily, 'No, by Allah, magic belongs to *Shaitan*.'

'That is the magic called *Jadu*,' said one expert. 'There is also *Sihr-i-Halal*, which is legitimate magic. *Nari* means "of the fire", and is evil; *Nuri*, however, means "of the light", and is legal.'

'Yes,' said a third, 'Nuri's a form of new enterprise, with mechanical devices such as the water-clock devised for the Caliph Haroun El Raschid of Baghdad; and it is called, in infidel languages, *Tiknoloji*. They teach it, even in Kabul, at the Pohantun, the university.'

That was all right, then.

'*Subhanallah* – Praise God!' they breathed with relief.

But 'Noah' refused to experiment. He was too old, he said, to risk a drink from such a vessel. Everyone laughed when one humorist said, 'Perhaps, on the contrary, you are the only one, Father, to drink from it. After all, you'd be losing fewer years than the rest of us if it killed you!'

The bus stopped for a time at the roadside. The driver walked up and down to stretch his limbs. The road was narrow and stony. We had passed the worst of the precipices and now trees were to be seen, reaching from the road into the valley.

The air was clear and keen. The far hills rising, range after range, were shrouded in bluey-purple mist.

A discussion was now taking place between the passengers about the importance of some holy man. 'Noah' listened, taking no part in the argument. Then he said he would like to tell a story. Everybody murmured encouragement.

'One day,' the old man began, 'a certain man said to himself, "I must be of great importance, because Allah has created everything for man. Everything on earth. Even Allah must consider man of the highest importance. I must begin to think more of myself than formerly, and see that others do the same. I have been much too humble."

'The man was allowing his thoughts to flow in this pleasing manner when – notice, my brothers, the greatness of The One! – a gnat landed upon his nose and said, "Why dost thou boast, O Man. Has not Allah created thee also for my benefit? Is not therefore, my importance greater than thine?"'

There might, I supposed, be a moral here in connection with my thermos flask. I received it back, thinking too that there were places more suited to its use, but none more needy.

Several hours later a nearby passenger asked quietly whether I had more hot tea in the 'can'. On my replying that there was none left, he turned to his companion, with both palms upturned, and said, 'Brethren. There is no magic in that receptacle, otherwise it would fill itself with more hot tea. The *Khaliq* – Creator, may be invisible, but he is nevertheless The One.'

After two hours, we stopped once again at a cara-vanserai. The place was crowded with camels, dromed-aries, fat-tailed sheep, goats, and donkeys, and the effluvia thereof. Their tired owners were snoring deeply, bedded down nearby.

As we got down from the bus our painful joints ached. There was no feeling in our feet, and we walked bent from the waist. The caravanserai was in a large, walled enclos-ure. Servants lay asleep outside and across the open sleep-ing quarters of their masters.

Newcomers found unoccupied places for themselves. I entered the first vacant cubicle in the women's quarters. The floor was bare earth, but there was the mercy of a rough bedstead. I remember lying down as carefully as my aches would allow, and wrapping my blankets around me.

Never do I recall slipping so comfortably into uncon-sciousness. The bed might have been down, and my sur-roundings peaceful as a first-class Western hotel, around which sweet-scented zephyrs blew.

By morning, the wind and rain had stopped; it was early spring, and presently our bus was on its way and ap-proaching the opening of the gorgeous valley of Bamian, the world centre of Buddhism for at least a thousand years.

Nothing really prepares you for the sight, however often you may have heard it described. The valley itself is lush and peaceful, with windbreaks of graceful poplar trees and – on one side – an immense towering cliff, with the immense Buddha statues hewn from the living rock.

When Buddhism migrated from India, unable to stand the challenge of Hinduism, the site selected here must have been – as it still is – something unexcelled in Asia.

There is little doubt that the Buddha statues were carved in these niches to impress, rather than for priestly worship. They are on the same side of the valley as the thousands of monastic cells which honeycomb their cliff.

The famous Chinese pilgrim Hsan-Ysang, seeking the roots of his faith, journeyed here as long ago as 632 A.D. He found several colonies of hundreds of cells burrowed out from the rock, and artistically decorated with polychrome figures.

The standing Buddha figures, the two largest 35 and 53 metres high (there are three altogether), are of such striking appearance that they far overshadow such sights as the Pyramids and Sphinx in Egypt, or the rose-red city of Petra in Jordan.

Originally covered in red and gold, they are yet more important to archaeologists and historians as the models for the draperies and styles seen in virtually all Buddhas in China and Japan. When it is remembered that the Buddhism of Tibet, far better known, is recent and heavily admixed with local, Bon-ist superstitions and practices, the importance of Bamian may be sensed.

The draperies and ribbons, as well as the crowns and other decorations, point to an unique culture-mixing of Persian Sasanian and Greek. There is very little of the Indian influence which is so evident in the Graeco-Buddhist culture of Gandhara (250 B.C. to 800 A.D.), which straddles Afghanistan and Pakistan to the south and is almost as striking as that of Bamian.

According to ancient records, there was a huge festival here every five years, with 80,000 monks and 500 Greeks. Pilgrims paid to have paintings done for them, according to a strict tariff. A pious act was to commission a poly-chromatic Buddha or *bodhisattva* on the rocks. There were also such exotica as winged horses: but the most expensive commission was to have a portrait painted of oneself as a Buddha. Even Buddhists, abhorring show and believing that all reality was imagination, seemed not to have over-come the vanity problem.

Art certainly travelled from Bamian to Europe and Japan, and everywhere in between. The three golden crescents which form the crown of the local king at Ba-mian, and which figure on the Buddhas there, migrated to China and Japan.

Bamian has not yet been thoroughly studied. The first scientific examination was made in the 1920s. M. Hackin, the eminent French archaeologist, discovered that there were two distinct 'layers' of Buddhist occupancy: the earlier with its 'primitive' grottoes near the smaller stand-ing Buddha, and the later one: elaborate decorated sanc-tuaries which encircle the Great Buddha.

I was interested to find that local people, at first dis-couraged by their monotheistic Islamic faith to speak of the Buddhist period, have retained in oral tradition a great deal of legend about the previous inhabitants.

According to them, the Buddhists had been 'great ty-rants'. One man said, 'In the name of religion, they were really exploiters. They made as many people as possible into monks, who did not work. The fertile valley floor was tilled only by their slaves, and all crops had to go to the monastery or the monks, so that prayers would be said to make sure that people were reincarnated properly.'

'They were chased out,' said one ancient bard, 'by the

soldiers of Subuktagin, father of Mahmud the Turk. The rascals then went to Kamboh [Tibet].'

I was shown what the locals claimed was the actual skull and teeth of Buddha himself. 'They didn't get away with those, we stopped them!' The people hereabouts call him *Isakyamani* – Isaac of Yaman – presumably a corruption of Buddha's real name, Sakyamuni.

The legends in present-day Bamian were amazingly detailed. One dealt with the way the new Great Chief of the Buddhists was reincarnated soon after death and recognised.

'It was most interesting, and is still carried out for other reasons in India, by gipsies,' said my informant, Yahya Khan. 'First, the priests find a compliant family with a child of the right age. Then they take to its hovel a number of small items which belonged to their late spiritual leader. These they mix with other trifles and reward the child with sweets if he hands them the ones belonging to the dead man; his own previous "incarnation". Of course, the child soon learns which items will earn him sweets, and he hands the priests these.

'Then the priests return, with witnesses, to discover that the child must be the reincarnation of their old spiritual leader, since he infallibly chooses his former property.'

I asked how the gipsies in India profited by such a trick in a different setting.

'Easily. They obtain small articles from a family where an old and *rich* man has recently died. Then they take these to a poor family and train a child of the right age to "recognise" them. Meanwhile, priests are searching for the "reincarnation" of the deceased. When these items are produced to the family by the priests – in collusion with the gipsies – the child is adopted with rapture. The gipsies share the reward with the priests.'

I had lived in India for years, and had heard of the discovery by priests of supposed reincarnations of old men

– always, it must be admitted, rich ones – but had never heard how the trick was performed. Or even that it *was* a deception...

Such stories, of tiny children in India who seemed to show a knowledge of things and people who preceded them, even figure from time to time in the Press of Europe and the U.S.A. They would not have found space, I realised, in a newspaper of Bamian, if such a thing existed...

I stood, after a really stiff climb up the idol, on the head of one Buddha, and filmed the valley below – the people looked like ants. From ancient times, the long caravans passed along the road far below, merchants and outriders banded together for mutual protection, bringing merchandise from China and India to Iran and the West.

Climbing down, I saw a wall on which there is a really beautiful example of ancient sculpture. When the sun rises and its light strikes the wall, it seems freshly painted, even after all these centuries, so glowing and bright do the colours appear. At sunset the effect is still wonderful, but different. The tints now appear to be in oils, deeper, more glowing, dazzling yet luminous. All over it there seems to be superimposed, by some trick of painting, a deep gold effulgence.

The Bamian River races madly along, with immense splotches of foam, like whipped white of egg, riding the dark waters. The sky is a deep, clear blue, and there is no sound except the chatter of the river. At night the moon was full, bright as a new gold piece. It added a silvery-yellow, almost ghostly glow, to the ancient Buddhist walls, and the silent rock-cut figures took on an unearthly radiance.

I have been in Bamian in three of the four seasons of the year. In the winter the winds are steel-spiked, but when summer comes and the tall trees are clothed in green, one emerges from the deep shade of their shelter to look, bewitched, across the sundrenched valley.

To the right are towering sandstone rocks. To the left, across an uneven carpet of flowers in all the possible blendings of blues, yellows and pinks, flows a calm river. By its sides, immense, moss-covered boulders invite one to sit and think of nothing: perhaps a Buddhist emptying of the mind. It is an invitation hard to refuse.

The river, now less than half its winter height, flows softly past, as if keeping time with tranquillity. The beauty of Nature is all around: everything complements everything else: yet here and there the eye notes contrasts, which in some way manage to flatter rather than make discord.

Here there is nothing artificial. The eye wanders to where the sun burnishes the river to the colour of a glossy chestnut. The eye travels up the cliffs, and farther on, to the wealth of subtle shades of the myriad trees.

What a background for that far-flung carpet! To the left lies a forest, through whose greens the pale, satin-like trunks shine. It feels as if one was seeing beauty for the first time. Teahouses, caravanserais, the early-morning starts with stiffened limbs, are all forgotten.

Our burly, six-foot kinsman, Amir Ali Shah, met me the following day, and insisted that I see a veritable fairyland, 'not so far away'. He meant the five famous coloured lakes, some sixty miles away, beyond the ranges.

Wonderful horses with yellow manes, surely ancestors of the Spanish palominos, were waiting for us with their grooms; and we turned their heads westwards, through the fertile plains. A few hours later we were under the frowning walls of the *Koh-i-Baba* – Father Mountain – range which joins with the great Hindu-Kush: the farthest projection of the Himalaya system.

The ranges are called the 'Hindu-Killer' because, so goes the legend, a caravan of Hindu merchants, returning to India from Samarkand, were overtaken by an early fall of snow and later found quick-frozen to death on the slopes.

After many a further long and gruelling uphill mile, which the horses negotiated with great skill, our host stopped at the summit of a mount, on which had been found the remains of a Buddhist stupa. We followed his pointing finger as he said, with all the panache of a showman: 'Behold! The Lakes of Band-i-Amir!'

I gazed at a vague shimmering in the distance which, from where we stood, overlooking a patchwork of valleys and plains, looked more like dewdrops on a lawn. Interesting, rewarding, but, well . . .

Politely agreeing that they were magnificent, I suggested that we might increase our pace, to reach shelter before the mountain twilight fell.

He heard the request with a grin. 'How far would you say we were from the nearest house?'

Taking one look at the distant lakes and the uninviting rocky walls which loomed over us like an enclave of black marble, I muttered, 'Too far'.

Again a smile played around his lips as he gave his horse a quick nudge with his knees: and the rest of us followed at a gallop to the nearby bend which would give us entry into the valley. There, lo and behold, like the answer to a prayer, I saw a large stone farmhouse with turret and a welcoming wisp of smoke spiralling from the chimney.

'How far?' queried Amir Ali, face now wreathed in smiles.

Dismounting in the tree-sheltered courtyard, we entered the house and stretched our limbs luxuriously on the soft *toshaks* – mattresses, which the hospitable farmer had brought us.

He asked no questions as to who we were, whence or where bound. To him we were travellers; entitled to claim his protection and hospitality, which is even extended to enemies if sought in the Name of Allah. This is an essential part of the Afghan Code of Chivalry, to which all subscribe, the *Nanawatri*.

The farmer's wife said, 'Do not ask, take! If you do not, we shall be disgraced, by the command of Allah!'

The supper was sumptuous. There were lamb kabobs, roasted on skewers over an open fire of aromatic wood, with rice. There was saffron-flavoured palao, with pine-kernels, savoury sauce, pigeon pie with almonds and raisins, mulberry juice and yoghurt and piles of fruit. There was more, but the feast seemed to clog my memory about itself. Eventually, we were led, comatose with food, to the turret, where beds had been prepared.

The coverings were quilts of padded cotton, decorated with embroidery depicting roses in red and pink on a bright yellow background.

As he wished us goodnight, our host assured us that, as is customary, his son would sleep across the threshhold, to fetch anything that we might need during the night.

Morning in the hills here – hills, as it were, upon hills – is something to be seen rather than to be described. Even photographs, film or video, cannot capture the atmosphere. If you are up early enough to see the first tinge of wild-rose-pink across the pigeon-grey of the sky, you will feel as one watching an artist deftly changing the pink to an ever-subtler hue.

Soon quick strokes of salmon, and a rare blue between cornflower and larkspur, are deftly added; then a glorious light is flung at the base and gradually envelops the many colours, which merge into iridescence. The sun has risen.

All around, the hills take on unexpected colours, a few early birds call from a distance; the farmyard cocks crow, and the spell is broken.

In the higher land, there is only one crop a year, but here there are two harvests: one sown in late autumn is reaped in the summer, the other sown in spring is reaped in autumn. The first is wheat, barley, and lentils – the last known as 'Hindu food'. The second harvest is millet and maize, 'animal fodder'.

The farmer explained these facts as he showed us the

way to the *ziarat*, the shrine where a local holy man was buried.

Then breakfast: with the whole of the ground floor converted into a breakfast-room for our sake. I thought, in spite of the feast the night before, that I was seeing things. Fresh, warm, golden bread, newly-made butter, balls of white cheese, fruit and delicious *bolani* – thin bread, fried and made into rolls stuffed with spinach. 'Just ordinary food', grinned the farmer; but his wife and daughters, happily smiling at our delight, must have been up and about long before daybreak to prepare such a meal. Two pots of straw-coloured green tea were placed beside each of us.

We sank down on the cushions and enjoyed a perfect meal, appetites keen with the mountain air, thanking our host and hostess for their wonderful kindness.

'We must show by actions the thanks which *we* owe: for your having honoured us with your presence, rather than that you should give thanks – which in any case are due only to Allah, for making us the channel of his favour accorded to your eminences by him,' replied the farmer. I wondered, fleetingly and perhaps not too charitably, what man of his kind and education in the West would be capable of such a speech.

Setting off again, we urged our horses through steep, winding paths through the valleys, passing among great trees and many picturesque waterfalls. Khamenil, between Bamian and Band-i-Amir, is named after the words *Kham* – a large jar, and *nil* – blue, used for whitening or bleaching.

The highest point was at Karghanatu, 3,100 metres (over 10,000 feet) above sea-level. From here the panorama of the mountains bordering Band-i-Amir is breathtaking. Around the lakes there is a reddish-yellow band, adding startling, very unexpected colour. On the horizon, to the south and south-west, tower the lofty peaks of the Koh-i-Baba Range.

As we approached, we found the road descending sharply until suddenly, like a mirage, there appeared in the distance a lozenge-shaped area of water, the colour a deep blue as of the finest lapis-lazuli. It gave the impression that a piece of jewellery, perhaps a brooch, had been set in the earth. The lapis effect is of the blue stone mounted with sparkling pink, with sapphires and rubies.

Further on we met a fairyland of small water-wheels, and small, foaming cascades of icy liquid crystal.

Band-i-Amir consists of five lakes which, over a period of thousands of years, have been formed from the calcium-bearing waters of the Kaprak spring, some sixteen kilometres away: the scene looks, at first, almost too colourful to be real.

The first lake came into view: 'The Band-i-Zulfikar, named after the great double sword of Hazrat Ali, son-in-law of the Prophet,' said Amir Ali Shah, pointing it out. The second was Band-i-Pudina, from where the waters meander into the Band-i-Panir – so called because the surrounding cliffs look exactly like *panir*, Afghan white cheese.

But, to my eyes, the most beautiful lake was the Band-i-Habat: semi-circular, tremendously deep, blue like a sapphire. All around it rise perpendicular cliffs of rose-red, virgin rock. At its base, many water-wheels revolve, and from its sides come leaping cascades of water.

20

Mountain Caravanserai

For the last three days our caravan had crept slowly through the rocky defiles, swept at times by icy blasts which tore at our clothes and screamed defiance and rage at all travellers.

We had safely negotiated the high boulder-strewn passes, and successfully evaded the masses of rock which, loosened from their anchorage away up on the rocks above, deposited themselves at times but a few feet before or behind. If the momentum was sufficient, they continued their hectic race over the precipice, which bordered the road on the other side.

If the rock stayed put on the road in front, the entire caravan had to halt until it was pushed over, when it crashed and tore its way and seemed never to be going to reach the bottom. Dozens of times my heart came into my mouth on that road where Nature rules. Whenever the tearing sound of an approaching avalanche from above came to our ears, we huddled against the safety of the barren hillside and hoped for the best.

It is said that when one is threatened with death all sins and shortcomings rise up, magnified. Later, when we reached safety, the members of our group discussed what we had thought about when threatened by seemingly certain death. Some said they prayed, thinking only of the forgiveness of God.

Others said they wondered who would plunder the caravan; and a very holy-looking man said he wished he had spent his money years before!

We had not spoken much on the road, which was so narrow that we had to travel single file; and if any traffic such as nomad or any other group passed us, we had to draw close into the hillside. Camels prefer to get into the middle of the road, and even if they are pulled right or left, they insist upon turning sideways. There is no room on these roads for this predilection of theirs, because the side to which they may turn is the edge of the precipice.

Three days before, at the last serai, we had formed a caravan for mutual protection and company, and the etiquette at such times is that no questions be asked; therefore none knew the name of another, whence he came, or his business. Fate had thrown us together, a band of miscellaneous travellers.

All that was required of one another was that we all managed our own, individual affairs, and that all presented a united front to the dangers known or imagined. Breath was kept for the original purpose for which it was given.

Eventually, dusty, hungry and exhausted, we reached the caravanserai. All we wanted to do was to wash as best we could, have a meal of whatever there happened to be, and lie down, – especially the last, even in preference to eating or washing.

Before we had time to do any of these, one of our companions, a Mulla, said that since only the mercy of Allah, The One, had led us safely through, prayer must come first.

We chorused agreement with him, adding that there was no God but God, and that Mahommmad – on whom be peace and prayer – was His prophet.

After what passed for a wash, we collected in a warm room. The food, we were told, would be ready soon, which we knew meant that everything had to be cooked, and that meant at least two hours; but no comment was made.

We were glad to see the fire. It consisted of a wide hearth on which the wood (branches and logs) were thrown. Most of the smoke chose to circulate around the room, which made the habitation thereof difficult until the fire burnt clear, but it meant warmth and safety.

Each one of us staked a claim to a part of the floor. I was addressed only when necessity demanded, and even then as 'sa'ib', a courtesy which meant that no notice was taken of the fact that I was the only woman.

My cushions, which had travelled all through the East with me, were still doing good duty. These luxuries were placed in my 'claim' with my baggage, against the wall. The others put bundles at their places, which did the same duty. There was no furniture in the room. On the floor was a country-made carpet, rather thin and worn.

To sit on the floor in the warmth, leaning against cushions, was a luxury one wanted to savour to the full. The thought of a few hours of rest was as a benison upon us. At present we simply sat and ached.

As we all arranged our person and belongings to our own satisfaction and to the convenience of the neighbours, the strict minding of one's own business continued. The safe anchorage after the rigours of the road gave none the privilege of indulging in any interest regarding the affairs of any other traveller.

This is appreciated when one is the only woman and conscious of the opinion one's fellows have of foreigners, and particularly of ones travelling alone with uncovered face, in the company of strange men.

Later, no doubt, conversation would come, possibly after the meal, but the preliminary settling-down was a completely exclusive affair. Anyone who removed coat or boots or even stockings, or untied one or more of the mysterious bundles, was perfectly at liberty to feel that the action was completely private and personal.

Food was now announced. I asked to have mine brought. The men left for the dining-room. The meal consisted of *palao*, mutton roasted on skewers, meatballs, a bowl of delicious yoghurt, and an immense oval flat 'cake' of bread, deliciously crisped golden, and newly baked.

My portion was easily sufficient for three hungry men. The savoury scent of the meat and rice mixed with the wood-smoke was not unlike the scent of oily kippers, or even fish which had been kept too long, but the taste was wonderful.

The men were a long time coming back. The food and warmth caused me to nod for how long I do not know, but I started and woke when they returned.

Conversation now seemed to be general, and as they reclaimed their places I knew they took for granted the fact that I kept my eyes circumspectly upon the ground. I stole glances now and again as though seeing my fellow travellers for the first time.

No doubt – I mused – a servant would eventually announce that our sleeping accommodation was ready and there was nothing to do but wait – waiting is the most difficult thing to learn in the East.

The room was baking hot, and the men began to remove their big coats. There was a hard frost outside, reported the fire-tender, and the water-pipe started on its round. This broke the silence, and polite but guarded conversation started up. I was not included.

In spite of the warmth, the Uzbek trader – one knew the type – drew his padded coat more closely round him. It created a cheerful splash of colour against the white-washed wall. Broad stripes of emerald green of his long *chapan* were superimposed on purple and pink lines. His high hat was of grey fur; felt boots reached almost to the knees.

Round his waist, as though taking the last chance of indulging in more colour, he wore a broad green cummer-bund. His features were practically hidden in whiskers. A beard in Afghanistan is usually trim, but these were simply whiskers. His eyes had the slant at the outer corners, typical of his people. He made a rather startling but handsome picture, which would have been quite at home in an illustrated Christmas story-book.

His neighbour looked as an Anglo-Saxon always imagines a German will look. Though short, he was, stout, square, with closely cropped straight hair and a ruddy complexion. He added to the appearance of his shortness of stature by wearing a very long red fox-fur coat, lined with crimson cloth.

That coat was so startling that it seemed to belong to a dream instead of reality. The fronts were velour, and showed several inches of the red lining. His boots were large, thick-soled and laced, the tops wide enough to admit the trousers.

He seemed ill-at-ease and his eyes, of a piercing blue, darted here and there as though this were the only way in which he could use them. His stubbly hair gave his head the appearance of a new brush. His arms were mostly folded across his chest, as it were, defensively.

The Uzbek asked him whether he were *Europoi*, to which he replied 'ja,' which did seem rather odd, since, if he understood Dari, he surely knew the word for 'yes' in it...

The German then asked me, in English, whether I came from England, I said that I did. He asked whether I had been there during the 'discord' which struck me as being a better word than our hackneyed 'hostilities'. I said that I had. Did I know Dresden? I did, and said so.

'If you once knew Dresden, in the days of its beauty, take out your handkerchief and weep, because Dresden was mutilated beyond recognition by your people.' With that his eyes shuttled towards me a few times, then he got up and marched out of the room, his immense coat billowing round his squat figure. The war's bomb stories had followed us even to the heart of Central Asia.

There were several Karakul-skin merchants, and a few tall fair Hazara merchants. These travellers talked in their own dialect, laughing a great deal among themselves. The laughter brightened up the rather tense feeling, at least for me, but I think I am right in speaking only for myself.

Some of the others still seemed to be weighing up those into whose company they had been thrown. They spoke guardedly, as though they did not feel competent to judge and therefore doubted the motives of the others. Two fur-booted and fur-hatted travellers told stories of Frankenstinian quality about so-called human apes who had committed murders so recently that 'the blood of the victims was not yet dry'.

After listening a while, I for one began to blame myself for being, at such a time, in a mountain caravanserai with the night yet to be passed. These tales subdued the others, and there was no sound for some time except for that of the water bubbling in the *chillum* pipe as it went the round.

Outside, donkeys brayed in what is surely the most unmelodious cry of any animal, and the camels, remembering the long hours of their loads and the rough roads, added their grunts to the disharmony.

A servant came to put more wood on the fire. He was wearing a number of ill-assorted garments, and walked as if in a dream. His breath, as he entered the warm room from the frost outside, was like steam from a fast-boiling kettle. Most of the several coats he wore had pieces torn from them as though he had been attacked by dogs. He had on a pair of long boots so worn at the heels on the outsides that the uppers touched the ground, while the insides were not worn at all. This caused him to lope in a peculiar manner.

On his head, pushed well down on his brow, he wore an Uzbek black fur hat. He made startling and strange noises in his throat. His eyes were large and staring, as though he could not close them. Over the hat he had tied a woollen scarf, fixing the structure by tying the scarf under his chin. He had an astonishingly thick red beard, and had a startling way of blowing out his cheeks and lips, followed always by the throat noises.

289

The people round him seemed to have no interest for him, and when he threw the rough wood on the fire his eyes became immense and he muttered what seemed to be some words in anger, to judge by his expression.

It was like a scene which one might have expected in Europe – but of the Middle Ages.

People were now getting ready to sleep, casting off of coats and in most cases boots. Everything taken off was neatly folded and placed close beside the owner.

The boots in all cases seemed immense, but so were the feet. Many toes, too, were on view which is an ordinary sight on long caravan treks. The fat Bokharan merchant appeared much relieved to be without his boots and spread out his feet. He twiddled his toes until he fell asleep. Every now and again his head, surmounted by its huge fur hat, fell to one side. Each time this happened he jumped nervously, took a quick suspicious look around, and reached down to examine his belongings.

The old Mulla fell asleep too. Occasionally he drew a long shuddering breath, and said in a deep voice 'God is greater [than all else], *Allah-ho-akbar*,' which words were automatically repeated even by those who appeared to be asleep.

The Mulla's *tasbih* – rosary, kept falling from his fingers, and for a few seconds the amber beads lay on the floor, a yellow stream on which the firelight played and animated. But only for moments, because with a loud semi-conscious snort its owner started up and fixed his eyes belligerently upon the harmless little man beside him, as though blaming him for the interruption.

In time, the looks proved too much for the little man who, as soon as the Mulla slept again, slipped to a place farther away. Next time the rosary fell the Mulla jerked himself awake as usual, saw the empty place, traced the erstwhile occupant, and fixed him just the same, while muttering holy expressions, which were echoed eerily through the room by the devout.

The empty place roused some suspicion in his mind, and he closed his eyes tightly, as though with considerable effort. For a short while he held them like this, then with startling suddenness he opened them and looked craftily round in all directions.

It was obvious that he did not approve of me. He had looked at me when he came in at first, as one would look at a particularly miserable specimen of anything. Most Mullas dislike unveiled female faces. They think that foreign women are all of the same type, which is as bad as they can imagine and worse than anybody could possibly be, allowing for everything. Besides, they think that foreigners give their countrywomen ideas of freedom which is not the Mullas' idea of progress. The place for all women, in their minds, is in seclusion, and so long as the Mullas have any power the women are going to stay there. Thus they think that any trouble is stayed. One wonders.

As the night wore on, most of the men slept. Each one snored loudly in a different key. At one time it sounded like a thunderstorm at its height, while the leaping flames played the part of lightning.

My long Turkestani boots felt tight and I considered the moment auspicious for their removal. A struggle ensued because my feet were sore. I had preferred to walk long stretches of the road rather than run the risk of being pushed helplessly over the precipice by a hurtling boulder. The result was that I discovered blisters on both heels.

The fire-stoker became human and noticed my problem. He went out and returned with a mess of red clay which he assured me was the panacea for all ills. Not to offend him, as things were, I took the stuff, hiding it in a much-used handkerchief, and put it in my pocket.

Then I began to wonder what would happen if robbers attacked us. How would it be possible – provided there was a chance – to run outside in stockinged feet on the iron-hard roads? Blisters or no, those boots would have to go on again.

The fire-tender now returned with a piece of cloth, none too clean, and offered to wrap up the heels. Seeing this was already done, he assisted me in getting into my boots, which now seemed at least two sizes too small. Eventually, between us, we succeeded.

Had my heels been cut off the feeling could not have been worse. I asked the man whether there was not a night watchman, and if not why not. He replied that up to a few years ago there had been one but they were usually dismissed, having been accused too often of murdering the travellers.

The man continued that in his opinion the best plan was for the travellers to look after themselves, and to catch their own robbers. When he said this he threw back his head and laughed, displaying very large long teeth, the sight of which added something sinister to his already peculiar appearance. He said that his philosophy was that if a name was written on a robber's knife, the rest was *Kismet*. He told me the story of the Sultan Ibrahim. Here it is:

One day the Sultan Ibrahim of Balkh, was holding a durbar, when a beggar, who had walked a long distance demanded entrance.

'Allow me to pass into the caravanserai,' he demanded of the guards.

'You are mad,' the guard said and barred the way. 'This is the palace of the Sultan Ibrahim, who will have you boiled in oil for using such words.'

The loud voices reached the Sultan, and he asked that the man be brought before him.

'Mendicant,' said Ibrahim. 'This is a palace, my palace. Why do you persist in calling it a caravanserai?'

'May I be permitted to ask a few questions of thee, Ibrahim?' When the courtiers heard the beggar address the Sultan in such familiar terms they expected the man to be dragged away forthwith, but the Sultan gave permission for the questions to be asked.

'Whose house was this to begin with?' enquired the beggar.

The Sultan replied that it was built by his grandfather.

'When he died, who lived here?'

'My father.'

'When thy father died, who came?'

'I did.'

'When it pleases Allah to call thee to thy account, who comes?'

'My son.'

'Then, Ibrahim, a place which one enters after another, and leaves to someone else, is a caravanserai, even although those who occupy it call it a palace.'

For some time the Sultan sat quietly thinking, then he replied.

'Ah! Brother traveller, the words to which I have listened are indeed truth, of which there is too little in this world. Although you must have heard that none may speak such words to me without suffering torture, yet you have shown the quality of courage. Because you have shown these two qualities, which I admire most and see seldom, I invite you to remain at my court as long as you please. Clothes and food are to be given to you, and you are to be treated as a guest. Few have the courage to tell Sultan Ibrahim that he is mortal.'

Such are the people of Central Asia, that an illiterate, underprivileged oaf could quote such material . . .

Now and again a sleeper awoke, trying to stretch cramped limbs. Each one, as he awoke, became sufficiently conscious to give a searching look around. The servant said that most of the travellers had had hashish. It was good, he said, in its place. He asked whether I had

had any. I said no, and he pointed to the little man who had been frightened by the Mulla, and said he would tell me about it. The little man, he said, was a wealthy hashish merchant.

If I had been told that he had murdered the merchants the night before, my surprise could not have been greater. Nobody could have been less like what I imagined a rich hashish dealer to be. Where were the gold rings and watches, and the aura of well-being, the finished polish which wealth alone can give?

Sometimes a little conversation started, somebody would ask if it was prayer time, or whether it were midnight? The wide-awake frontier chief was explaining at great length to his neighbour that the Devil made all the sinners who fell to his lot collect wood in the Black Forests of *Jehunnam* – Hell. This they did during the spring, when the fires were stoked up.

So big were these fires that they did not blaze fully until June, when the weather here became hot. The sun, he said, sank down into the regions of the Devil every night to be reheated, so that man would be able to understand how hot those regions were, and so make up his mind not to behave in such a way that he went there for eternity.

The neighbour ventured that the 'people of the Book' (Muslims, Jews, and Christians) had full directions on how to live.

The Mulla said this was so – and he asked pardon of God – but that was no reason why those who did follow the teachings should go to Paradise.

When any of the company left the room, the others appeared uneasy until their return. There were enquiries where the *khariji* – the foreigner, the German of the fox coat, had gone. The fire-stoker was called in, and said he was asleep in one of the rooms 'where the inhabitant of last night had received the attentions of the robbers.'

The room was now stuffy and smelt of camels, which is scarcely bearable. My limbs ached, and my blistered heels which were resting on the hard floor felt as if the blood in their veins was playing drumbeats.

The longing to go out into the keen, frosty air became my constant thought. I agreed with myself to wait until everybody was asleep before venturing. It was a long time before everybody settled down.

Just as I was on my feet, the Mulla and several other men woke up. Perhaps they thought there was no need for me to go outside. Perhaps they thought that I, being a woman, and added to this misfortune, a foreigner, had some other sinister motive. Anyway they awoke fully, and became vigilant. Aware of this, but taking no notice, I went out. At once Red Beard appeared, and directed me where I wanted to go. He waited until I emerged and conducted me back to the communal room.

Before entering I drew in long breaths of the sparkling air. The Mulla asked the servant where I had been, and the man told him that naturally I had been where they had all been from time to time since their arrival. The Mulla then asked whether I had visited the German whom he called the Khariji. The servant replied that I had not. There seemed much satisfaction at this reply.

The atmosphere of the hot and stuffy room after the frosty air was choking. Outside there had not been a sound, but a stillness such as is never experienced where men congregate. It was as though everything with life had ceased to be. I had been careful to wish peace upon the gathering on entering the room. They returned my greeting but there was a very perceptible air of suspicion everywhere on my return.

The Uzbek in the Jacobean coat watched the door for some time, as though expecting some robber or gang which had received my signal.

The Mulla, as I could see from his hostile glare under the beetling brows, could not think of a woman separated from trouble. He ran his podgy fingers through his long black beard, and started to intone a *sura* (of the Koran).

Everybody earnestly repeated '*Allah-ho-Akbar.*' It is quite startling the emphasis which can be put on the word All-ah; all of the hope, trust and faith of which sinful man is capable, and perhaps – sometimes – a little of the hypocrisy.

The man who tended the fire confided in me that his name was *Khirs* – Bear, and that he was suspicious of people who kept calling on Allah. 'Allah is always here: you do not need to call Him!' Then he imparted a story to make his point.

> There was once a man, called Mulla Nasr-ud-Din, very wise while appearing stupid. He ordered a shirt and went to the tailor to collect it after a week. The tailor said, 'It will be ready in another week, Inshallah – God willing.'
>
> So the Mulla returned, again to be told the same. Week after week he went, but the shirt was not ready.
>
> Finally, in exasperation, he cried: 'How long will it take *without* the "If Allah Wills"?'

It was then 3 a.m. Dawn was not far away, yet not by any means near enough to ensure a feeling of safety. Three o'clock in the morning, under such circumstances, seems to be zero hour. One is half afraid, suspicious of everybody and everything. Travelling companions look their worst, and the lack of sleep adds a final touch to existing un-easiness. The only comfort of which I could think was the repetition of all the poetry I could remember.

An hour later we had breakfast. Green tea, bread and huge white grapes, followed rather unexpectedly by a tremendous plate of scrambled eggs. The German appeared, still wearing his handsome coat, looked at nobody, failed to return our greetings, and wolfed the food. Afterwards he asked for more eggs.

Now that everybody was awake, fear receded. The grumbling protestations of the camels as they were pre-pared for the road was as music in our ears. The dawn prayers were said, and Red Beard saw us safely off the premises. His last words were that as the robbers had not come that night, he hoped the blessing of Allah was sufficiently upon all of us, that they might not be hiding for us along the road.

We had covered many dreary miles along the hill road, with little to relieve the drabness. The ravines were deep and far down in the valley; the mountains seemed to go up and up, without end. The stone-strewn road was narrow and rough. It was easier to walk than ride, despite the fact that the stones slipped and slid under the feet, and only the very toughest leather can withstand the cutting edges.

The supply of pebbles and fragments of rock for this road surface is kept up, because the loose rocks continually hurtle down, splitting themselves into jagged fragments. Earthquakes too are numerous, and these add their quota to the road rubble which comes trickling over the wayside rocks on to the road. Sometimes a rock has been dislodged and completely blocks what is called a way, rather than a road.

Suddenly, round a corner, a little nomad, *Kochi*, family appears. They seem to blend into the surroundings, but the chief interest is that they are human beings, of whom one has not seen any others for nearly two days. They seem like superhuman beings, after the absence of a sight of one's kind.

The woman and her husband are on foot. She is driving a rather thin, dreary-looking camel upon whose back, snugly wrapped up in many shawls the same colour as the camel, and placed in a basket, is a child of about two years old.

The sun has just risen. It is only 6.30 a.m. The Eastern sky is that soft glowing fire-opal, which seems to be the colour most complementary to the grey surroundings.

The child is wide awake. It surveys us with intense

interest. It is beautiful, a flower 'born to blush unseen'. Its whole face is a deep pink; its eyes large, brown, and almond-shaped. Its tiny nose looks like a small cherry. Its small head jerks from side to side, as the camel jolts along carefully, and practically silently, on its flat-soled pads. This movement of the head is the only one the child is able to make, in its cocoon-like wrappings.

A younger child, which looks about a year old, is securely tied upon his father's back. He also is wide awake and from over his father's shoulder peers at the goats which are being driven, with many admonitions, behind the camel which the mother is driving.

She wears a long black cotton jumper, lavishly embroidered down the front and around the neck. When the garment was new – which must have been long ago, perhaps for the wedding – the embroidery will have been snow-white and beautiful against the dark background. Underneath she wears a pair of black, full trousers; over her head, and thrown back over her shoulders, a thickish scarf.

Her features are good. She might be the very spirit of the mountains, so healthy does she look. Her face is perfectly oval, deeply tanned by the sun, the wind and the outdoor conditions under which she lives, and was certainly born. She walks upright as a debutante is supposed to do.

She has achieved the skill to negotiate the rough track with seeming ease: because she does not stumble, as I do repeatedly. Her shoes are coarse and thick, but they cannot detract from her grace. She must have been lovely when she was younger, although she is probably not more than twenty-three even now.

She does not seem to be interested in anything but keeping the camel and flock away from disaster, such as slipping over the precipice, or turning at a sharp right angle in front of our horses. As usual, the camel is only thinking about being perverse. The husband shouts at the woman. He says he might have known that she would be the ruin of the family, and probably the death of the camel. She replies something unprintable, and continues on the same subject, with rising emphasis. Her voice stops eventually. The husband is completely silenced.

I reflect that this is the couple's only way of breaking the terrible tension of their situation.

The dog which accompanies them is a breed never seen outside Afghanistan, though they are similar to the terrible animals owned by the Turks on the high Anatolian plateau. He would scarcely merit a glance, except of surprise, from other dog owners. His size is immense, as is his seeming ability and desire to be disagreeable. He is almost as big as a donkey, legs long, thick and strong. His face and whole being express the belligerence of which he is capable. He is covered with thick wiry hair of a nondescript colour, something between putty and camel.

He looks what he is, a capable watch-dog. He takes a serious view of his responsibilities, which are to guard the family and animals at any of the many stopping-places on the upward or downward journeys.

His coat is somewhat matted; one can imagine there is no time to brush him. In any case, he would look all wrong in that little group if he were sleek. His head is immense. His eyes give no sign that he has ever looked gently upon anything. His teeth, which are unpleasantly evident, are long, strong and sharp. Sometimes he retrieves a wandering goat. The herd seems to realise that while he is on duty, it pays to keep together circumspectly. He would be a formidable enemy.

The head of the family gives orders to the woman, the camel, the goats and the dog, perpetually. He does not bother about the children. Knowing that they are safe and out of harm's way, he completely ignores them.

He is tall and muscular, and much tanned by the sun. This appears all the more evident because his eyes are green, possibly inherited from his ancient ancestors, the

Aryanni, who some 5,000 years ago populated the valleys and hills of the Hindu Kush. The Iranis and Arya Hindus both also claim this ancestry. It was subsequently and mistakenly adopted by an English eccentric and later filched from his writings as an idea by Germans, especially during the Hitler period.

The Kochi man wears a securely-tied but careless look-ing dark blue turban. His trousers are of the same colour, peg-topped, and caught in at the ankles. His coat is a *posteen* – sheep-skin worn with the wool inside, lavishly-embroidered with red, behind which, the yellow back-ground contrasts cheerfully. The coat is edged all round with goats' hair, which looks like monkey fur. No rain or hail, snow or wind has the power to penetrate those weather-cheating coats. When wet, as many a buyer in London's King's Road during the 1960s discovered, the cheaper ones can smell like old sheep.

His shoes look uncomfortable in the extreme. They are thick and large and clumsy, although he does not seem to notice any of these disabilities. Naturally they are his own Kochi footwear, and he steps out easily in them. They are curly-toed boots, and closely resemble those worn by the soldiers of the Middle Ages who hailed from these parts and conquered neighbouring empires.

To an onlooker, the problem posed by such shoes is how to walk in them at all, because it is impossible to bend the sole. They look like the lower half of a bowl, with a clumsy heel on one end; the other part of the semicircle points well up into the air.

Taking into consideration the fact that shoe leather quickly wears out on the Central Asian roads, which are sometimes flooded, these travellers must have solved the problem. It is said that these shoes are good in all weath-ers and wear indefinitely, and that there is only the diffi-culty of getting used to them.

I stand watching the little family until a bend in the

road hides them. They are not in the least interested in me, after a fleeting glance.

This little group is one of many hundreds, perhaps thousands, of their kind to be met with on the endless roads of Central Asia. No distance is too great for these hardy travellers. Their home is where they put up their tents, and that is where there is probably sparse wayside grass for their animals.

Perhaps they are going to sell the goats many weary miles away. Perhaps they are moving to the highlands for the summer grazing there.

Whatever their destination, they will allow nothing to stop them until they reach it. All unawares, they have given courage to me, a negligible foreign woman who at that moment needed it badly – someone whom they just possibly envied for a moment as they passed by.

21

Seeking the Seer of Panjshir

Winter in the Afghan uplands presents some of the most spectacularly beautiful scenery imaginable. It is a mixture of Switzerland and the Scottish Highlands, but on an immense scale.

The air is sharp and crackling, and even the horses become winded on the gradients of the passes. Every now and again they rest, snorting loudly, while we are glad to walk, trying to get some circulation into our feet and legs, usually without success, because we cannot get up enough speed to produce results. Our fingers feel lifeless, like smaller sticks tied to large ones.

On this occasion I was heading north and east from Kabul, with a small string of donkeys as my caravan, through the Valley of the Panjshir (Five Tigers). One of our body-servants, rifle slung, and two grooms completed the party.

This is one of the richest areas of Afghanistan for minerals and gemstones. The first minted silver of the Afghan kings was mined here. The valley is also enchanting and tremendously fertile.

Autumn had turned into winter, and we caught sight of pairs and coveys of grouse, which with their ruddy plumage made an attractive picture against the grey and cream of the rocks.

All around there is peace, a peace which, an archaeologist said, is 'as of God'. Away in the far distance lies the glory of the grand snow-covered Hindu Kush with the Anjuman Pass still to negotiate as the valley ends. The sky is a cold clear blue, making a fine background for the sparkling snowy peaks, some of which look like colossal mounds of crystalline sugar.

The night is spent at a caravanserai, where blankets and a blazing fire as well as roast chicken, tasting of coriander and some delectable marinade, are supplied and most welcome. How good the hot freshly-baked *nan* tastes, dipped in the rich gravy; how right this way of eating seems to be.

There are still apples, apricots and other autumnal fruits, together with goat cheese and the largest, most enjoyable, selection of pickles – nuts, peppers, fruits, vegetables, celery – I have ever seen.

It is possible to be cosy under a *sandali*, an ancient Tatar arrangement, which consists of a low table under which a *mankal* – container of glowing charcoal, is placed. Over the table a thick quilt is spread, and those who feel chilly take their places upon cushions on the floor. The quilt is drawn round legs and feet, or, if extra luxury is required, it is possible to slide well under the table, warming the body as well.

With many other unexpected items (including mint sauce, domesticated carrots and windmills) sandalis were introduced from hereabouts into Arabian Spain in the Middle Ages.

The sandali can be an immense comfort when snow lies deep, a most delightful way to warm oneself in out-of-the-way places. All you need is a small mankal filled with glowing charcoal. This keeps the heat for a long time and can be sited wherever you want to sit. Thus one misses the billowing smoke entailed by a middle-of-the-floor fire – as well as smoke-stung eyes and a cough.

I decided against the sandali, however, having had a few enlivening experiences while discovering that it was not only humans who appreciated the arrangement.

Next day we were off early. Those who had used the sandali felt the cold on the bare hillsides more keenly, but the valleys were sheltered. Down, down we went until it felt almost as if we were descending the side of a well. The horses sprawled and we slid.

The hills catch all the snow, and it rarely falls in the valleys. Isolated village people came out of their houses to gaze upon what must to them have been rare specimens of humanity.

They stood in silent wonderment, with uncomprehending eyes, and mouths more than half open. When I dismounted, they took a few steps backwards nearer the safety of their homes, all the while looking intently at my jodhpurs, boots, and coat.

Gradually overcoming their shyness and doubt, a small group began to edge nearer. When we prepared to have a snack from my hamper, they watched every movement. The sight of the strange cakes and sandwiches, the fruit and thermos-flasks, caused a great deal of chattering.

The children seemed to find the way we ate a matter for the closest inspection. When we offered them sweets they took refuge behind their elders, who were now remarkably numerous, considering the few cottages in sight.

When we continued eating and took no notice, the little ones began to come near, step by step. Like children everywhere I noticed the boys pushed the girls first. They were dressed exactly like their parents, and their baggy trousers and shirts were clean, although much patched, and of rough quality. The children looked healthy and attractive, and the coloured skull-caps showed up their red cheeks and mischievous eyes. They wore tiny coloured boleros, heavily embroidered.

They were now very interested in us, and no doubt wondered where we came from, and why we were there. As soon as they discovered we spoke Dari, they began a conversation at once.

The first question was where we came from. When I said Kabul, a woman asked whether all the Kabul ladies had short hair? A groom told them that I was 'Europoi', which is a widely-embracing word, and accounted, no doubt, for all my peculiarities. All nodded, as if this were what they had expected all along.

By now a small girl with very bright eyes was examining my hair. She called out to the onlookers that I had 'round hair', curls, and that she would like the same. She ventured to say that the *sherini* – sweets, were funny. I asked her to taste one, upon which she clutched what I gave her and darted away to the back of a house, pursued by the other children.

None of the onlookers seemed to feel the cold as we did, nor were they wrapped up or even warmly clad.

Throughout my travels and residence in Afghanistan one thing was particularly noticeable; however poor or ill-clad the people were, there was no begging.

The Afghan pride goes right through to the poorest: and often when we were seated by the wayside eating, and poor people passed, they had to be persuaded to accept a little food.

How very different from some places farther east! They always apologised for being so poor that it was impossible for them to return anything. Sometimes the humblest produced dried fruit and nuts tied up safely and securely in their turban-ends, against the rigours of a long journey, and presented them with politeness.

There were times when people in houses by the wayside insisted upon leaving their warm rooms for us that we might be more comfortable. If we offered them money, they always refused it. 'The wayfarer is the guest of God,' they said, with a shy smile.

As we were preparing to leave, after eating lunch by the wayside, the small girl who had received the sweets returned with a lamb a few months old. This, she said was hers, and it was a gift from her to me. It was out of the question to transport a lamb but I asked her to keep it until it was older.

She asked whether we would promise to return; if so,

the lamb could be cooked and made into a pulao for us. The earnest little face demanded a reply, and it would have to be a truthful one. Remembering the cragged heights and depths of the road, I said that return would not be possible until next year. By that time the lamb would be big enough for all of us to have a pulao.

The father replied that that lamb was to be kept at all costs. Finally we agreed that the animal could be shared out, as our contribution, *in absentia*, to their post-Ramadan feasting, and honour was apparently satisfied all round.

We thanked the little group, shared out among the half-dozen children, food that we had unpacked but not eaten, and prepared to go. Our going emboldened them, and they gathered round, smiling broadly. They wished peace upon us, and we upon them. They stood waving as long as they could see us.

By and by, we came upon a cave which we had been warned to expect, beyond a single fir-tree close to the mountain-track. As we approached we saw an old man, standing erect, wearing an immense long quilted coat, and a fur hat. Over the hat he wore a thick shawl, the ends of which were crossed in front and fastened under his thick white beard.

He looked rather like one of the etchings one sees of an old-time alchemist – long-bearded, beady-eyed, with hunched shoulders. He seemed oddly out of place. We greeted each other. He spoke high-class Persian, and when the preliminaries were over, told us that he was a traveller.

Passing through that part of the country he had found the peace for which he sought, and he spent much time in contemplation. He was able, he said, to concentrate sufficiently to converse with Nature, and he was trying to understand the language of the birds. He offered us sour milk and *qurut* – porridge made of maize crushed to flour between stones and mixed with yoghurt, but we declined the offer with flowing thanks.

He asked me after a time whether I liked Egypt, and whether the Arabian desert was not a difficult part to traverse.

This was undoubtedly the Seer, because we had spoken only of Kabul. I replied that present-day Egypt appeared to be going through a chaotic time and that the Arabian desert fully deserved every shade of the meaning of the adjective he had applied to it.

I asked how he knew of my travels. He replied that he had asked those questions that we might observe that he had progressed in his subject. 'The pictures rise in my head, and names and words rise in my ears.'

Like many another seer, including those in the West, I realised from what he said that he was able, in a somewhat uncontrolled way, to read thoughts in my mind or memory. Mostly, as with seances and clairvoyants elsewhere, he only imagined that he could penetrate the future. I confirmed that later: all the predictions which he made, and there were several, were wrong in the event.

He was a fascinating figure and I realised that, in that strange scenery, and faced by such an impressive creature, people in need of emotional stimuli might well wonder whether he were human.

When we reached the great Pass, we had a meal of good mutton, hard but palatable cheese, thin bread, and a bowl of milk. The local people are cheerful, hardworking, and willing. After the meal was finished, as we thought, they brought dried mulberries, green tea and blocks of marzipan. The latter is composed of ground mulberries, honey, rosewater and walnuts. It is extremely palatable but also equally medicinal: the mulberries are a powerful aperient.

It is well to take but a little. Refusal is considered rudeness. All travellers in the East should memorise the only phrase which will work: 'I very much wish to have some – unfortunately my doctor forbids it . . .'

The women were spinning a thick brown cloth which

makes their winter coats. The people are tall, slim and fair-complexioned, originating from the Nuristani (formerly Kafiristan) tribes.

Called Kalash, these people are variously thought to be ancient Iranians, lost Aryan tribes or descended from the soldiers of Alexander the Great. Many are fair-skinned and have blue eyes. Some of them make wine, forbidden by Islam, and they live in wooden chalets like Swiss ones, as well as in clay and wattle houses. They were not amalgamated into Afghanistan until the nineteenth century, when Amir Abdur-Rahman Khan made a pre-emptive strike to prevent the British arms, always aimed at his country under the 'Forward Policy', from approaching Kabul from the north.

The children have round red cheeks and look well-cared for and happy.

Three immense grey-white dogs guarded the place. They were long-limbed with long sharp wolf-like fangs and large belligerent eyes.

Further along the road we saw a family of cave-dwellers, who looked like survivors from pre-history. They seemed busily engaged in various activities and, although the weather was extremely cold, they had bare arms. Their dwellings or shelters were composed of branches stuck in the ground, covered with an assortment of cloths of all colours and considerable antiquity.

The ground was littered with footwear, pieces of bone and other odds and ends of rubbish. A noisy goat was tied up to a stout tree nearby, and hating it. It bleated all the time. The children's clothes were simply pieces of cloth fastened around them, making them look like untidy parcels. The young people marry the one chosen for them from within their own tribe and, if either partner dies, the one left may marry again but not outside the tribe.

They seemed quite healthy, if somewhat grim and distrustful. One old crone, bent almost double, was attending to a handleless pot over a stone-built fireplace. Her eyesight had obviously been bad so long that her face was screwed up until she was quite hideous. Age seemed the time here for responsibility, because while we watched, a small child was brought for her to mind. Without ceremony she tucked it into her capacious coat and went on attending to the pot. The smoke from the fire seemed to have no effect on her or on the infant.

Meeting this fresh variety of people was as worthwhile an experience as the journey itself: though for real revelations of the strange and supernatural, I had to wait for another time, and go in a quite different direction.